About Island Press

Since 1984, the nonprofit organization Island Press has been stimulating, shaping, and communicating ideas that are essential for solving environmental problems worldwide. With more than 1,000 titles in print and some 30 new releases each year, we are the nation's leading publisher on environmental issues. We identify innovative thinkers and emerging trends in the environmental field. We work with world-renowned experts and authors to develop cross-disciplinary solutions to environmental challenges.

Island Press designs and executes educational campaigns, in conjunction with our authors, to communicate their critical messages in print, in person, and online using the latest technologies, innovative programs, and the media. Our goal is to reach targeted audiences—scientists, policy makers, environmental advocates, urban planners, the media, and concerned citizens—with information that can be used to create the framework for long-term ecological health and human well-being.

Island Press gratefully acknowledges major support from The Bobolink Foundation, Caldera Foundation, The Curtis and Edith Munson Foundation, The Forrest C. and Frances H. Lattner Foundation, The JPB Foundation, The Kresge Foundation, The Summit Charitable Foundation, Inc., and many other generous organizations and individuals.

This project is supported, in part, by an award from the National Endowment for the Arts.

The opinions expressed in this book are those of the author(s) and do not necessarily reflect the views of our supporters.

Schools That Heal

Schools That Heal

DESIGN WITH MENTAL HEALTH IN MIND

Claire Latané

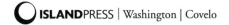

ISLANDPRESS | Washington | Covelo

All rights reserved under International and Pan-American Copyright Conventions. No part of this book may be reproduced in any form or by any means without permission in writing from the publisher: Island Press, 2000 M Street, NW, Suite 480b, Washington, DC 20036.

Library of Congress Control Number: 2020947252

All Island Press books are printed on environmentally responsible materials.

Manufactured in the United States of America
10 9 8 7 6 5 4 3 2 1

Keywords: ASCEND School, biophilic design, Bridges Academy, B. Traven Community School, collaborative planning, COVID-19, Daniel Webster Middle School, developmental disabilities, ecological health, Eagle Rock Elementary School, empathy, Environmental Charter High School, equity, funding, George C. Marshall High School, green infrastructure, inclusion, Kesennuma Shiritsu Omose Primary School, Los Angeles Unified School District, nature-based design, outdoor classroom, public health, Redwood Park Academy, renovation, restorative justice, safety, Sandy Hook Elementary School, school design, sustainable design, social connectedness, teacher retention, violence prevention, well-being, wildlife habitat

MIX
Paper from
responsible sources
FSC® C008955

For Felicity, Jacob, and Levi.
You are my heart and inspiration.

Contents

Foreword

This is a time for reckoning and reimagining. Our world is being reshaped by a pandemic, and multinational, multigenerational protestors are insisting that the United States finally fulfill its promise of equality and racial justice for all. Before June 2020, it would have been hard to believe that our country—one of the most heavily militarized nations, with the highest rate of incarceration on this planet—would rigorously debate public policy to defund police and redefine community safety. But, in the wake of shocking tragedy, we have begun to do both.

We have an opportunity to re-envision and change the course of the unjust systems that have lasted far too long.

This book is a tool to help us do just that. Claire Latané provides us with stories and data that clearly demonstrate that the current dominant practices in school design harm our children, mentally and physically. Claire helps us take a good, honest look at how we've built, designed, and maintained our schools for decades. But, more than that, *Schools That Heal* is a key to help us unlock our imaginations. Claire provides teachers, parents, administrators, students, and designers with inspiration and examples to help us reimagine what is possible. Through expert interviews and primary research, she demonstrates how designing, building, and maintaining schools to foster health and to respect the environment can make our children truly feel safe, welcomed, loved, and respected. High-functioning, well-designed schools can stand as a bulwark against systemic racism, police brutality, and environmental injustice. The design strategies in this book can help schools become beacons of hope, providing a sense of community safety and serving as ecological sanctuaries.

This is the time to apply the wisdom in these pages—in all of our schools. This is the time to heed the lessons from this and other, similar instances in our history. Our responsibility is to place a laser focus on investing public and private resources to improve conditions in the most heavily impacted schools. All students need and deserve schools that heal. This need is especially urgent for our Black and Brown children.

Make no mistake, transforming our schools will not be an easy task. But we can create schools that heal. It is not too much to expect or demand that our schools stand as models of restorative justice and environmental stewardship that support physical and mental well-being. They are, after all, an embodiment and a reflection of our commitment to educating future generations. In healthy schools, we set up more of our youth to blossom into leaders who we hope and expect will guide our country toward our highest social ideals: health, prosperity, equality, and justice. Administrators and teachers cannot make this transformation alone. Designers, parents, students, and community advocates are essential partners in ushering in new models, demanding greater inclusion, and insisting on transparency and accountability. Our schools are hubs for the practice of democracy, messy as it may be.

As Claire so clearly details in the pages that follow, mental health, physical health, and the quality of the environment are all intimately connected to one another, to performance in school and in life. What we've learned time and again from past public health scourges—from tobacco-related lung cancer to lead-induced learning delays—is that we won't succeed if we limit our approaches to services and counseling that deal with one person at a time. We need to fix environments, transform institutions, and move mindsets to create real change on the scale that's needed. With examples and insights from research and practice, *Schools That Heal* shines a light on a practical path forward.

This book is a call to action for all of us. As the up-and-coming stewards of our society and our planet, our children deserve nothing less than environments that cultivate their mental health, safety, and well-being. We know children are resilient. But just how resilient do we expect them to be? The school environments too many students inhabit are devoid of life or inspiration and are arguably unsafe. In order to face the challenges that this generation will be called to confront, students need and deserve nurturing, nature-filled schools that help them grow and inspire them to learn. We owe it to them, to their children, and to their children's children.

Manal J. Aboelata, MPH

Deputy Executive Director
Prevention Institute
Los Angeles, May 2020

Preface

It is hard to make healthy schools. Even in neighborhoods that have plenty of resources, most school environments fall short of supporting students' mental and physical health and well-being. Too few school decision makers know that decades of research show that nurturing, nature-filled school environments improve mental health, lessen crime, give a sense of safety, and improve academic success.

I was a lucky winner of excellent public education in Upper Arlington, an affluent 1920s suburb of Columbus, Ohio. The informal experimental program was student centered and full of opportunities for learning the arts, sciences, and vocations. My elementary school was a cluster of buildings set amid parklike lawns scattered with trees. There were no fences, there were no playground rules that I can remember, and there was lots of grass. We were free to walk out for lunch starting in seventh grade, or in elementary school if we had a note from a parent and went home to eat. My strongest recollection is of lying in the cool grass under a maple tree, prompted by our teacher to "think of a poem." I lay there watching the birds fly by, puffy clouds dotting the blue sky, and felt the earth's dampness seep into my T-shirt. I felt peaceful. This was a big feeling for me. In first grade, I struggled with such severe shyness that my sister had to come from the next classroom over to talk me out from under the teacher's desk. Through elementary, middle, and high school, my social anxiety prevented me from speaking up in class. If I was called on, I either froze or stumbled through an answer. Despite this, I felt a sense of belonging in my schools. There was a variety of programs and activities I could participate in, and the teachers and principals greeted us warmly every day. The schools were surrounded by the wide lawns and trees that are typical of suburbia. It never dawned on me to think about just how special my school environments were . . . until my own children started school.

They had mostly positive school experiences in the suburbs of Charlotte, North Carolina, and then in east Los Angeles County, where we moved so I could attend graduate school. In the middle of the 2005 housing bubble, our landlord gave us notice to move. Priced out of nearly every neighborhood with highly ranked schools, I found a little rental house in the city of Los Angeles. The neighborhood was mixed socioeconomically and culturally, a positive in my mind. Eagle Rock was known for its good schools. And yet my children and their peers struggled in crowded classrooms and limited outdoor space with a lack of grass or trees. Many of their classrooms were in windowless modular boxes. When their father and I divorced, and especially after he moved away, their stress and anxiety bloomed. They were not alone in this. As my children grew, I learned through them and their friends about commonplace bullying and self-harm, the perilous use of cell phone cameras, and the compelling pull to self-medicate despite regular conversations about our family's addictive tendencies. I grew to hate the sound of the school's automated truancy phone call: "Your son was either tardy or absent from one or more periods today." We nearly lost my daughter to suicide when she was seventeen. One of my sons seemed compelled toward self-destruction. He pushed every boundary and landed in jail and rehab more than once. Phone calls became traumatic. Was he hurt? Or worse?

My children's schools were not the cause of most of their issues . . . but they didn't help. I saw my children and their peers suffer emotionally and academically in uninspiring and often hostile environments. I knew my kids had it better than many others who struggled with racism or poverty or who had lost parents and loved ones to jail, drugs, or violence. I dreamed of schools that could help parents support and inspire their children in the face of such adversities, especially in neighborhoods barren of fresh food, health services, trees and parks, and viable careers.

My work in landscape architecture let me design school landscapes. I saw many other K–12 campuses and noted the patterns they shared. I participated in behind-the-scenes conversations about high costs and high maintenance of living landscapes in public schools. We had to fight for every tree or square foot of nature. Even when the district supported nature in schools, the budgets seemed to evaporate by the time it came to build the campus landscape. I worked on others—mostly private schools—where we created enriching, supportive academic environments. I knew from personal and professional experience that school could be a warm and inviting and nurturing place. As I became aware of the startling numbers of young people struggling with learning differences, stress, and anxiety, depression, and other mental health disorders, I began designing school landscapes with a focus on supporting mental health.

In 2017, the Landscape Architecture Foundation launched its Fellowship for Innovation and Leadership. As one of six inaugural fellows, I explored the connection between school design and mental health. I visited public schools and school districts in Los Angeles, Oakland, and Pomona, California; in Virginia; and in Berlin, Germany. I spoke to experts in school administration and education, mental health and kinesiology, environmental economics, design, law enforcement, and restorative justice. I interviewed students and parents and community members about school environments and their effects on mental health. I read books and dissertations and articles. Many of these conversations and resources are referenced in the pages that follow.

This exploration brought to light some alarming statistics. Today's students are experiencing record rates of mental health disorders. Because of a variety of economic, environmental, and social factors, children and teens aren't getting the ample access to nature or deep sense of belonging that they need for well-being. Equity is an issue. The research shows a clear connection between neighborhoods with the worst environmental and health conditions and high rates of trauma. As became particularly poignant during the 2020 protests against police violence, our public systems—including education—play out the injustices born from centuries of racist policies and practices. This exacerbates the devastating conditions of neighborhoods where federal policy denies bank loans and city policy underserves and overpolices. But schools everywhere—rural, urban, suburban—need improvements to support the mental health and well-being of students from all socioeconomic backgrounds and cultures.

Roger Ulrich's groundbreaking 1980s study found that hospital patients recover faster when given views of nature. This work permeated the realm of hospital design with a movement toward therapeutic gardens and environments. There is no parallel initiative to design schools with mental health in mind. It is time to start that movement. As we grapple with how to improve environmental justice and equity and how to safely keep our schools open in a pandemic age, school design for mental health provides some strong solutions. Schools are spread throughout communities. Children and teenagers spend most of their time at school. Most children and adolescents don't get the mental health services they need. Schools and districts struggle to find resources to support counseling, mental health, and restorative justice programs. We can support all of these initiatives by designing schools to become environmental and social safety nets for all students, families, and communities who access them.

This book is an attempt to bridge the gaps between research and the designers, administrators, and facilities managers who shape schools today. *Schools That Heal* provides resources to help parents, students, and educators advocate for school design that supports students mentally, socially, physically, and academically. Included are design strategies, communication tips, and examples of schools to help you reimagine today's schools with mental health in mind. It is written to help parents, students, teachers, administrators, and school designers find common language around the multiple issues facing us today. Students suffer greater levels of anxiety, stress, and fear now, compounded by the isolation and loneliness caused by the COVID-19 pandemic. It is time for a new social contract for public schools. We must rethink school environments to give students, teachers, staff, and community members safe and restorative places to heal, commune, and learn. Our young people need and deserve this. Teachers, staff, and parents do, too.

CHAPTER 1

Nine Reasons Why We Should Design Schools with Mental Health in Mind

What would schools look like if every design decision were made with mental health in mind? We might see them as the essential public goods that they are. We might design them so they could remain open in times of pandemic and social distancing. The physical qualities of schools impact mental health as well as public health. The schools students attend affect how they see and treat themselves, their peers, their futures, and the world around them. As the hearts of communities, schools connect people. They can reverse the feelings of isolation and overwhelm so many children, teens, adults, and seniors have struggled with even before the outbreak of COVID-19, the novel coronavirus. When designed as nurturing, nature-filled environments, schools can give students a sense of belonging, soothe their anxieties, reduce their fears, and elevate their moods.

Mentally healthy school design is good for people, animals, plants, and ecosystems. It's good for economies, too. Schools that heal work with nature and natural processes to need fewer materials for less money and less maintenance. They provide ample indoor and outdoor connection and space to alleviate crowding, noise, and physical contact. Supporting students' mental and physical health through design helps them thrive academically and socially. Nurturing school environments promote positive behavior, safer schools and communities, and better lives for students during school and over their lifetimes. Because schools are an essential public resource, the way they are funded, designed, and managed impacts environmental and social justice and equity.

Very few schools today are designed to support mental health. Most don't support physical health very well, either. More often than not, school environments are made up of hard institution-grade materials that reflect noise and light, limit choice, heighten stress and anxiety—and, as a result, aggression—increase heart rates, and reduce students' sense of belonging and ability to learn. Reduced school funding and a desire to harden schools against potential external threats have created schools that are little more than walled testing centers of students' intellects and teachers' patience. And this is in the wealthier neighborhoods. In lower-income communities, they look and feel like prisons. The way schools are policed often lands students of color in a juvenile justice system that impacts the rest of their lives. Most public school environments offer little to spark the imagination, engage curiosity, or invite quiet reflection or kind interaction. Stark wide-open spaces and fenced grounds invite boredom, competition, or aggression. Teachers beg for relief. And students struggle and suffer.

Children and teenagers who go to school in classrooms with ample fresh air flow, big windows looking out to trees, and opportunities to play freely in nature are kinder to one another, are better behaved, do better in school, and are more likely to go to college. Students of all ages are calmer, less stressed, and less likely to act aggressively or criminally in schools and communities with more trees, places for people to gather outside, and opportunities to play creatively and be active. There are many reasons to design schools with mental health and well-being in mind. The following sections explore nine.

1. Children Need Healthy Environments to Develop Healthy Nervous Systems

As a somatic psychotherapist, Sergio Ocampo works with the mind-body-environment connection. He specializes in trauma therapy. For three years Ocampo worked with children suffering from trauma and related conditions in Los Angeles public schools. "A student's surroundings affect the part of the autonomic nervous system which is associated with feelings of safety and calm," he told me. "A school designed with soothing surroundings, visual depth, and varied interest signals to the brain to let go of hyper-vigilance and defensive or self-protective responses. The brain and nervous system can rest."[1]

Soothing surroundings are full of tree leaves and tall grasses swaying in the breeze, birdsong, and butterflies—scenes and sounds and scents that take us away from everyday stressors. With resting nervous systems, students are more open to interacting with other people, have a greater sense of well-being, and have better brain function. Schools made up entirely of hard surfaces separate children from the natural environments that they need to develop a healthy nervous system. Ocampo said:

> Many schools, especially in urban areas, are devoid of nature . . . the opposite of the places humans evolved to live in. The result can be a nervous system which is unable to settle down and self-soothe. This can present itself as an inability to control emotions and impulses or achieve higher cognitive functions. The consequences can be learning difficulties, disruptive confrontation, and even violent behavior. Or the opposite can emerge in the form of shut down emotions and social interaction.[2]

We have to begin treating nature and the services nature provides as essential and precious resources in urban schools and communities. Our bodies, minds, and spirits work better and last longer when we are immersed in healthy natural environments. Nature provides the air we breathe, the water we drink, the food we eat, and the complex ecosystem that we all inhabit. Expanding research illuminates a web of benefits between healthy urban ecologies, public health, social and environmental justice, and educational outcomes. Nature is more than just window dressing. Students thrive when they can see, hear, smell, and feel the natural resources that sustain us.

2. Mentally Healthy Design Supports Public Health and Works toward Justice

"School facilities aren't welcoming places for communities," said Manal Aboelata, deputy executive director of Prevention Institute in Los Angeles. "People and communities are not just our clients—they are the benefactors or receivers of harms."

Planning and public health practices are beginning to adopt this idea. "We need a lot more work to reframe mental health not as an individual problem that lives inside someone's head but as a community-wide problem.

"There is still a stigma around mental health—we don't internalize our community situation, privilege, and resources as connected to mental health and social connectedness," Aboelata told me. But they are. "Connectedness and reversing isolation is important, especially for seniors. Street design, benches with shade . . . there are gaps and opportunities in every system."

Loneliness doesn't hurt just seniors. Before the coronavirus pandemic, a study by the health insurer Cigna found that nearly half of young adults in the United States felt loneliness and that millennials and Generation Z-ers were more likely than older generations to feel lonely.[3] One in three people between fifty and eighty years of age reported being lonely. Loneliness is connected to depression, anxiety, and risk of heart attack, stroke, and early death.[4] More and more, our lives are devoid of communal and multigenerational activities and full of isolation, independence, and loneliness. The best antidote is to engage in meaningful social contact, pursue purposeful work, and build strong relationships. Schools can be designed as nature-filled community centers where senior citizens, artists, businesspeople, and others can find and nurture meaningful relationships through volunteering time and resources and mentoring young people. This benefits students and the entire community.

These strategies boost ecological health and social cohesion as well as physical health. This in turn reduces the need for medical care, psychiatric care, and the subsequent economic stress that often leads to food insecurity, homelessness, and hopelessness. It is those things—not the inherent desire to commit crime—that lands most in the criminal justice system. We cannot expect young people or adults to thrive in neighborhoods overshadowed by schools that look and feel like detention centers. Public schools are positioned well to become community centers for health and resilience—a beating heart for the neighborhood. We can start repairing those injustices in public school neighborhoods with the least resources and the most to gain. Designing schools as healing, restorative, community-building places can build physical health, mental health, and resilience in the face of the next pandemic, recession, or natural disaster. While some physical improvements can take years, engaging students and the community in reimagining their school can have immediate benefits.

3. Designing with Empathy—Not Fear—Increases Students' Sense of Belonging and Safety

Sometimes positive intentions have negative consequences. In the aftermath of the 1999 shooting at Columbine High School in Littleton, Colorado, school districts around the country began implementing "active shooter drills" to train students and teachers what to do in case of this type of emergency. This sets up the classroom and school as a place where fear undermines learning. Children as young as three and four come home after active shooter drills worried about being shot at school. While the threat is terrifying, the likelihood of a student experiencing an active school shooter is 0.003 percent.[5] Drilling students to prepare for this unlikely tragedy leads to anxiety and trauma. The Pew Research Center found that 57 percent of American teenagers worry about a shooting at their school. The drills place undue fear in students. For example, having students "arm" themselves with pencils and rulers and barricade the door is an approach that isn't even grounded in empirical evidence. A more effective response would be nurturing each student with student-centered learning environments that meet students' unique and individual needs. A 2020 study by the US Government Accountability Office found that current or former students were the shooters in over 80 percent of school-targeted shootings between 2009 and 2019.[6] Design solutions can also be an important part of preparing for the unimaginable—and less frightening. HMC Architects designs classrooms with bolts of color on the floor marking safe zones. Teachers instruct students to get into the safe zone, out of sight of doors and windows, for an "emergency drill." This allows schools and districts to practice for emergencies—including earthquake, tornado, or lockdown—and avoids frightening children with mental images of guns and shooters and other extreme emergency language. Schools can include safe zones as a part of student training on how to handle the most common emergencies.

One of the most inspiring examples of how design can provide protection and support emotional well-being is in evidence at Sandy Hook Elementary School, the site of a horrific mass shooting in 2012. It was redesigned not as a fortress but as an embrace. Architect Barry Svigals told me:

We selected fifty people including consultants. The opportunity was clear—that they needed to be able to reset emotionally where they were. We started with what they loved about their community, a remembering and a re-visioning with what their community could be. This community engagement process is essential—even in schools that are already built—in order to reimagine what safety/wellness is and think about it holistically. It's comprehensive, broad, deep.[7]

The whole hub of public health professionals, mental health professionals, law enforcement, social workers, parents, teachers, students, and the local community worked together to reknit the reasons for school back into the community.

4. Design Can Amplify Existing Restorative Justice and Mental Health Programs

Many school districts are replacing punitive discipline with restorative, relationship-based methods to bring people together around forgiveness and healing. Others have established robust mental health frameworks by providing services, social workers, and other systems to support students' individual needs. Some, such as California's Oakland Unified School District (OUSD), do both.

"Restorative justice is a really great way to help humans feel safe because it allows them to connect to one another, and build relationships, and do it in a way the student values can be present," David Yusem, the director of OUSD's Restorative Justice program, told me.[8] Few schools, if any, see restorative justice as a design issue. But physical changes to schools can amplify the effects of restorative justice programs by creating calming, quieting environments and places where students can go alone or in small groups when they need to decompress. Creating an environment that invites rest and helps teachers and students nurture one another and themselves will reduce the likelihood of students acting out. Designing healing places to hold community circles—the center of many restorative justice initiatives—can facilitate the restorative justice process by providing inviting environments where people feel safe and comfortable. The more comfortable students, teachers, and community members are, the more likely it is that they can fully participate in the process of healing wounds and righting relationships.

Seeing an opportunity well over a decade ago, Deanna Van Buren founded Designing Justice + Designing Spaces. She acknowledges that people rarely understand the importance of design. "I believe and expect that people are not going to value design very much. These are working communities who are traumatized, and doing a design workshop is not their top priority," she told me. "That doesn't mean design and the environment is not a hugely important and impactful thing that needs to be addressed. But it's not their responsibility to address it. It's ours, as designers, and architects, and whoever else to be finding ways to ensure that people have healthy, nourishing, supportive environments for their life."[9]

5. Boosting Children's Physical Ability and Immune System with Nature Play Increases Long-Term Health and Physical Safety As Well As Mental Health and Well-being

When we talk about student health and safety, we need to think about students' long-term health, over the course of their lives. Many school design and policy decisions are made to minimize the risk of students hurting themselves in the moment. My children went to elementary school during a time when running wasn't allowed, for fear that a student might trip and fall. Other parents and advocates tell me the same rules apply at their schools. And yet most will agree that running and other vigorous physical activity is essential for students' long-term health and well-being. One of the most impactful ways to benefit students' lifelong physical and mental health is by letting them play freely in nature-filled environments.

"How do you define safety?" Sharon Gamson Danks, cofounder of the International School Grounds Alliance (ISGA), reminded me of a concept called beneficial risk. The ISGA's Risk in Play and Learning Declaration calls for school grounds to be as safe as *necessary*, not as safe as *possible*. This call to action came from the enormous amount of evidence connecting beneficial risk—such as climbing trees, swinging from ropes, jumping off logs and boulders, running across uneven surfaces—with stronger minds, bodies, mental health, and social skills, even if it comes with skinned knees and other hurts.

After months of closed schools due to the coronavirus pandemic, rethinking priorities for school facilities is even more crucial. Pediatricians and public health experts recommend being outside instead of in recirculated air-conditioned rooms to reduce the spread of disease. Decades of research point to the health benefits of being in or looking at nature. We can transform schoolyards into outdoor classrooms, learning laboratories, restorative gardens, and nature play areas. This will support immune system health, reduce infection rates, and allow teachers more options for experiential learning. Opening outdoor classrooms will also help schools reduce class sizes during times of social distancing. This commonly brings concerns about protecting students from cold, heat, snow, rain, and wind. The traditional response from the forest school movement (popular in cold and blustery Denmark and Scotland) is "There's no such thing as bad weather, only bad clothing." For underresourced schools, the National COVID-19 Outdoor Learning Initiative recommends that schools provide rain and snow gear kits for students through donations or grants funding public health solutions.

6. Ecological Literacy Helps Students Thrive in School and Gives Them a Sense of Optimism and Purpose

While teaching an introduction to landscape architecture course at East Los Angeles College, I took my children with my students on a field trip to several nearby parks and natural areas. At the north end of the Lower Arroyo Park Area in Pasadena, we walked upstream to where the shallow water lapped along a sandy beach. Sycamores, willows, and mule fat lined the stream and shaded the water with a protective canopy. My children, adept at negotiating natural terrain, climbed the boulders and concrete retaining wall along the edge and made their way down to the water. My students stood still, nearly all of them dumbfounded.

"How did you find this place?" one asked.

"I can't believe this exists," another said. They were awestruck at the natural beauty we were immersed in just a stone's throw from the Rose Bowl. We were less than ten miles from their college.

Too many students in metropolitan areas live within a few miles of nearby beaches, mountains, and natural areas yet have never experienced them in person. Lack of transportation, awareness, parental time, or resources are real hurdles to connecting students to the restorative qualities of nature.

I was transformed by overnight science camp in elementary school. I will never forget the magic of sharing the woods with my classmates and a few instructors who knew about the plants, animals, and rock formations all around us. Learning about nature while being in nature was life changing. Too few students get this opportunity. It requires the interest of the teacher and school principal as well as available funding and space. Los Angeles Unified School District's administrator of environmental and outdoor education, Gerry Salazar, told me there is a six-year waiting list of schools wanting to participate in fifth-grade science camp.[10] The district prioritizes Title I schools and students who might not otherwise experience camping. Filling schools with natural systems can relieve the demand by bringing some of the magic of science camp to school sites, especially in cities. Salazar has seen this work. Leo Politi Elementary School in Los Angeles's Pico-Union neighborhood made headlines when its National Wildlife Federation habitat garden was followed three years later by a massive improvement in science test scores.[11]

Natural landscapes on campus can support environmental literacy as well as create places for students to go when they need to reduce stress and restore their ability to pay attention. Changes in school environments can also support the recent interest in project-based learning. Outdoor classrooms, wildflower gardens, ethnobotany gardens, urban forests, food forests, and visible rain- and energy-harvesting systems are all opportunities for living laboratories. These hands-on environments compel students who might be reluctant in a classroom setting to become curious and learn through exploration life science, ecology, watershed health, agricultural and horticultural science, history, and green infrastructure. Outdoor classrooms and gardens can be designed to support myriad activities. Theatrical arts and music, fine arts, history and literature, and the hard and soft sciences can all benefit from outdoor learning environments that also support mental health and well-being.

7. Nature-Based and Community-Led School Design Nurtures Teachers, Too . . . and Might Help Keep Them in the Profession

The only people who spend more time at school than our students are our teachers. They deserve work environments that are welcoming, nurturing places to teach. Research connects green views, soft materials, access to gardens, and a choice of environments with higher job satisfaction, fewer sick days, and people staying in jobs longer.[12] As more states face teacher strikes and teacher shortages, improving teachers' work environment is a concrete approach that can address many issues. In the pandemic age, designing classrooms that open to the outside and outdoor learning environments will be critical in supporting teachers' physical and mental health as they return to the physical school site.

As nurturing environments reduce student stress and aggression, teachers gain more time to teach. After one-quarter of their asphalt schoolyard was replaced with trees, living grass, and a habitat learning garden, Eagle Rock Elementary School teachers told Principal Stephanie Leach that their students behaved better in the classroom.[13] This made their jobs easier, giving them more class time to teach, with less time devoted to redirecting attention. The students came in from recess and lunch reregulated and ready to learn. Teachers know that green space in schools makes a difference. The 2019 United Teachers Los Angeles strike ended with an agreement that included a request by teachers for a green task force and more green space at schools. Teachers want, need, and deserve greener, healthier school environments that support their students' well-being and their own.

8. Including Students in an Inclusive, Collaborative, Multidisciplinary Design Process Is Essential for Creating Mentally Healthy School Environments

Contrary to some design egos, no single person or profession can design a good school, let alone a mentally healthy school. We need mental health professionals, public health professionals, social justice experts, educators, contractors, designers, ecologists, regenerative designers, and resilient community experts working together to plan and design schools for a new era. Students and their communities are central to the process. Without including students in the design process, it is impossible to honor and reflect them in the school design.

Moving beyond the idea of designer as expert toward a model in which designers are facilitators can create design processes and outcomes that exceed everyone's expectations. This can also free the designer from the pressure to know everything. Instead, design teams can focus on emotional intelligence and the ability to represent, understand, and listen to the school community. To be successful, this model depends on clear project parameters (timeline, budget, scope of work) and consistent and transparent communications.

An inclusive, collaborative design process will benefit students long before a design is implemented or evaluated. The very act of involving students and asking them what works and what doesn't gives them a voice in a process that usually excludes them. For me, the most powerful moment of the school design process is when students realize they are being heard. No matter how old they are, when students notice you are writing down their observations and ideas, their facial expression shifts as if to say, "Wait. What? You're writing that down? You're *really* listening to me?"

Students care about the design of their school and the safety of their community. Including them as experts in designing nurturing, nature-full schools communicates to students, "You matter."

9. A Community-Led, Nature-Based Design Approach Can Support Justice, Equity, Diversity, and Inclusion in Communities and in the Design Professions

One of the strongest ways to support communities in design is to engage design teams who represent and understand them. But these professions are overwhelmingly White and male. The landscape architecture, architecture, planning, and engineering professions struggle to attract and support underrepresented minorities. Working with and hiring students and community members as codesigners of their schools and neighborhoods will build equity in a number of ways. Community members will be able to advocate for what they want and need in their schools and neighborhoods. Students and community members will learn about the potential for the planning and design process to improve their neighborhoods. The codesign process can bring communities together to build social connectedness, strengthen the ability to advocate for change, and increase community resilience. Design professionals will have the opportunity to introduce students to the planning, design, and engineering disciplines and encourage and support them in entering into those careers.

During a conversation about designing for resilience, Gabrielle Bullock, director of global diversity for architecture firm Perkins&Will, said:

> The response to George Floyd's murder and the civil unrest and protests . . . has ripped the mask off the structural and institutional inequities of our society. As urban planners, architects, and designers we have the opportunity to strip those barriers, identify what they

are, and figure out how they can positively impact communities instead of destroying them. If we lead with justice and equity, cultural competency, and using the community as a design partner then we can truly embrace social infrastructure—and thereby the people—in providing a more resilient society.[14]

Students and communities around the country are demanding that school districts and cities focus funding and attention on schools, preventive health, food security, and community building instead of allowing punitive discipline and policing to be the default response to our societal breakdowns. How else might we imagine our broken, racist systems? We are not the only nation to provide dismal public school environments. Around the world, children and teenagers suffer in public education systems that get less funding, less design attention, and less priority than our students need and deserve. In the United States, transportation, prisons, police, entertainment, sports, and advertising are more important than our youth. At least that's what our budgets say. We could improve the lives of hundreds of students every year by renovating a school and its grounds for the cost of one thirty-second Super Bowl ad.

Public school is an undeniable and necessary public resource. We have an opportunity to rethink school environments (inside and out) to nurture students (inside and out) for the good of each individual and the good of society. Each school will look different, depending on the communities who create it and the ecologies that support it. This is the beauty of community-led, nature-based school design: it embodies the people and places it serves to allow healing, growth, and learning to occur.

CHAPTER 2

How School Environments Shape Mental, Social, and Physical Health

"There is no such thing as a neutral environment."
—Sarah Williams Goldhagen

The average American spends 15 percent of his or her lifetime in primary and secondary school. Children and adolescents spend the majority of their waking hours there. Where we live, go to school, work, and socialize shapes how our minds and bodies function and how we relate to the world. Children and teenagers need positive and supportive school environments as they struggle to navigate their lives and futures. Overwhelming anxiety now affects nearly two-thirds of young adults.[1] It has surpassed depression as the number one reason college students seek counseling. And suicide is now the leading cause of death for children and youth aged ten to eighteen.

In a recent survey of Los Angeles public school students, 50 percent of students screened suffered from moderate to severe post-traumatic stress disorder.[2] Trauma-informed education is growing as a teaching approach as more school districts acknowledge that the majority of students today have experienced at least one childhood trauma impacting their ability to learn. A groundbreaking study by the Centers for Disease Control and Prevention found that nearly two-thirds of participants had endured at least one adverse childhood experience.[3]

The school environment—the organization and physical materials that make up a school—offers a powerful yet overlooked way to support everyone who learns, works, or otherwise finds themself there. Plenty of evidence shows that nature-filled environments support mental health and well-being. But few designers, and even fewer school decision makers and educators, appear to be aware of the research. Instead, schools too often present harsh environments with imposing fences, locking gates, window grates, and security cameras. These types of places don't feel safer—they amplify students' stress, anxiety, and trauma.

Supporting Trauma-Informed Education

Scientists' understanding of the human brain has changed in recent decades to reveal a vital connection between our minds, our bodies, and the environments we inhabit. This mind-body-environment relationship means our mental health is connected to our physical health and the health of the environment we live in. All three shape who we are and how healthy we can be.

Psychologist Stephen Porges's polyvagal theory explains why. His work connects post-traumatic stress disorder, autism, depression, and anxiety with the autonomic nervous system through the vagus nerve. This principal nerve transmits feelings of emotional well-being through our bodies to regulate our heart rate, breathing, and digestive rhythms. It also works in the other direction: when our breathing and heart rate are regular and calm and our stomach is relaxed, the vagus nerve conveys feelings of safety to our brains. When we are overwhelmed or stressed, our heart rate goes up, our breathing quickens, and our stomach feels tight. And in reverse, when our stomach aches or our heart rate goes up, we don't feel safe.

Often, our bodies react to trauma and anxiety without our being aware of what is happening or why. We jump at the slightest noise or movement. We feel on edge while riding in a car, waiting for an accident to happen. We can't sleep or relax. These signs of hypervigilance—being supersensitive to our surroundings—are symptoms of anxiety, post-traumatic stress disorder, and other anxiety-related disorders. Even if we don't identify or remember the cause, our bodies do. Children and adolescents live with trauma that builds up in their bodies over time. Sometimes they remember the original physical or emotional trauma or traumas, and sometimes they don't. Many remain unaware of the cause for their entire lives. We see the effects of trauma as aggression, irritability, skipping school, or "checking out." This is our bodies' "fight, flight, or freeze" response. While it is easy to visualize what a fight-or-flight response might look like, a freeze response is harder to recognize. Freeze is a state of numbness or of feeling stuck in one or more parts of the body. People in freeze often seem cooperative, quiet, or contemplative. Or they might have a hard time hearing you. Students who get in trouble for not paying attention could be in freeze. Since the likelihood is that students have endured one or more childhood traumas, trauma-informed educators suggest supporting all students as if they are impacted by trauma.[4]

We can help children and teenagers by creating calming places where they have opportunities to both be alone and connect with other people or living beings to settle their fight, flight, or freeze response. Environments that help calm the nervous system help students feel safe.

Breaking the School-to-Prison Pipeline

In *Welcome to Your World*, Sarah Williams Goldhagen states that characteristics of a school's built environment account for 25 percent of a student's learning progress. The higher the quality of a school's design, materials, and maintenance, the better students learn and succeed in school. If the quality of a school's environment accounts for one-quarter of learning progress, imagine the difference between well-designed and poorly designed environments on mental health in general. Students living in higher-poverty and higher-crime neighborhoods suffer from both more trauma and environments with fewer natural resources such as trees and gardens that can reduce stress and provide respite. These same students, more than anyone, need calming, welcoming school environments that build community around them. Yet schools with high numbers of traumatized students, who often act out their trauma in the fight response, become easy targets for reactive and punitive measures to control students rather than nurture them. Inequitable planning, financing, policing, and education decisions have led to today's inequitable school conditions. Students in marginalized communities attend overcrowded, overpoliced, and fenced-in schools where the most common descriptors from students, teachers, and community members alike is "It feels like a prison."

This creates a cycle of trauma. Students living in neighborhoods overwhelmed by exposure to noise, light, and pollution are more likely to attend schools with harsh environments. They come to school tired, on edge, hypervigilant, and more prone to reach the limits of their stress and trauma thresholds and act out. Their school environment makes things worse. If they act out or skip school or behave in the least bit unruly, the school police are there to take them to juvenile hall. Students are ticketed for being late to school, skipping school, or possessing cigarettes, vape pens, marijuana, or alcohol. What could be seen as common teenage behaviors become life-changing events for students and their families when the juvenile justice system stands in lieu of mentoring, counseling, restorative justice, or health interventions.[5]

The design of school environments is an important, and too often overlooked, aspect of working toward racial and environmental justice and breaking the school-to-prison pipeline. The physical environments we move through and inhabit every day are just one piece of a complex mix of factors that determine our mental health and well-being. But they make an enormous impact on the quality of our lives. Public schools make up the most stable and widespread land use and serve diverse and vulnerable populations. They are an important place to start reversing social and environmental injustices.

Applying Evidence-Based Design

Nature-filled schools with hands-on and active learning and play opportunities calm students, reduce aggressive behavior, and improve learning outcomes. Being in nature helps students play cooperatively and creatively. Neighborhoods and schools with more trees have less crime and stronger social ties than neighborhoods and schools with less.[6] By remaking schools to become welcoming, healthy, safe, and productive, we create models for students and the community to experience, learn from, and emulate in the larger world. While it sounds like common sense, these design solutions are not commonly applied. Too often, concerns about cost and long-term maintenance of supportive school environments take priority over student needs. Tight school budgets set up feelings of scarcity and competition for limited resources. Yet we can create safer, nature-filled, more beautiful school environments for the same or less money than hardened facilities and with greater chances that students and the community will take better care of them. Schools can become social and physical safety nets at the heart of our communities.

Environmental psychologist Roger Ulrich first coined the phrase "evidence-based design" in his 1984 study showing that hospital patients healed faster and needed less pain medication if they were in a room with a green view. This is one of many studies that connect nature-filled environments or exposure to nature with mental health and well-being as well as physical health. Expanding on his hospital view study, Ulrich went on to discover that the environmental conditions of psychiatric facilities impacted patient aggression. His theory of supportive design suggests that perceived control, social support, and positive distraction are integral to a patient's well-being. The study proposed a bundle of design elements to reduce patient aggression. Primary factors are nature-filled environments and a sense of belonging.

Attention Restoration Theory

For over fifty years, psychologists Rachel and Stephen Kaplan studied which environments people preferred and how those environments affected them. Their attention restoration theory aligns with Ulrich's work, finding that access to nature reduces stress and supports mental health and well-being. It sheds light on the types of places that make people feel most comfortable or most at home. Working with landscape architect Robert L. Ryan, the Kaplans translated their research into designable themes and spatial patterns for restorative environments—those places that best restore people's minds after stress or mental fatigue.

The following are examples of restorative environments:

- Places that offer quiet fascination
- Places that separate us from distraction
- Places that allow us to wander in small spaces
- Places that contain materials with soft and natural textures, such as cloth, wood, stone, or weathered old materials
- Indoor places that have windows with views out to nature

To be most effective, these places should give the sense of being far away, in a setting that is large enough or designed in such a way as to hide its boundaries. A restorative place offers fascination, such as a natural setting where we can see or hear leaves or water moving or watch wildlife. And the place needs to be designed or situated so that it allows us to do what we want to do there, for instance, sit, think, eat, read, walk, or be alone.

The design strategies that support students' mental health and well-being can be organized around three general themes (which are explored in more detail in the next chapter): nurture a sense of belonging, provide nature-filled environments, and inspire awe. While these themes overlap and intersect, they help us to begin visualizing specific opportunities to create more supportive school environments.

Nurture a Sense of Belonging

Belonging happens when we feel valued as part of a community. We cannot thrive in places that don't make us feel welcomed, valued, and as if we belong. University of Illinois landscape architecture professors Ming Kuo and William C. Sullivan studied two enormous and infamous Chicago public housing developments—Ida B. Wells Homes and Robert Taylor Homes—to look for the differences a landscape can make. Ida B. Wells Homes was made up of 124 two- to four-story apartment buildings laid out in a grid. Robert Taylor Homes had 28 identical sixteen-story apartment buildings laid out in a single three-mile-long line. The buildings in each development were exactly the same, and people were randomly assigned to each apartment. The only differences were whether the common spaces had trees or not. "Compared to residents living adjacent to relatively barren spaces," they concluded, "individuals living adjacent to green common spaces reported that they had more social activities and more visitors, knew more of their neighbors, felt their neighbors were more concerned with helping and supporting one another, and had stronger feelings of belonging."[7]

The common areas with shade trees invited people to come outside, make a place for themselves, and get to know their neighbors. The more trees there were and the closer the trees were to the apartment buildings, the more people gathered beneath them. This gathering led to stronger community ties and safer neighborhoods. There was another effect that strengthened with the number of trees: both in homes and in the neighborhood, aggression dropped as the number of trees went up. The safest neighborhoods were those with the most trees. The most barren neighborhoods had the most crime. Similar patterns are seen on high school campuses.[8]

Once we understand the relationships between environment and mental health and behavior, we can design schools that support students instead of sabotaging them. Trees and gardens and outdoor learning can support academic success, too. Not all students learn well from classroom lectures. Students who struggle to learn from lectures and reading often thrive in hands-on learning experiences and outdoor settings. An important outcome of experiential or outdoor learning is that it gives teachers a chance to see students who struggle in a classroom succeed and even thrive when they learn outside or in another hands-on environment. This allows both student and teacher to see the student in a new light, with strengths in different contexts. Teachers' positive or negative perceptions of a student can affect a student's self-esteem, motivation, and academic behavior.[9] See box 2.1 for evidence of how outdoor learning can change teachers' perceptions of students.

Imagine the lifelong impact on students once defined by their challenges to feel and be perceived as successful. Students who don't perform well have incredible strengths that simply don't show up in traditional classrooms.[10] Providing a variety of places where students can interact with and learn from the environment in a variety of ways will give more students the sense that they belong in school. A stronger sense of belonging could improve attendance, high school graduation rates, and the number of students who attend college. Supporting and encouraging teachers to learn to teach in outdoor classrooms and experiential learning environments will help even more.

Provide Nature-full Environments

As mentioned at the beginning of the chapter, the benefits of outdoor learning extend far beyond changing teacher perception and creating a sense of belonging. Nature-filled environments improve mental and physical health as well. Just fifteen years after Ulrich's first study, the therapeutic garden movement took hold in health care, helped in large part by Clare Cooper Marcus and Marni Barnes's book *Healing Gardens: Therapeutic Benefits and Design Recommendations*. The Chicago Botanic Garden's Healthcare Garden Design Certificate program drives a growing number of gardens in

Box 2.1: Changing Perceptions of Students by Teaching Outdoors

In her 2019 landscape architecture master's thesis, Lisa Strong asked nineteen teachers to participate in an outdoor learning intervention.* Strong designed the intervention to determine how outdoor learning might change students' learning outcomes as well as teachers' perceptions of students and students' perceptions of themselves. The outdoor learning intervention consisted of teaching a thirty-minute session outdoors twice a week for twelve weeks.

Statement	Before			After		
	True	Sometimes	Not True	True	Sometimes	Not True
Learning in the outdoors could help students become more academically engaged at school.	78%	22%	0	100%	0	0
Learning in the outdoors could help struggling students become more engaged at school.	50%	50%	0	100%	0	0

Question	Bounce Back	Work Harder	Give Up Too Quickly	Get Overwhelmed
How do academically struggling students face setbacks? (Before teaching outdoors)	0	0	100%	0
How do academically struggling students face setbacks? (After teaching outdoors)	60%	40%	0	0
How do academically struggling students face setbacks? (After returning to the classroom)	75%	12%	0	13%

*Lisa Strong, "Classrooms without Walls: A Study in Outdoor Learning Environments to Enhance Academic Motivation for K–5 Students" (master's thesis, California State Polytechnic University, Pomona, 2019).

hospitals, nursing homes, and other health-care settings. The same qualities of nature and natural views that aid healing and make for faster recovery times also support students' mental and physical health and well-being. Research specific to school and community environments points to the poignant effect of trees and nature on students and community members. See box 2.2 for design principles for healing gardens.

Inside and outside the classroom, building materials affect how well a student learns, behaves, and socializes. A 2015 study by the University of Salford in Manchester, England,[11] found that students in the best-designed classrooms were a year ahead of students in the worst-designed classrooms after just one year. Accounting for nearly half of the students' progress was classroom "naturalness," including quality of light, air quality, and room temperature. Other factors were whether students felt a sense of owner-ship in the room, room flexibility, color, and the visual complexity of the room. Another study found that larger classroom windows with views of trees helped students recover from stress and do better on tests than smaller classroom windows or views of buildings, parking lots, or grass fields.[12] A study of high school environments connected campuses with plenty of trees breaking up the large spaces with less student crime, less disorderly conduct, and more students planning to attend a four-year college.[13] And a before-and-after comparison of Eagle Rock Elementary School's schoolyard improvement project (see chapter 7) showed that more students engaged in physical activity, creative and collaborative play, and positive social behav-iors in new nature-filled schoolyard spaces than they did when the school-yard was mostly asphalt.[14] It's important to note that schoolyards with living grass—unless the grass is also planted with trees—didn't invite cre-ativity or collaboration or reduce disorderly conduct and student crime.[15] Wide-open spaces, whether they are made up of grass, asphalt, concrete, or synthetic turf, don't provide a sense of safety or comfort.

Inspire Awe

The third theme in the research connecting place and mental health involves that elusive quality that sparks the imagination and curiosity: awe.

"When it comes to the built environments people inhabit, there is no such thing as neutral," Sarah Williams Goldhagen wrote. "If a park, or a hos-pital waiting room, or a streetscape, or a neighborhood, or a workplace isn't

Box 2.2: Design Principles for Healing Gardens

According to landscape architect Clare Cooper Marcus, emeritus professor at the University of California, Berkeley, and an expert on healing gardens, some things require special attention when designing for places for healing. I've adapted the following design principles in Marcus's article "Healing Gardens for Hospitals" for school environments.*

Marcus begins with a brief summary of Roger Ulrich's theory of supportive design.

- Create opportunities for physical movement and exercise. A looped pathway with choices of a long or short walk is ideal.
- Provide opportunities to make choices, seek privacy, and experience a sense of control. The ability to make choices helps patients feel a sense of autonomy.
- Provide settings that encourage people to gather together and experience social support. People with strong support networks feel less stressed than those who are isolated.
- Provide access to nature and other positive distractions.

"Nature attracts our attention without depleting the body of energy," Marcus writes. "A healing garden can have the effect of awakening the senses, calming the mind, reducing stress, and assisting a person to marshal their own inner healing resources." She then distills decades, worth of her own research, observations, surveys, and interviews to create a list of strategies to bring a garden to its fullest healing potential:

- Visibility. Make sure people know the garden is there.
- Accessibility. Consider the needs of all users, including visiting parents and grandparents, people pushing strollers, and users of wheelchairs—make sure there is room for two wheelchairs to pass on a path.
- Familiarity. Base the garden's aesthetic on the local ecology or culture to bring familiarity and comfort to the garden.
- Quiet. Air conditioners, traffic, and maintenance equipment will disturb users. Welcome birdsong, wind chimes, or water sounds.

- Comfort. People need to feel physically and psychologically secure. Carefully plan handrails, seating, and paths for safety and convenience, and make sure paving and furniture do not create glare. People should be able to sit in sun or shade and feel they could take a nap undisturbed.
- Unambiguously positive art. Any art or sculpture should be positive, such as images of water, landscapes, or nature, and should help relieve stress.

*Clare Cooper Marcus, "Healing Gardens for Hospitals," *Interdisciplinary Design and Research eJournal* 1, no. 1, *Design and Health* (January 2007), accessed July 31, 2020, https://intogreen.nl/wp-content /uploads/2017/07/cooper_marcus.pdf.

designed in a way that inspires users and bypassers, that doesn't support what they need or what they do, then they are quite literally inhibiting cognitive development, eroding people's sense of well-being, compromising their physical and mental health. Poorly designed built environments impoverish people's lives."[16] Nowhere is this more important and impactful than in schools. Environments that reach beyond the ordinary and invite a child to wonder at the world invoke awe. This is the realm of sunsets and mountain peaks, silvery slug slime glinting in the sun, or a trumpet and trombone serenade over a foggy field. It can manifest as anything that we marvel at, awestruck. Richard Louv—author of *Last Child in the Woods*—calls it the wonder of nature, drawing out the curiosity within us. The Berkeley Social Interaction Laboratory found that awe—feelings of reverential respect mixed with fear or wonder—has the power to inspire, heal, make us happier and nicer, and connect people to one another. Project Awe found that 75 percent of awe is inspired by the natural world.[17] Nature and its processes provide that critical sense of wonder and awe that sparks creativity and imagination. But music and art can bring it, and so can live sporting events, uniting us in amazement over human agility and performance.

Beauty awes us. Landscape architecture scholar Elizabeth Meyer wrote of the "somatic, sensory experiences of places that lead to new awareness of the rhythms and cycles necessary to sustain and regenerate life."[18] She named this "sustainable beauty"—the phenomenal beauty created by places that are ecologically aligned with the natural, cultural, and historical processes that frame them. Rather than superficial qualities of applied order, sustainable beauty occurs when design taps into and works with natural flows and processes instead of against them. Sustainable beauty can be achieved in a number of ways. John T. Lyle—founder and designer of the Center for Regenerative Studies at California State Polytechnic University, Pomona—advocated for deep form "shaped by the interactions of inner ecological process and human vision, which make the underlying order visible and meaningful in human terms."[19] Planning facilitator James Rojas supplies toys and small everyday items such as hair curlers, small containers, and silk and plastic flowers to help workshop participants visualize and build their ideal communities. He starts by asking people to build their favorite childhood places. In the decades he has run these workshops, he said, "they are almost always outside in nature."[20]

Nancy Striniste, author of *Nature Play at Home: Creating Outdoor Spaces That Connect Children with the Natural World*, gets to the heart of the matter. "I've been thinking a lot about joy," she told me.[21] Striniste's public play spaces are full of small whimsies such as leaf prints pressed in pathways, child-sized tunnels, and tree parts "arranged" for climbing. We were working on the National COVID-19 Outdoor Learning Initiative, a partnership of Green Schoolyards America, the San Mateo County Office of Education, Ten Strands, and the Lawrence Hall of Science at the University of California, Berkeley. Even for the temporary outdoor classroom and learning areas the initiative advocates for, it is important to consider how a design will spark joy, creativity, imagination, or awe. You never know how long a temporary classroom or other structure will be on a school site. So many schools still house "temporary" modular classrooms placed there ten, twenty, and even thirty years ago.

When was the last time you felt joy or awe in a school environment? What if schools were full of places that could become favorite childhood memories?

I've discussed remaking the physical environments of schools to support students' mental health and well-being with many people over the past five years. Usually, they say, "Of course! This makes sense." And then they wonder why they hadn't thought of it before. We all want to be in places that make us feel welcome. We crave human connection and beauty. We need places that let us orient to our surroundings, make sense of where we are, and feel that we belong.

Occasionally, I hear a different response, usually from those deeply entrenched in school district administrative roles or responsible for the thankless task of budgeting school improvements. They might say, "But children are resilient," or "I played on asphalt as a kid, and I did fine." The overwhelming evidence is that while children and adolescents are resilient, they are up against astonishing amounts of stress and trauma in their lives today. And, for many students in marginalized groups, going to school means an entirely different set of social and physical school standards: unjust, inequitable, less nurturing. While healthy children under normal amounts of stress might do well academically in stark school environments, they will do even better in schools designed to support them. It is frankly a wonder that so many students succeed at all in the environments we give them. Imagine how many more would survive, succeed, and thrive in beautiful, welcoming, calming school spaces.

It is hard to overstate the potential impacts that mentally healthy public schools could have on children, families, communities, and the future of our society. Ninety percent of students go to public schools. In the United States, over 50 million students attended nearly 100,000 public schools in 2019. While they are still few and far between, more and more schools, districts, and public agencies around the country and the world are working to create calmer, more restorative school environments. Designing schools that heal works in cities, suburbs, and rural areas, in small schools and large, and in poor and wealthy places serving any number of students. The following chapters share evidence-based design strategies that have worked in the biggest metropolitan school districts—such as New York and Los Angeles—to smaller suburban schools healing from unimaginable loss, such as Sandy Hook Elementary School. Students deserve nurturing, nature-filled, and inspiring school environments that can help them heal, learn, and flourish.

CHAPTER 3

Site Design Strategies to Support Mental Health, Safety, and Well-being

The principal design idea behind schools that heal is to work with nature and natural processes to create healthier places using fewer resources. (This approach has been called sustainable design, ecological design, regenerative design, biophilic design, design with nature, and nature-based design, among other terms.) Nature-based design works with and renews or regenerates nature's gifts instead of ignoring or working against them. For instance, buildings designed to bring in natural breezes and sunlight, as well as absorb heat during the day and radiate warmth at night, use less energy for heating, cooling, and lighting (and thus result in lower electricity bills). These same design elements give people access to nature's healing properties.

Strategically planted trees can intercept and absorb rainwater, filter air pollution particles, increase habitat for birds and pollinators and other animals, shade streets and outdoor places, store carbon and nutrients, reduce noise pollution, build soil health, improve human health, cool neighborhoods, bring people together, and reduce stress and aggression. These examples demonstrate the multiple benefits of nature-based design strategies. Similar to nature-based strategies that build on and renew natural systems, strategies that come from within the community they serve build on existing social ties and networks and take less energy and fewer resources to keep

27

going. Community-led solutions harness the deep knowledge of community members to build strong relationships between people, nature, and design solutions. I'll use the terms "community-led" and "nature-based" to convey these ideas throughout the rest of the book.

This chapter introduces community-led, nature-based design strategies that support mental health, safety, and well-being. These strategies are organized into the three themes introduced in chapter 2: nurture a sense of belonging, create nature-filled environments, and inspire awe. They were developed for existing schools in landlocked city neighborhoods, but they will work for new schools and those in rural areas and suburban communities, too. Any school, no matter when or how it was designed and on what budget, can improve its environment to support students' mental health, feelings of safety, and well-being. The strategies that follow overlap, intertwine, and can be difficult to draw clean boundaries around. This is because community-led, nature-based systems are integrated and holistic. They address multiple issues. I've selected examples and images that best convey each strategy while providing multiple, layered benefits—an intended outcome of community-led, nature-based design. Each strategy includes examples arranged in order of their level of physical change. For instance, if a design strategy can be implemented through shifts in thinking as well as in small- or large-scale physical changes, the examples are listed in that order: shifts in thinking, small-scale physical changes, larger-scale physical changes. If a strategy includes only one or two levels of intervention, it is listed as such. For readers outside of the design fields, see the Resources section after chapter 9 for additional guidance on design approaches and processes.

Nurture a Sense of Belonging

Designers can nurture a sense of belonging by engaging people in the design process and by designing places that bring people together and meet their individual needs. The physical environment can be designed with welcoming and easy-to-navigate places that provide comfort for anyone who might use them. Schools that nurture a sense of belonging support positive social interaction to help build a community around each student. They also provide decent and appropriate places for all students to learn, rest, play, eat, socialize, and be alone.

1. Conduct an Inclusive Design Process
Shifts in Thinking

Typically, school planning and design leaves out those most impacted by the design. We need to include the people who are in school every day to design solutions that will support and nurture them. For many designers, the community engagement process is the most challenging and stressful part of design. Few design programs offer training in community engagement or participatory design. When done well, participatory design honors the deep knowledge and unique experiences of the community to give the design team broader and more meaningful information to consider in their design. Success depends on entering the process with a humble attitude, free from assumptions of what the school needs.

Most public schools serve students with a wide range of learning and developmental differences and mental and physical health conditions and abilities, whether in integrated classrooms or in separate areas of the campus. It is important to identify and understand any prevalent patterns or conditions that are present in your school community. The design team should seek out and collaborate with those working closely with students, including school psychologists, social workers, occupational therapists, trauma therapists, special education teachers, and other experts in educational and mental health practices. An inclusive, community-based process gives students, teachers, parents, and the entire school community a design voice and has the greatest chance of creating a school environment that supports students' mental health, safety, and well-being.

Architect Gabrielle Bullock, director of global diversity for Perkins&Will, advised making sure the design team represents the community you are working in. "And if you can't," she said, "do your research and engage the community as a design partner."[1] No matter who you are, it is important to educate yourself on your biases when it comes to school environments, student and community populations, and design aesthetics. This can be difficult, especially for designers with strong and established styles. Ego needs to take a back seat to students' needs.

Start with a community engagement plan. Make a schedule, organize your team and materials, and plan activities to invite community participation and gather knowledge in a meaningful way. Have a backup plan (or two) in case things don't go according to plan. They never completely do. Whether you conduct large community workshops, small focus groups, digital surveys, or one-on-one interviews, start by listening. Engage students, teachers, administrators, facilities and maintenance teams, and anyone else who regularly uses the campus. School nurses, occupational therapists, special education teachers, and others who support the socio-emotional well-being of students can offer crucial insights into student, teacher, and staff needs. Often, school projects begin with a community or parent group trying to improve the conditions for their own children. Sometimes, parents who are architects, landscape architects, designers, or contractors lead or are invited to join the process. In this case, it is especially important to engage students, teachers, the principal, and a broader sample of parents and community members to make sure improvements have champions after the children of the parents who originally participated in the plan age out of the school.

Parent and community groups can invite environmental or community nonprofit organizations to organize and lead the design process. They can help define the project area, program, budget, and timeline and often can employ community organizers to lead the process. They can also help identify and apply for grant funding. If you are leading the community engagement process yourself, as a member of the school community or as a designer with little to no community engagement experience, research participatory design or codesign methods. (See the Resources section after chapter 9.)

If the improvement project came through a consulting contract between a school district and a design team, request and build in a community process. In all project types, be transparent and open with the reason for the new design, the areas it will impact, the budget and timeline, and other information you might have. Share whether the improvements center on accessibility, or building code updates, or stormwater management, or other goals. Be clear about the main project goals and the decision process for including other goals. Convey optimism but don't overpromise. This can lead to disappointment and resentment if improvements don't come through or are delayed.

Once you've heard from the community, share your findings. Find the patterns and themes in their statements and share them back to the community to make sure you've heard them correctly. Then you can begin honing the design goals and strategies that will best serve your school community. Maintain the community's participation, interest, and trust with clear and consistent communication throughout the design and construction process. See box 3.1 for an inside look at codesigning with three different school communities.

2. Create a Welcoming Entry and Edges

The way a school looks and feels on the outside is a signal to students, teachers, and the broader community of what happens inside. For David Yusem, Oakland Unified School District's Restorative Justice program manager, the first word that came to mind when asked what the students' ideal school would look like was "welcoming." He said, "From the second you approach the school, whether you're a student or a parent, it would have to feel welcoming, and there would have to be opportunities for people to welcome you."[2]

Shifts in Thinking

Inviting community members to participate in supporting students can promote a sense of pride and ownership in the school for the entire neighborhood. There are a number of ways schools can leverage community volunteers to benefit students, the volunteers, and the community as a whole:

- Partner with local senior centers to send volunteers to read to younger students and tutor older students.
- Schools that have community gardens or horticulture gardens or quiet, out-of-the-way spaces may need support in supervising those areas in order to let students use them. Encourage community members to volunteer on campus to provide more adult oversight and introduce themselves to students who appear lonely or in need of positive guidance. Note that it is important to train campus volunteers and playground monitors on your school's approach to creating a sense of

Continued on page 38

Box 3.1: Designing with Students: An Inside View

Our Cal Poly Pomona (CPP) Master of Landscape Architecture (MLA) program focuses on regenerative, nature-based planning and design. In the spring of 2020, we partnered with three schools to create community-led, nature-based landscape master plans. I sent out a call to local nonprofit land trusts, public health organizations, school district administrators, and others working to improve school environments asking for schools that were seeking design help. Selected schools had their principal's approval, at least one teacher champion, and students committed to a healthier school environment. In the first week of our semester, teams of three or four CPP graduate students introduced themselves to their school communities over e-mail or Zoom videoconferencing and set up their first in-person meeting dates.

We used *Design as Democracy: Techniques for Collective Creativity** to shape their step-by-step plans for working with their school communities. The book is a collection of methods developed by experts in participatory community engagement. In addition to using strategies from the book, some students selected qualitative and quantitative research methods from Professor Susan Mulley's research methods class to test over the course of the semester. The CPP teams worked with three Los Angeles County schools: Willard Elementary School in East Pasadena, Cleveland Charter High School in Reseda, and Bridges Academy in Studio City. The two public schools are in high-need, predominantly Hispanic neighborhoods. Bridges Academy is a private fourth- through twelfth-grade school serving

FIGURE 3.1A: Cal Poly Pomona (CPP) Master of Landscape Architecture (MLA) student Jose Guadalupe Gutierrez interviews Willard Elementary School Green Team students about what they like and don't like about their campus.

FIGURE 3.1B: CPP MLA students (from left) Adrian Chi Tenney, Phil Gann, and Robert Douglass work with Bridges Academy students and teachers to analyze their school campus.

"twice exceptional" students—those with high academic ability coupled with learning or developmental differences such as attention deficit hyperactivity disorder (ADHD), autism, dyslexia, or sensory processing disorder.

The teams completed their site visits (see figures 3.1a and 3.1b) and were able to work directly with the students at least once before the coronavirus pandemic sent us all to work from home halfway through the semester. Follow-up questions, teacher surveys, and some student-driven analysis happened over e-mail and online surveys. At the end of the semester, CPP students shared their draft campus landscape master plans via videoconferencing with their school partners. After they received feedback and revised the plans, we connected the schools with local nonprofits that might help them look for planning or implementation grants.

Willard Elementary School

The Willard Elementary School Green Team of first through fifth graders is led by second-grade teacher Ingrida Grabis. The CPP team asked the Green Team for a tour of their most favorite and least favorite places on campus. On the tour, the CPP students took detailed notes of the Green Team's observations about their campus: the gopher holes that riddled the play field, the hot and smelly cafeteria area, the favored bouncy piece of the play set, and many more. Back in the classroom, the CPP team guided Willard students through a paper survey. The survey asked them to write and draw what they liked best and liked least about the campus (see figure 3.1c). Students colored maps by marking the places they liked green and the places they didn't like red. Then they drew pictures of their most and least favorite places, talking through

Box 3.1: Continued on next page

Box 3.1: Continued

AREAS STUDENTS LIKED MOST AND LIKE LEAST

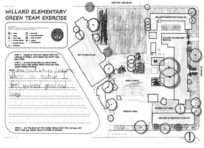

FIGURE 3.1C *(left)*: CPP MLA students created a survey to collect the deep knowledge, experiences, and preferences of Willard Elementary students. Image: CPP MLA/Willard Elementary students.

FIGURE 3.1D *(below)*: The diagram displays the compiled responses of students surveyed. Image: Michelle Shanahan, CPP MLA.

AREAS STUDENTS LIKED MOST AND LIKE LEAST

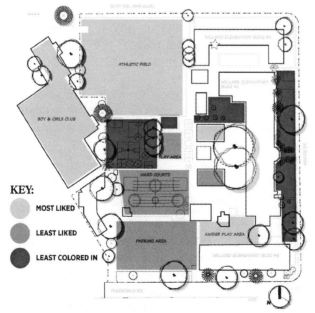

their decisions with the CPP team. At the end of the exercise, the CPP team led a class conversation so that students could share what they wrote and drew. Mrs. Grabis was vital to the process, rewording phrases she thought might be difficult for the elementary school students and asking questions to clarify as needed. After the student surveys were collected, the CPP team drafted a teacher survey which Principal Angela Baxter sent via e-mail. The CPP team analyzed student and teacher survey responses to find patterns and opportunities. They then presented a draft site analysis, community survey results, and design concepts to get feedback before creating their master plan (see figures 3.1d and 3.1e). Environmental non-profit Amigos de los Rios applied for grant funds to make the proposed improvements.

TEACHER RESPONSES

Which elements would you like to see in Willard's schoolyard?

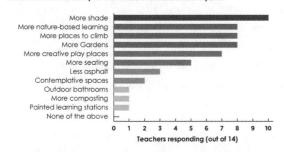

Teachers responding (out of 14)

FIGURE 3.1E: Willard Elementary teachers overwhelmingly asked for more shade, more gardens, more places for climbing and creative play, and more opportunities for nature-based learning. Image: Linley Green, CPP MLA.

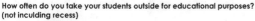

How often do you take your students outside for educational purposes? (not inculding recess)

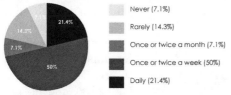

Never (7.1%)

Rarely (14.3%)

Once or twice a month (7.1%)

Once or twice a week (50%)

Daily (21.4%)

If given the right settings, how often would you take your students outside for educational purposes? (not inculding recess)

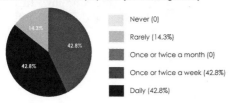

Never (0)

Rarely (14.3%)

Once or twice a month (0)

Once or twice a week (42.8%)

Daily (42.8%)

Box 3.1: Continued on next page

Box 3.1: Continued

Cleveland Charter High School

Fifty or so Cleveland Charter High School student leaders and advocates from several campus environmental and social justice groups came together to form a Green Ribbon Coalition. Their goal was to improve their school environment and for their school to become a Green Ribbon School—a designation awarded to schools with high levels of environmental sustainability and environmental programming. The Cleveland students were especially interested in how their campus could better support mental health, bridge two distinct student populations—community students and students attending the Humanities Magnet within Cleveland Charter High School—and connect ecologically and symbolically to the adjacent Aliso Creek Wash. CPP students worked with the Green Ribbon Coalition's six core student leaders and two faculty advisors. They toured the campus and gained student insight into the primary physical and programming issues. A major issue was the lack of shade in a place that gets brutally hot many days of the school year, with an expected increase in days hotter than 100 degrees over the next twenty years.[†] The CPP team conducted interviews and surveyed students about

FIGURE 3.1F: Cleveland Charter High School students led CPP MLA students through their campus to point out issues and opportunities for improvements. Their survey answers helped CPP MLA students map the emotional geography of the campus. Image: Sarah Fisher, CPP MLA.

their perception of existing campus spaces and their dreams for a healthier future campus (see figure 3.1f). Each CPP student developed a draft campus landscape plan focused on increasing tree canopy and habitat and addressing flooding issues with nature-based stormwater design. The designs also created new places for students to seek respite, learn outside, and gather in shady spaces.

Bridges Academy

Bridges Academy was founded in the 1980s and remains one of the few schools devoted to creating a learning environment that encourages twice-exceptional students to explore their creative and intellectual curiosity on their own terms. The CPP MLA team worked with a seventh-grade sustainable campus design class and a high school architectural design class, several teachers, and a parent liaison. The seventh graders provided important insights into how students used campus places and how they felt about them. They conducted sun and shade studies, created water flow and flooding diagrams, and showed us where they ate lunch and hung out with their friends. Noise was a big issue. In the center of campus, a metal climbing dome acted as the main play feature, and older students complained of younger students playing too loudly there during classes. Traffic noise was a major deterrent for some students who wanted to use the generous tree-shaded north and south lawns. Students were also upset that a good portion of the north lawn had been replaced by mulch while they were on winter break, with no explanation. This is a good reminder of the importance of preparing students and teachers when a change is going to happen, preferably before it takes place. Most of us need a little warning when our world is going to shift, even when the shift is positive.

Southern California's Mediterranean climate means months of no rain are followed by several months in winter of sometimes intense rain. It is always important to ask students and teachers what happens year-round and throughout the course of a day to get a better understanding of campus dynamics. If we hadn't specifically asked about flooding, we would not have discovered that one of the interior stairwells floods as deep as two feet during heavy rains.

Box 3.1: Continued on next page

Box 3.1: Continued

TEACHER AND STUDENT RESPONSES

Students Like:

Students Dislike:

Teachers Like:

Teachers Dislike:

FIGURE 3.1G: Bridges Academy student and teacher survey answers were organized into word clouds to highlight the most frequent responses. Image: Adrian Chi Tenney, CPP MLA.

CPP students gathered opinions from students, faculty, and staff through an e-mail survey sent out after the coronavirus pandemic sent students home (see figure 3.1g). They completed campus master plans that focused on creating a quieter campus edge and a diversity of spaces where students could play, learn, gather, and find respite throughout the day. (Bridges Academy is one of ten schools shared in more detail in chapter 7.)

*David de la Peña et al., eds., *Design as Democracy: Techniques for Collective Creativity* (Washington, DC: Island Press, 2017).

†Fengpeng Sun, Daniel B. Walton, and Alex Hall, "A Hybrid Dynamical-Statistical Downscaling Technique. Part II: End-of-Century Warming Projections Predict a New Climate State in the Los Angeles Region," *Journal of Climate* 28, no. 12 (2015): 4618–4636, https://doi.org/10.1175/JCLI-D-14-00197.1.

belonging. Research shows that reducing or eliminating rules regarding play areas fosters greater student responsibility and positive social behavior. See strategy 10, "Make Space for All Students (and Everyone) to Play Freely in Nature."

- Develop partnerships with city parks and recreation departments so that school playgrounds, athletic facilities, swimming pools, and fields can double as community parks to serve the community year-round.
- Encourage the school and the greater community to use the school grounds at all hours of the day and all days of the week.
- Hire local artists, craftspeople, and business experts to work with and

mentor students by building and creating together. This will create a support network around students and their families, connect them to the greater community, and give them an inside look at potential careers to strive for.

The more students and the community feel a sense of belonging and ownership in the school, the more they will take responsibility in caring for and watching over it. Senior community members of Littleton, Colorado; Kitsap, Washington; Avon Grove, Pennsylvania; and other school districts get a tax break by volunteering in their local public schools. In Washington, DC, the United Planning Organization runs a federally funded Foster Grandparent Program, which gives low-income residents over the age of fifty-five a small stipend to volunteer as mentors in area schools. The program requires an annual physical examination and training on how to recognize children who need help—those who are stressed or upset. Students and teachers win with Grandparents helping in classrooms, and Grandparents win by gaining vital community connections.

Small-Scale Physical Changes
Make sure students, families, and community members can see and identify the main entries from the surrounding neighborhoods. For entries located off the street, create signs or paint directional arrows with inviting words around the perimeter of campus. Improved visibility of entries and clean, well-tended entries and edges send a message to the community and the students entering that they matter.

Larger-Scale Physical Changes
When renovating an existing school or designing a new school, think about first-time students and their families trying to navigate unfamiliar territory (see figures 3.2a and 3.2b). A large entry facing the community can invite students and families into a lobby designed with clear directions to administration and attendance offices. Minimize fences and the appearance of security controls. Clear windows from spacious and warm entry halls convey a message of invitation and hospitality. Think about design strategies for the school perimeter that convey

FIGURE 3.2A: The original 1920s-era Eagle Rock Junior/Senior High School campus faced the community with a generous and clear entry sequence. Image: Eagle Rock Valley Historical Society.

FIGURE 3.2B: Eagle Rock Junior/Senior High School campus, 2017. A campus renovation in the 1970s to improve earthquake safety resulted in the main entry moving to the back of the campus and construction of a community-facing edge lined in chain-link and steel pipe fencing.

warmth and spark a feeling of "I want to go there!" in children of all ages. We want the smallest children to dream of going to their neighborhood school when they're old enough, and school-age children to be proud of their school and excited to attend.

3. Organize Space Logically, Legibly, and Humanely

Small-Scale Physical Changes

Students struggling with overwhelm, stress, or sensory integration are sensitive to noise and visual chaos and need clear pathways and transitions between activity levels. As with creating a welcoming entry and perimeter, aim to make it effortless for students, parents, and visitors to navigate into and through campus. Signs, color-coded paths, and symbols can guide people to the main office, auditorium, community rooms, and athletic facilities. Carefully consider navigating the school from the perspective of a new student or someone experiencing overwhelm. The easier it is to find the front office, classrooms, the library, the lunchroom, and the other places they see on their schedules, the more at ease students will feel navigating campus. As students get older and need to find their way to different classrooms on their own, this notion of a wayfinding system is just as important. Try to remove any obstacles to students and families getting where they want to go.

In existing schools where these rooms are located away from the perimeter, create visible pathways and signs to community spaces and event entries. A simple, inexpensive, and immediate method might be to paint footprints or follow-paths on walkways or walls, color-coded by their destination.

Larger-Scale Physical Changes

Egyptian architect Magda Mostafa developed the Autism ASPECTSS™ Design Index, an evidence-based design criterion for autism. The index can be used to design schools and other facilities to be welcoming and inclusive of all community members. Rather than excusing harsh school design as "preparing students for the mainstream," we need to mainstream comfortable, homey schools where all students feel they belong. Mostafa's seven criteria are Acoustics, SPatial sequencing, Escape space, Compartmentalization, Transitions, Sensory zoning, and Safety.[3]

A main idea of ASPECTSS is to arrange indoor and outdoor programs

FIGURE 3.3: The School of Arts and Enterprise rehabilitated a series of industrial and commercial buildings in downtown Pomona, California. The design is full of warm, homey details such as this wood and brick entry hall that opens into a student art gallery and music room.

by activity and noise level. For instance, place classroom buildings near the library and quiet gardens and away from athletic facilities, sports fields, music rooms, and the cafeteria to help students concentrate during lectures and tests. If lunch times are staggered, it is especially important that cafeterias and outdoor eating areas are located away from areas where students need to focus. Provide clear transitions between zones of different activity levels to ease sensitive students from one noise level to another.

Locate community rooms, auditoriums, and athletic facilities along perimeters, where they can be easily opened up after hours for events, recitals, and community gatherings. Sometimes the architecture itself can give students hope. Architect Nina Briggs specializes in humane design for health and well-being. She told me that certain things can bring on instant depression. A dead-end hallway, for example. Or a classroom with no windows. Design classrooms, corridors, and other indoor spaces with the intention of providing hope. "Clerestory windows give us hope," Briggs said. "Seeing natural light in unexpected places gives us hope."[4]

When I asked her to describe how she would design a school to best support mental health and well-being, she said, "It already exists . . . the Waverly School in Pasadena." The high school is a little cluster of six California Craftsman bungalow houses moved from elsewhere around Pasadena and placed around a central garden courtyard that is used for events and as an everyday student hangout. The school design is homey, student centered, and welcoming. No fences separate students from the outside world, and yet there is a feeling of enclosure and warmth that embraces you as you walk into campus. This is how school should feel: comfortable, personal, humane. If you think about school design the way you think about designing a home, Nina suggested, it opens up a new paradigm in your mind. Imagine all the positive messages you'd like students to be able to receive at school: to embrace lifelong learning, to love and care for one another and themselves, to tend to the natural world. How could a school be designed to convey those messages?

Major renovations and new schools can also be designed with consideration of long-term health and the possibility of long-term or frequent need for social distancing. Designing schools to handle the next pandemic will better serve students' and communities' mental health, physical health, and resilience.

4. Honor Students' Lived Experiences and Abilities

Students and community members of all different abilities and backgrounds need comfortable and appropriate learning and gathering spaces in school buildings and outdoor areas. One out of six children has a developmental disability. One out of six people has some form of visual disability. One in seventeen has deafness or hardness of hearing. And one out of one hundred requires a wheelchair. One out of seven people worldwide experiences disability in some form.[5] If the student population doesn't reflect these numbers, it is likely because the school's design or services neglects the needs of its disabled community.

Shifts in Thinking

Honoring students' lived experiences and abilities includes recognizing and reflecting students' unique and diverse identities, learning strengths, and physical abilities. In addition to including the school community in the design process, designers can research and develop cultural competency for the school communities they serve. Heterogeneous Futures founder Diana Fernandez writes that her work "is defined by 'unlearning' and making space for inclusive futures that embrace and celebrate our differences in the physical manifestation of place."[6]

The mostly Hispanic students and families in the Christopher Columbus Family Academy community didn't see the school's namesake, Columbus, as a hero figure. Architect Barry Svigals told me the neighborhood is "a largely Hispanic community with not so warm feelings about Columbus, unlike the largely Italian community that used to live in the neighborhood." Svigals facilitated a school advisory committee made up of community members.[7]

"They couldn't believe they were in the room," he said. This was the beginning of a process and design that honored the community and resulted in a deep sense of belonging and ownership in the school.

Similarly, engage the disabled community to develop site-specific universal design strategies. Create spaces that are accessible, comfortable, and predictable for students and community members who navigate with sensory, developmental, or mobility challenges. Work with the local disabled community, teachers, universal design experts, occupational therapists, physical therapists, and movement experts to understand the ways in which environments can include as broad a community as possible.

Most cities are home to people from many different places, races, and cultures, with different gender identities and abilities and nonconforming bodies. A person's identity is often layered and complex. This heightens the importance of inclusive design processes that honor students' lived experiences and provide safe spaces and processes to protect and nurture students' maturing and evolving identities. Those of us in older generations can learn from young people's embrace of gender identity, fluidity, and nonconformance.

Small-Scale Physical Changes

Occidental College health researcher Marcella Raney spoke with me about the big impacts simple changes can make. At Eagle Rock Elementary School, the grassy field with trees invites students to do many things that they couldn't do before, when it was asphalt. They cartwheel and somersault and run and jump. But Raney pointed out the simple act of sitting in the soft grass and then standing up as an important strength and skill to invite. This move is a key focus in physical therapy, she said, especially for older adults. The activities, movements, and environmental relationships children establish at a young age are likely to stay with them through their lifetimes. Understanding this may prompt teachers and school administrators to open or make use of campus areas that were previously underused, such as the grassy front or side yards of many campuses. Eagle Rock Elementary School gained use of a large, tree-shaded lawn on the side campus by asking the school district to fence the perimeter. (See chapter 7 for more detail.)

Larger-Scale Physical Changes

Remember the dramatic changes in teachers' perception of struggling students when they took students outside to learn, shared in chapter 2, box 2.1? Outdoor classrooms, arts and crafts studios, and indoor and outdoor laboratories engage students in hands-on, experiential learning suited for a broad range of learning styles. This educational approach isn't new. Friedrich Froebel's first kindergarten class in 1897 took place in a garden. Children cultivated their own little plots and were free to do with them whatever they liked. They learned science, math, the arts, social studies, and social responsibility through gardening.[8] Cal Poly Pomona, like many polytechnic universities, prioritizes this "learn by doing" approach for all subjects. Physics professors at Pomona College in Claremont, California, dreamed up a number of ways they could teach physics by engaging their students in physics demonstrations. They worked with landscape architecture firm EPTDESIGN to create a garden full of human-scaled physics experiments (see figure 3.4). In addition to teaching physics to their own students, the physics department hosts K–12 student field trips in their Physics Garden. Students learn how levers work on a bench that unlocks to become a seesaw. They see the difference an arc length makes by swinging on swings with shorter and longer chains. And they experiment with centrifugal forces and momentum on two spinning platforms designed to put students in motion to feel the forces at work.

In the case of the Christopher Columbus Family Academy, the community participation process led to a design that reframes Columbus and his journey to "America" as a focus on the forces of nature that affect us every day.

FIGURE 3.4: The Physics Garden at Pomona College in Claremont, California, was designed to reveal the path of rainwater flowing from the roofs and pavement and to provide experiential learning. Pomona students and younger students from area K–12 schools experience the forces they're learning about in this living laboratory garden. Design by EPTDESIGN.

"The ship that brought him here was blown by the winds across the Atlantic Ocean," Svigals said. "The design honored the winds by positioning the school in the four cardinal directions and creating sculptural wind elements to help students learn from which direction they enter." The design features kites (and electricity), hot-air balloons, and lessons on how air travel began and how the world was mapped. A new canopy shaped like a ship's bow presents a welcoming face to the street, with big glass doors opening into a two-story entry hall. The terrazzo flooring is patterned in constellations, furthering the narrative about navigation by stars.

"What's important is that Columbus Academy is in a setting that has ubiquitous violence," Svigals said. Unlike many schools that respond to neighborhood violence or the fear of violence with solid walls and fences creating a barrier between the school and the community, Columbus Academy fronts the street with large, clear windows and a welcoming entry, signaling to the community that this is their school. The design connects to the community by creating a transparent edge and by changing the narrative about Columbus from a powerful explorer to one whose voyage was steered by the winds, not him. School districts and parks departments might go a step further to honor communities by renaming places to reflect notable figures from or representing the community.

We can also honor students' lived experiences by designing to protect them from the harms of erasure, bullying, racism, and cultural blindness. For instance, bathrooms can be an issue in a number of ways: accessibility, gender fluidity, privacy, lack of visibility. The new Beacon View Primary School in Portsmouth, United Kingdom, was designed without closing bathrooms to eliminate a place where bullying frequently occurs. Mentally healthy bathroom designs improve visibility and safety, with trough sinks placed in a corridor rather than behind doors, and gender-neutral bathrooms. Restroom design, sanitary supplies, and maintenance are key to both emotional and physical health and can reduce the number of students who miss or skip school.[9] Mentally healthy design meets students' basic needs and helps remove any distractions that might prevent them from being able to learn. Efforts to improve access to basic needs include searching the campus to find opportunities to add fresh drinking water stations (fountains and bottle refill), rehabilitated bathrooms, lunchtime food share tables, private shower rooms, laundry stations and services, free clothes closets, and so forth. Anything that can support students' health, hygiene, and access to school supplies will in turn support their mental well-being and ability to learn.

5. Create Calming, Quiet Places and Cozy Spaces
Shifts in Thinking
Once children outgrow nap time at school, we tend to underestimate the importance of rest. Quiet spaces are probably the scarcest, most important places on school campuses. Students, like the rest of us, need places to go during times of stress, anxiety, or overwhelm to calm their systems and restore their ability to learn. Schools can provide places students or teachers can go to feel away from it all—the quality the Kaplans promote to restore well-being. It is important to remember that students often feel (and are) powerless over their environments and whether they attend school or not.

FIGURE 3.5: One of the quiet corners in every Beacon View Primary School classroom. In this one, the teacher hung fabric and leaf strands to give students the feeling of being in a forest fort.

Many students seek out and find small hidden corners, cozy spots beneath or behind trees and plants, or places a little out of the ever-present gaze of other humans, only to be told they aren't allowed to be there. Given the freedom, students of all ages will choose all kinds of places where teachers and supervisors usually ask them not to go. They stand on or in things such as trees or walls, tables, chairs, or desks where they can survey the landscape. They crawl under branches, shrubs, tables, desks, or benches where they can feel protected. They hide behind plants, walls, buildings, tree trunks, boxes, furniture, or other students where they can feel privacy. Bridges Academy art teacher Caroline Maxwell took a series of photos of students inhabiting such places, including in boxes and inside cabinets. We can support students by simply allowing them access to those out-of-the-way places. We can go a step further by creating spaces like this on purpose. At Beacon View Primary School, every classroom includes a quiet corner (see figure 3.5).

Small-Scale Physical Changes

Calming the visual environment helps, too. Though it's a common practice, classrooms cluttered with posters, visual aids, and years' worth of student work heighten anxiety and reduce calm. Try to reduce visual clutter inside classrooms and throughout campus. Remove competing posters, bulletins, and unnecessary classwork from the walls. Sliding, overlapping boards or flip charts can allow teachers to pull out pertinent exhibits when needed and store them when not in use to minimize visual chaos.

A simple change of color makes a difference. Inside and outside, public schools often scream "institution." Don't let your district management team mandate paint colors based solely on affordability. Use color theory and community preference to select colors that calm students and speak to their unique identities. Some colors universally evoke a sense of calm. The greens and blues of plants and trees and sky and sea convey a sense of calm and tranquility. While classrooms tend to need more order and calm to soothe nerves, exterior walls are a natural place to paint large, vibrant murals telling stories relevant to the neighborhood. This can be a way to invite local artists into the school to work with students on conceiving and creating a new identity for school buildings.

In 2016, the New York City Department of Health and Mental Hygiene (DOHMH) led a pilot project to promote mental health in public high schools. The initiative was part of an effort to tackle the racial and income disparities in both quality of school environment and mental health needs of students. Mental Health by Design (MHxD) engaged students from fifteen high schools spread throughout New York City (see figure 3.6). The students collaborated with DOHMH and design experts from Hyperakt in a three-week student-centered program to teach students how to advocate for mental health in their communities. The program culminated with an awareness campaign poster and a special place designed by students for students to decompress at each school. The program was conducted, and posters and places installed, over a six-month period and varied by school. "Projects included six exterior spaces (three gardens, an outdoor classroom, an outdoor mural, and a green space) and nine interior spaces (three mindfulness/meditation centers, an audio booth, a student artwork display, a mural, a student lounge, a restorative/

MENTAL HEALTH CHALLENGES
NYC MENTAL HEALTH BY DESIGN SCHOOLS

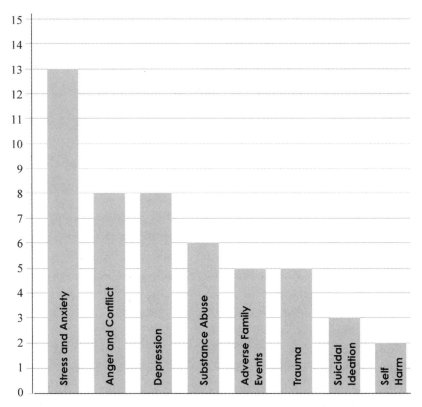

FIGURE 3.6: The graph presents data shared by fifteen participating schools as requested by the Fund for Public Health in New York City as part of its 2016 Mental Health by Design (MHxD) program. Adapted from New York City Department of Health and Mental Hygiene.

retreat room, and a lobby redesign) with specialized programming to help students pursue wellness-promoting activities such as mindfulness, physical activity and self-expression."[10]

Design places where students feel comfortable if they don't know anyone. "Our body requires the presence of another . . . that's who we are, that's who mammals are," Stephen Porges says. "Social media or Skype may be helpful, but it's not a replacement. We evolved with the help of others and we continue to need the help of others to live our life. Our bodies are asking for good friends, support, help." For students who don't feel comfortable with people, designers can include smaller, intimate places where sitting or playing alone or with one friend feels safe. Some schools make places for pets, chickens, rabbits, or other animals for students to care for or spend time with.

Larger-Scale Physical Changes

Test the classroom acoustics. Engage the help of an acoustical designer to dampen and absorb noise inside the classroom for an environment more conducive to learning. Porges points to the big role the sounds we hear play in our feeling safe.[11] Lower monotone sounds, such as noises from freeways, ventilation systems, or stern low voices, mimic the sounds from a predator and trigger defense mechanisms. Higher-frequency sounds, such as birdsong, wind rustling leaves, or singsongy sounds of nurturing caregivers soothe students' nerves. Outside, small hills or berms or rammed earth walls can absorb sound coming from play areas and adjacent roads.

6. Include Places to Sit, Rest, Swing, Rock, and Walk

Shifts in Thinking

Swinging, rocking, and walking bring focus away from our minds and anxieties and back to our bodies. This type of rhythmic, swaying movement helps us feel calm and grounded in who we are and will benefit teachers and school staff as well as students at all grade levels. As with the quiet, calming places, children and teens will seek out activities that engage their bodies if allowed. Students who might be scolded for walking along a tall wall, hanging or spinning over railings, rocking or twisting in their seats, or pacing the halls are engaged in important work. Balancing, climbing, spinning, swinging, pushing, pulling, rocking, and walking develop the vestibular and proprioceptive sensory systems—both vital for healthy physical and mental development.[12] Creating a school culture that encourages these kinds of activities during free time will help children and teenagers regain calm and the ability to learn during class time. Teachers and staff will also benefit emotionally and physically from having these opportunities available, which in turn will strengthen their ability to support students.

Small-Scale Physical Changes

Walking can be meditative, restorative, and social. Schools can develop or simply mark out measured walking paths through and around campus to give students, teachers, and staff places to walk together or alone. Groupings of hammocks or bench or chair swings can provide opportunities for people to rock or swing together while ensuring social distance. Rocking chairs are good for places with space constraints and the need for flexibility. Seating is a simple, yet surprisingly meager, resource in many schools. The lack of enough decent seating options sets up a competition and hierarchy of those who get the good seating—or any seating—and those who don't. Ask students where they need and would like more seating. It is likely that their responses will include seating along corridors, along outdoor walks, in courtyards, under trees, and in small out-of-the-way spaces that might invite a student or a small group of students to sit and rest. A survey of over a thousand students at Eagle Rock Junior/Senior High School found that students requested seating and shade in almost every area on campus, as well as around the campus perimeter, in a nearby park, and on an adjacent hillside. Make sure there is enough seating in the cafeteria, library, auditorium, and amphitheater and around informal athletic fields for students, parents, and community members.

Add a variety of seating options in different configurations in classrooms and outside to give students who need to stand or rock choices of places to be without calling attention to themselves. Choose classroom furniture that gives students the most choice of position—desks with separate chairs, for example, or both seating-height and standing-height tables with stools so students can sit or stand. Stools with swivel seats are even better. Create spaces in each classroom that feel homey, comfortable, and safe for students to escape to if they need a break. An armchair with a reading lamp, beanbag chairs, an area rug give students of all ages a sense of comfort and calm.

Design different-sized outdoor places, flexible gathering areas, and walking paths that offer quiet fascination, separate people from distraction, and allow people to wander. Outdoor seating can be made from a variety of natural or salvaged materials. Straw bales, stumps, crates, and boxes can provide affordable or free seating that students can move to where they want to be. Salvaged construction materials such as wood, brick, concrete block, concrete paving, boulders, and other materials can be used for impromptu or formal seating. Rammed earth seat walls can be made by students, parents, or local community members with guidance from an expert in sustainable construction methods. Stumps and logs can be requested from local arborists, or from the school district when damaged or sick trees need to be removed from the school site or nearby properties. Tree trunks can be cut into seat-sized stumps, or logs can be flattened on one or two sides to make quick seating. Include opportunities for students to lie down and relax their entire bodies.

Benches, hammocks, cots, and folding lawn chairs can invite rest and respite before and after school or between classes or activities, especially for older students. A donation program can invite students, parents, teachers, and community members to bring in any extra or discarded potential seat to school. In many neighborhoods (at least in mine), people leave chairs and furniture by the curb; these can be repaired by a school shop class or a parent volunteer. Local freecycle websites can be used to request donations from the larger community. Another option is to contact local or regional office or furniture suppliers to ask whether they have seconds or overstock items they would be willing to donate or sell for a fraction of the retail cost to their local school. Some schools and districts keep stockpiles of older furniture in storage and may be willing to let school communities reclaim it for good use.

Larger-Scale Physical Changes

A bigger change could integrate elements of nature play around campus to allow students of all ages to engage their bodies in balancing, rocking, swinging, and other physical challenges. This could look like an adventure course made of natural materials. Or a 1950s-style metal structure with pull-up bars of all heights (including lower bars to allow spinning over), rings or places to hang, swings, monkey bars, parallel bars, balance beams. The Cal Poly Pomona campus has a wood and rope challenge course used by the kinesiology department for trust building. Imagine a similar setup made of all natural materials where children, preteens, and adolescents could scramble up rope netting or swing and spin on ropes or take a nap in a cozy hammock.

Create Nature-Filled Environments

7. Design for the Health of All Species

Building equity in schools includes equity among species. Make sure your design provides healthy places for birds, pollinators, and insects to live and thrive. Human health depends on animal health and soil health as well as clean air and water. Insects, reptiles, amphibians, and other animals thrive in a healthy web of plant life, fungi, and microscopic species that live in healthy soils and water habitats.

No matter what the climate, take advantage of any and all outdoor space to create habitat gardens and living laboratories. Outdoor spaces are opportunities to collaborate with wildlife biologists and researchers to create wildlife gardens where students can experience and study the potential for schoolyard habitats to attract and protect wildlife. This will give students firsthand experience with natural processes and life cycles, which will support their emotional well-being as well as their academic success.

Shifts in Thinking

Native American ecologist Robin Wall Kimmerer wrote of the importance of teaching ourselves and our children that other living creatures, as well as natural processes, are beings worthy of protection: "The animacy of the world is something we already know, but the language of animacy teeters on extinction—not just for Native peoples, but for everyone."

> Our toddlers speak of plants and animals as if they were people, extending to them self and intention and compassion—until we teach them not to. We quickly retrain them and make them forget. When we tell them that the tree is not a *who* but an *it*, we make that maple into an object; we put a barrier between us, absolving ourselves of moral responsibility and opening the door to exploitation. [13]

Design that welcomes other species can also help students feel more at home. Students who are wary of other people might feel safe with a dog, a classroom pet, or nearby wildlife. When students appreciate the vulnerability of an animal (or a friend) and love them, this helps them feel connected and safe.

Chemical pesticides and herbicides, plastics, rubberized play surfacing, and other petroleum-based materials are toxic waste often disguised as eco-friendly products. They poison our children and youth as well as plants and animals (moreover, targeted species can become resistant to chemical pesticides; see figure 3.7). An alternative method to using chemicals for pest control and weed control is a nature-based strategy of monitoring and managing pests with the goal of long-term health of humans, other organisms, and the whole connected ecosystem. Called integrated pest management, this practice invites beneficial insects, pollinators, and a diversity of species

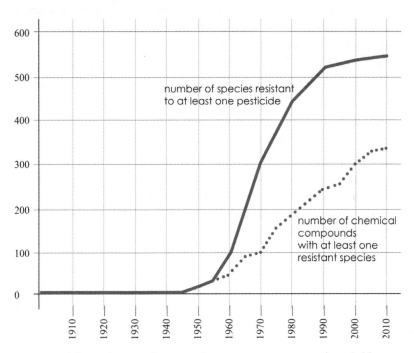

CHEMICAL USE LOSES EFFECTIVENESS OVER TIME ...
SO WHY USE IT?

FIGURE 3.7: The evolution of insecticide resistance over time: the solid line represents the number of insect, arachnid, and crustacean species with resistance to at least one pesticide; the dotted line shows the number of chemical compounds for which at least one species has evolved resistance. Source: Adapted from Randy Oliver, "The Pesticide Situation: Part 4—Pesticide Resistance and Changes in Farming Practices," Scientific Beekeeping, April 2019, accessed September 7, 2020, http://scientificbeekeeping.com/pesticide-situation-part-4/#_edn3.

to create an ecologically rich and healthy environment where students can learn from and understand animals and their habits.

I planted a rosebush in my garden once, and within days it was covered with aphids. Rather than using chemicals, I researched natural remedies to deal with them. After reading that aphids rarely killed plants, and that you could wash them off easily with water until their natural predators came, I simply left them alone. A few days later, ladybugs found their way to the rosebush and feasted on the little green bugs. Examples such as this present an opportunity to teach kids about life cycles and natural processes in a way you can't with chemicals.

Whether a school's buildings and grounds are healthy and energy- and resource-efficient depends largely on the school's maintenance and operations. Often, landscapes and buildings that are designed to use fewer resources end up using the same amount of energy and water as their conventional neighbors. This usually happens because the site management team isn't trained in or aware of the intent and manage- ment needs of the school's design. Include the site management team in your design process, and work with them to develop a realistic and healthy maintenance plan. Things to consider are using organic and integrated pest management practices instead of chemical pesticides and herbicides, establishing and watering trees and plants with long but infrequent watering to encourage deep root growth, and training management teams how to maintain and monitor the natural and built systems on-site for efficiency and health.

Small-Scale Physical Changes

The COVID-19 pandemic brought the inherent problems and inequities of a global supply chain into glaring focus. Materials that come from far away have negative shipping impacts. It is also difficult to know the poten- tial harm of many of the materials and manufacturing processes used every day in construction and maintenance. We have an opportunity to honor students' broad range of interests and abilities while making local, nature- based goods and incubating local nature-based businesses. Schools can offer vocational training, make-it and fix-it studios, and business classes. Home economics, machine arts, woodshop, and the like used to be offered to every student. The spaces are still present in many schools. Districts can hire local tradespeople and craftspeople, artists, horticulturists, and small business owners to teach and guide students in becoming entrepreneurs. Species-safe, nature-based product making could become a vocational program and funding stream for schools and students.

Larger-Scale Physical Changes

Organic materials and management processes support student health in many ways. The monotonous, featureless schoolyards so many students suffer in today came about largely from school administrators wanting to avoid potential lawsuits and maintenance costs. But they provide little protection from the elements and expose students to petroleum-based chemicals. Children's health advocates urge decision makers to provide places where children and adolescents can practice strength, balance, and coordination while also contributing to environmental health and education. Nature-based design can and should include places imagined by and for children and teenagers that allow them to challenge themselves physically and socially in safe, organic materials (see figure 3.8). The benefits to public and mental health far outweigh the costs and time of maintenance. The

FIGURE 3.8: This schoolyard in Berlin, Germany, features a stone climbing wall carved by students. All the playground elements are made by the community with natural materials. Sand and wood chips in the fall zones allow rainwater to percolate, invite digging and play with loose natural materials, and provide a safer surface for falling than rubberized playground surfacing. Image by Sharon Danks. Source: Marcella Raney, PhD.

International School Grounds Alliance's Risk in Play and Learning Declaration calls for school grounds to be as safe as *necessary*, not as safe as *possible*. This came in response to the massive number of lifeless, single-purpose school play areas found around the world. In schoolyards that are predominantly grass fields, this could be a smaller-scale physical change. Urban asphalt schoolyards will require larger-scale efforts to convert to natural materials and processes.

8. Work with Nature for Multiple Benefits
Small-Scale Physical Changes
Use Local, Natural Materials Wherever Possible
In classrooms, soft natural materials will absorb sound and lend a sense of comfort and welcome. This includes wood or cork floors or wallboards; wool, linen, or cotton upholstery or carpets; and straw, reed, willow, or grass tapestry wall panels or carpets. Outside materials could include rammed earth walls made with soil found on-site, adobe bricks, bales of grass or straw, and mats made from local plants. Engage local experts in natural processes and materials to harvest, design, and build art pieces and structures (see figure 3.9). Students can research how people made their homes and lived with the land before colonial times to find ideas for building and working with local nature. Local indigenous communities, ethnobotanists, nature artists, and cultural anthropologists are good places to start. Where a natural material won't work, create natural forms or textures. Local and native artists and craftspeople can work with students to create structures, sculptures, mats, tiles, photographs, or other elements designed with natural materials, textures, and forms.

Larger-Scale Physical Changes
Design with Nature and Natural Processes
A historic resources report conducted for the Los Angeles Unified School District states:

> Conventional wisdom held that window areas should equal approximately 40 to 50 percent of the total wall area of the room's longest side. Windows would extend up to 6 inches from the ceiling, to maximize light. In this way, the repetitive bays of windows, on each floor of the

FIGURE 3.9: Handcrafted branches of sycamore trees, such as those that grew on the site before construction, emerge from the walls of the West Hollywood Library. Art: *Platanus bibliotechalis* by David Wiseman. Architects: Johnson Favaro.

classroom space, become one of the trademark features of 1920s schools in particular. Views out the windows were also considered important, because students should have the chance to look out the window and "rest their eyes at times." Ceilings tended to be high, ranging typically from 12 to 15 feet, "a minimum standard that in many places was regulated by building codes." High ceilings helped with ventilation and accommodated tall windows, which provided the main light source until the advent of fluorescent lighting in the 1930s.[14]

Designing with nature aligns site and building design with the natural flows of water, wind, sunlight, soil, and natural-material resources. This supports our innate love of and need for nature while reducing energy, water, and resource use in construction, maintenance, and operations. No matter where you're located, look to local indigenous and vernacular design customs, early building styles (before electricity), and natural ventilation strategies for guidance and inspiration. Design and situate buildings and outdoor spaces to harness the breeze, capture natural daylight, and rely on other energy-free methods of cooling and warming interior and exterior spaces. Favor windows that open, screened doors, and other openings to draw in fresh air. Don't rely solely on mechanical air systems to move and filter air. As we've found out with the coronavirus pandemic, mechanical air systems in schools were often underdesigned to save money. And they're useless in the case of energy blackouts. There are natural ventilation strategies for buildings of all sizes and floor numbers. Use local building patterns and materials that are appropriate for the climate, renewable, nontoxic, and reclaimed. Hot desert climates with big fluctuations between night and day temperatures often feature homes made of thick adobe walls that take a long time to heat up in the sun. This vernacular building material keeps the interior spaces cool during the day and then radiates the sun's warmth inside at night as the outside temperatures begin to drop. Architects of the 1920s understood and applied design strategies for health and well-being, a response to the widespread Spanish flu and tuberculosis outbreaks. Many century-old school buildings still feel good to be in.

Material selections can also look to local, natural, renewable resources to benefit both students and ecosystem health. Every region has its own local renewable resources and cultural practices that connect students to recent and past histories. In 1892 my great-great-grandmother wrote in her diary about "picking pines" with her little daughter in Petersham, Massachusetts, to collect material to stuff her cushion and mattress with pine needles. They also celebrated the first dandelions of the season by eating the greens and picked wild blueberries in summer. In precolonial Southern California, acorns were a major food source, abundant in the dozens of oak species in the region and easy to store over winter. Fast-growing arrowweed and willow provided plenty of material for making shelters and baskets. If you live in pine forest country, pine should be relatively affordable and easily available. Pine flooring or pine timbers for an outdoor shelter would resonate with the school's surroundings. Pines could also be good trees to grow on campus. You could plant a mini pine forest throughout campus, strategically overplanting in a few places to thin and use for school furniture and play equipment in the future. Pine needles and cones make ideal materials for creative play and arts and crafts, as well as for learning natural and societal history. Indigenous people across the globe wove baskets and vessels with pine needles, grasses, and reeds, and many continue the practice today. Hiring indigenous foresters and craftspeople to teach ecosystem management practices and arts can honor and value their knowledge while teaching students and communities about local traditions and brutal histories. It could also be a way to begin rethinking what commercialized goods and foods we could replace with locally grown and harvested goods that nourish people, the planet, and the local economy.

Reveal Natural Processes on Campus
School buildings and grounds can be designed to reveal and celebrate the flows of nature, wildlife, and people over time. There are infinite processes to highlight and reveal. Seasonal change fascinates us and helps us feel connected to the world. Monsoonal rains can bring dramatic seasonal floods, flushes of growth, and sediment deposits. Winter snow dampens sound, its new surface a perfect stage for tracking small mammals and the pace of snowmelt. The subtler the seasons, the more important it is to teach students to attune themselves to seasonal shifts and changes. With the increasing destruction caused by hurricanes, wildfires, floods, and drought, schools can teach safe practices during and after emergencies. School campuses can also become testing grounds for climate-forward strategies to mitigate heat, flood, habitat loss, and food insecurity.

Schools can become living laboratories where students can explore natural processes and living systems. Learning gardens, outdoor classrooms, and nature playgrounds all offer experiential learning opportunities. Engaging students in designing and creating their own environments provides even more learning opportunities. Ideas might include designs for students to study watershed health by revealing the flow of rainwater through campus and incorporating places for students to take water samples before and after runoff enters rain gardens and biofiltration swales for treatment. Support the life sciences by building soil health and allowing students to collect soil samples to study under the microscope and search for small organisms. Plant native trees and plants and pollinator gardens to attract a variety of wildlife and give students the experience of being in nature (see figure 3.10).

Design in day-to-day opportunities for learning, respite, and awe. Think about seasonality. Plant trees and shrubs that bud and flower in different seasons and at different times of day. Deciduous species lose their leaves

FIGURE 3.10: Beacon View Primary School Forest Walk: even a small corridor of trees along a paved edge or a marshy field, such as the one pictured here, can emulate a walk in the woods.

during winter hibernation or summer drought, depending on where you are in the world. These provide winter sun when we need it and perches for birds. Plan for the joyful fall crunch of crisp leaves underfoot, morning dew shining on a grass field or dripping from a gutter downspout, and elongating shadows as the days shorten in winter. Engage students in planting trees, shrubs, grasses, and flowers found in your area before settlers came. Ask them to find nature clues on campus. Invite them to design creative ways to harness the flow of water, track the movement of the sun, attract and document migrating birds, and reveal other seasonal changes of plants and creatures.

Los Angeles principal Brad Rumble brought his bird-watching skills first to Leo Politi Elementary School and then to Esperanza Elementary when he partnered with the Los Angeles Audubon Society to apply for the US Fish and Wildlife Service's Schoolyard Habitat Program. Together, they created wildlife gardens in underused corners of campus, designed to reflect

FIGURE 3.11: The front lawn of Flintridge Preparatory School was transformed into a California garden attracting birds and wildlife. The mature coast live oaks that already graced the site create their own weed-blocking mulch when the leaves are allowed to stay on the ground. Design: Richard Grigsby, The Great Outdoors Landscape Design. Nature-based landscape management: Saturate.

what might have been there six hundred years before. High school students in the local Audubon education program served as restoration leaders for the schools, mentoring the elementary students and taking on the role of community leaders. The students contribute important knowledge of urban wildlife, tracking and documenting bird species that visit the gardens, including the rare burrowing owl, a favorite at Esperanza. Rumble wrote on the Audubon blog, "Every school campus, no matter how urban, has its own natural history just waiting to be reclaimed and observed."[15] (See figure 3.11 for Flintridge Preparatory School's approach.)

Capture, Clean, and Absorb Rainwater
More and more cities and school districts are mandated to manage runoff from streets and school sites. The federal Clean Water Act requires states to do so, with each state working on its own timeline. School districts

in states such as Virginia are adept at natural stormwater management; others have yet to begin planning. Schoolyards provide an opportunity to design natural water management systems that also create places for experiential learning and support environmental literacy. Design strategies include collecting rainwater in rain tanks, replacing pavement with planted or organic surfaces to let rain soak into the ground and refill aquifers, directing runoff into planted areas for soil microbes to clean it, and revealing streams that used to run through or near the school site. I've been surprised to learn how many schools sit on or adjacent to existing or former streambeds, marshes, wetlands, and the like. Sometimes remnant water-loving trees or patterns of thick vegetation can reveal where a stream used to run, even if it has been buried in a storm drain. School designers can use nature as a guide to reveal the smaller patterns that rain creates as it flows from rooftops onto pavement and out toward low spots or drains. Explore opportunities to intercept rain before it hits the ground and to use nature-based systems to manage it once it becomes runoff. Don't underestimate the power of trees to capture rain in their canopies, absorb runoff in their roots, reduce soil erosion, facilitate groundwater recharge, shade the earth to conserve soil moisture, and more. See chapter 7 for more detail on stormwater design strategies that support mental health and well-being in Eagle Rock Elementary School, Daniel Webster Middle School, and Environmental Charter High School. The Wetlands Learning Lab at Campbell Elementary School outside Washington, DC, transformed a perpetually muddy spot next to the playground by restoring wetland plants that might have once lived around the natural spring (see figure 3.12).

9. Increase Access to Trees and Nature

Shifts in Thinking

Uncover Windows in Classrooms, Cafeterias, Corridors, and Common Areas
Research shows us that views of trees and nature from classroom windows let students recover from stress, improve concentration, and improve test scores. Windows need to be free from obstruction for students to benefit from the trees and gardens outside. This is a far more important, and far less simple, strategy than it seems. Many urban schools have long-standing policies requiring security grates on first-

FIGURE 3.12: At Campbell Elementary School near Washington, DC, Nancy Striniste of EarlySpace designed the Wetlands Learning Lab to transform the natural springs and seeps into a nature play space and learning opportunity, rather than a source of flooding onto the playground. Photo: Lani Harmon.

floor or exterior campus windows. In other classrooms, such as in temporary buildings, there are no windows, or windows are located high above students' heads, providing no views of nature. And in rooms with windows, teachers—taught to keep student attention on themselves and the assignments—too often cover windows with blinds, curtains, or other materials, as shown in figure 3.13. Architects wonder why the windows they work so hard to design into classrooms end up covered. And yet they rarely go back to ask teachers why.

Engage teachers to find out how and why they teach the way they do. Educate them about the impact of natural daylight and views of nature on students' mental health and well-being. And then work with them to identify the obstacles to allowing views outside. The reasons will likely be a surprise. Advocate with the school and district decision makers to remove posters, paint, and security grates from windows in classrooms, cafeterias, and other school areas to provide access to views outside. Protect classroom windows from glare with awnings, trees, or louvers as needed to help teach-

FIGURE 3.13: It is all too common to find classroom windows—even those facing beautiful views—painted, boarded up, or blocked by curtains or blinds. In this case, several layers of coverings include district-mandated security screens to deter vandalism or theft. Image: Amanda Millett.

ers keep them uncovered and accessible to green views without the discomfort of direct sunlight. Work to understand view corridors from the outside and whether fear is keeping blinds drawn or windows covered. Refer to strategy 5, "Create Calming, Quiet Places and Cozy Spaces," for design strategies for calming classrooms while considering the safe zone approach described in chapter 1 for addressing emergency drills.

Stephen Porges's research suggests scanning our surroundings to help us reregulate. By orienting—moving our head, neck, and eyes to survey the world around us—we activate the vagus nerve and calm our systems. Orienting sends signals that our brains interpret as a sign of safety. When we orient our heads and bodies, scanning our surroundings, our brains know that we are not in fight or flight but at rest. Having something to look at outside a window (see figure 3.14) or in a garden helps us do this naturally. We can remind ourselves and students to take a moment to look around or outside every now and then. Other ways to relax the sympathetic nervous system include singing, playing wind instruments, breathing deeply, and engaging in cooperative play.

FIGURE 3.14: Eagle Rock Elementary School second-grade teacher Mirta Muscarolas keeps her large classroom windows uncovered to flood the room with natural daylight and allow students to look out into the trees.

Small-Scale Physical Changes

Bring Natural Materials, Patterns, and Scenes Inside

Some schools have classrooms, cafeterias, offices, or other rooms with no windows. In these cases, there are a few options that can support students' mental health. Study ways to relocate classrooms. Are there enough classrooms with windows on campus to accommodate all classes? Are there any windowed rooms used for storage or something other than a classroom that could be converted to a learning space? During this process, refer to future estimates of student population, to plan for changes in the number of classrooms needed on-site.

For rooms without windows, bring the feeling of the outdoors inside using one or more of the following ideas:

- Have students design and paint a large-scale mural, or hang a tapestry, or wallpaper with a natural scene, on one or more classroom walls.

- Locate indoor plants and trees, fish tanks, bird cages, hamster or guinea pig runs, or terrariums where students can see them while sitting at their desks.
- Place a mobile made of natural materials or forms near an air vent so it will move slightly in the breeze and provide a resource for quiet fascination and orientation.
- In classrooms with smart screens or projectors, play scenes from nature such as wildlife videos, nature cams, or audio of birdsong or calming music while students are studying or taking a test.

Plant Trees to Shade Gathering Areas, Break Up Space, and Provide Views
Trees are underappreciated and underused by school design architects, administrators, and even landscape architects. And yet they're inexpensive and relatively easy to plant. Rodney Matsuoka's study of one hundred Michigan high schools found that even the nicest school campuses with the most trees could dramatically increase tree canopy to better benefit students.[16] Schools as a rule are sadly underplanted and exposed to the elements. Rather than ask, "Where should we plant a tree?," ask, "Where are the places we *cannot* plant trees?" This will eliminate the places where underground utilities, regulated sight lines at driveways and street intersections, fire access lanes, and clearance distances around structures prevent tree planting. Everywhere else can and should be considered. Green Schoolyards America founder Sharon Danks recommends covering at least 50 percent of the school site that is open to the sky with tree canopy.[17]

There are myriad opportunities to break up large spaces with rows of trees to protect students from sun exposure and encourage activity on warm days. Divide large areas of athletic fields, lawn, paving, and parking with rows of trees or gardens or both to create separation and shelter from the sun. Provide shade trees in large elementary school play areas to encourage students to move and play in shade during mild and warm weather. While we tend to place chairs or benches under trees for the most comfort, placing benches under trees on school grounds may invite more children to be sedentary on even mild days.[18]

Plant trees in window sight lines to provide green views from classrooms and cafeterias. Plant them around sports fields and courts to break up vast areas, over outdoor seating areas and walkways to shade them, along south and west building sides in warm Northern Hemisphere climates to reduce buildings' energy use, and in parking lots to cool the pavement and vehicles, which increases energy efficiency. Trees are a valuable addition to rain gardens and along biofiltration swales because they absorb massive quantities of water. They are an important source of fruits and nuts for people and wildlife and offer habitat for all sorts of pollinators and other animals. Trees provide twigs, acorns, cones, needles, and leaves for nature play and mulch and compost. Their parts can be used to teach about life sciences, mathematics, patterns, design, and the arts. Trees give us beauty and inspiration in addition to the air we breathe. And when they are from the local region or a climatically similar one, they are affordable (or free) and easy to grow.

Larger-Scale Physical Changes
Add New Windows and Plan Major Improvements with Green Views in Mind
An option for rooms along an outer building wall is to engage an architect to explore the possibility of adding one or more windows to the outside. Study where windows can be added in classrooms, cafeterias, corridors, and common areas to give students, teachers, staff, and the school community views of trees and gardens. For major renovations, additions, and other improvements, keep in mind the importance of views of and access to nature in addition to the previous eight strategies.

Create Gardens That Serve Students, Teachers, and the Community
A large number of schools have nurtured gardens at one time or another. Some, like the twenty-year-old Edible Schoolyard at Martin Luther King Jr. Middle School in Berkeley, California, thrive with in-house educators and district support in place. Others are conceived and created only to fade away when the initial champion moves on. Raised planting beds once full of food lie fallow when program funding dries up. Work with the school community to plan, design, and install gardens that work with the school's curriculum and in alignment with student, teacher, and community interests and energy. While school communities are encouraged to create their own concept, the following are a few types of gardens that could serve schools well:

- Therapeutic garden, such as those being added to health-care settings, where the focus is on reducing stress or working with plants for their restorative properties
- Ethnobotany garden, to teach students and community members how indigenous communities have used local plants, trees, and wildlife for food and healing
- Edible garden or food forest to provide students and community members with opportunities to grow and eat fresh, healthful vegetables, fruits, nuts, and herbs
- Labyrinth or maze garden to provide a place for meditative walking or playful exploration
- Wildlife garden to attract and observe wildlife such as birds, butterflies, insects, and other species
- Rain garden to capture, clean, and infiltrate rainwater from hard surfaces while teaching students and the community about riparian habitats and healthy watersheds

10. Make Space for All Students (and Everyone) to Play Freely in Nature

Shifts in Thinking

Children, adolescents, and adults find inspiration and restoration in natural settings. Nature play—play or recreation in areas with trees, plants, and natural materials to interact with—encourages students of any age to orient and reset their minds and bodies in an environment that offers soft fascination, sensory activation, and physical challenge. Free exploration in natural settings fosters social, emotional, creative, and collaborative play while exercising senses.[19] This freedom lets students become their own advocates, relationship builders, mediators, and conflict negotiators. Removing or reducing playground rules brings even bigger benefits of free play in nature. When Swanson Primary School in Auckland, New Zealand, eliminated playground rules, there was more positive, creative, and social play by children of all ages. There were fewer injuries and fewer conflicts.[20]

Small- to Larger-Scale Physical Changes

As the nature-school and nature-play movement gains ground in primary schools, we can't forget our older students. Preteens and adolescents need and deserve nature play, too. Students who climb trees, scramble over boulders, balance on logs, walk over rough surfaces, and hang from branches learn their own physical limits through incremental risk. Small grassy mounds or hills allow children to scramble or climb up and run or tumble down. Logs, stumps, or boulders can be arranged so students can sit for an outdoor talk or performance and use them during free play to jump from one to another. A wide, shady spot covered in thick mulch at one school invites children to sit and dig and arrange toys in imaginative play. This kind of play builds fine motor skills in addition to the core strength needed to get down on the ground and back up again. Nature playscapes, such as the one shown in figure 3.15, welcome adolescents and adults to use them, too, unlike pre-engineered play structures that imply they are only for small children.

A top priority while planning nature-based exploration areas is to make sure they are designed to be welcoming and accessible to everyone. Students with developmental and physical differences need and deserve access to nature's restorative and strengthening qualities. See box 3.2 on bringing all children the benefits of nature through Universal Design for Learning.

FIGURE 3.15: The nature play area in Constitution Gardens Park in Gaithersburg, Maryland, invites children of different ages to work together in unprescribed play. Designer: Nancy Striniste, EarlySpace. Image: Nancy Striniste.

11. Plan for the Future

Planning for the future means thinking about the long-term health and well-being of the school environment and its human, animal, and plant inhabitants over generations. It also means addressing young people's deep concerns and anxieties about their own future and what quality of life it will bring. We can help alleviate students' fears by designing school environments that embody nature-based practices to create healthy, welcoming, living schoolyards. As we grapple with uncertainty in times of climate change, future pandemics, and changing priorities, we need to come to conversations about design with a completely open mind. As we learned in 2020, assumptions about school, public space, public health, and the economy can change almost overnight. What opportunities come with our new knowledge? How might our priorities around space and programming change?

Shifts in Thinking

Design with Time in Mind

Too often, especially in the landscape, designers plan for the first day or year and neglect to think of what will happen in five years or twenty years or one hundred. While buildings are generally completed by the day they open, school landscapes grow and change through the seasons and years. Understanding that schools are used very differently depending on time of day, time of year, whether school is in session, and from year to year as curriculums, teachers, and students change will help you create plans that can withstand those changes. The following are some ideas for designing with time in mind:

- Choose plants and trees that are native or adapted to your region to provide habitat for local birds, reptiles, amphibians, beneficial insects, and other animals.
- Understand the mature size of trees and plants to reduce the need for pruning and thinning as they grow in. Studying and taking advantage of a site's microclimates will reveal opportunities, such as using the shady sides of buildings to plant shade-loving species and the sunny sides of buildings to plant sun-loving species.
- Plant shorter-lived perennials around plants and trees that take a long time to grow to protect the roots and branches from running children as they grow in.

Box 3.2: Bringing the Benefits of Nature to All Children

By Kirsten Haugen

Increasingly, we hear the call to "Get outside!" How do we ensure children with exceptional physical, cognitive, sensory, or social challenges can fully participate in the outdoor opportunities we provide?

As a special educator involved in nature-based learning opportunities, I view the licensing and legal requirements of the Americans with Disabilities Act (ADA) and playground safety standards as essential, but not sufficient for children with unique challenges. *Accessibility*, or getting to things, is critical, but it's only a pathway to *participation*—being a part of things. Bringing together the Universal Design for Learning (UDL) framework with research-based principles for implementing nature-based outdoor classrooms helps us move much closer to supporting children of all abilities to be a part of things—and thrive—outdoors.

UDL is a framework guided by research and focused on the *what, how,* and *why* of learning to promote the development of flexible and responsive learning environments and activities.

- **What?** Include and allow for *multiple means of representation*. To help all children take in information, instructions, and ideas, incorporate spoken and written words, illustrations, diagrams, charts, hands-on models or materials, and physical demonstrations.
- **How?** Invite *multiple means of action and expression*. To fully understand what children think and know, support them to explore and demonstrate their ideas and knowledge with a variety of forms and materials: words, movement, large- and small-scale structures and creations, experiments, performances, and more.
- **Why?** Provide *multiple means of engagement*. To increase children's motivation, sense of purpose, and belonging, ensure your environments, materials, and activities reflect and connect with the diverse range of children's backgrounds, interests, and experiences—or are open ended enough to reflect the child's imagination.

Looking through this UDL lens, I understand why many children with additional, unique needs fail to fit in or engage appropriately in the limited play options available during conventional recess. Even if they meet ADA

Box 3.2: Continued on next page

requirements, playgrounds dominated by asphalt, turf, and manufactured equipment have a built-in bias toward competitive gross-motor play and "burning off steam," which compounds sensory overload, social challenges, and physical differences. Such playgrounds limit engagement, action, and expression, and can provoke or shut down some children as much as having to sit and complete the same worksheet, at the same time, in the same way as their peers. Supervising adults in this environment typically find their time taken up with intervening and redirecting children rather than observing and supporting their ideas, plans, and imaginations.

Learning and playing in nature-filled outdoor (and indoor) spaces, on the other hand, offers rich benefits for children and the adults who work with them. With a purposeful balance and arrangement of activity areas, the outdoor classroom engages more children. Visual, physical, and even sensory cues built into signage, pathways, plantings, surfaces, and storage provide multiple means of representation, allowing children to understand the space and opportunities available. Children experience physical movement, challenge, and exertion through climbing, running, and crawling; engage socially through dramatic play and music; explore STEM strategies with block building, water play, or loose parts investigations; and find quieter, contemplative moments for art, reading, or scientific observations.

In these diverse environments, children have the opportunity to thrive in different ways and to practice self-regulation by choosing the mix of physical, cognitive, and social activity their brains and bodies need. Time in nature with supportive, responsive adults promotes good health and fitness, enhances attention span and observation skills, promotes problem solving and resilience, and supports appropriate risk taking. Accessible spaces with a range of activity areas offer children more ways to exercise their motor planning and skills, their competence, and their confidence.

Look at the outdoor spaces available to children in your lives through this dual lens of UDL and research-based outdoor classroom design. How will you expand the activities available, include more open-ended materials, and increase opportunities for engagement, expression, and action?

Source: Kirsten Haugen, "Bringing the Benefits of Nature to All Children," *The Active Learner, High-Scope's Journal for Early Educators,* Spring 2019 (Ypsilanti, MI: HighScope), 12–13, https://highscope .org/wp-content/uploads/2019/05/HSActiveLearner_2019Spring_sample.pdf.

- Place rain-loving plants in low spots to allow rain to collect and feed their thirsty roots.
- Plan walkways and paved areas with rain gardens or other shallow bowl-shaped natural surfaces next to them so rainwater runs from the paving into the gardens.
- Place mulched areas and gardens or compost piles where you can sweep leaves off walkways right into them to become new soil.

Small-Scale Physical Changes
Specify Natural and Nontoxic, Reclaimed, Locally Made, and Regenerative Materials

Every school improvement, renovation, or addition presents an opportunity to make thoughtful material selections that support mental and physical health. As easy as this sounds, finding the specific ingredients and processes used by manufacturers can be incredibly difficult. Good qualities to look for when selecting materials are whether they are natural and nontoxic, reclaimed, locally made, and regenerative.

Untreated and local wood, bamboo, natural fibers, metals, stone, brick, and glass pose little risk of harming students and community members with chemicals. When weighing options, think about the environmental costs of energy used to make materials such as bricks, glass, and metals and the impacts of quarrying rock and other minerals. Trying to understand a material's life cycle—even that of a natural material—will help you make responsible and intentional decisions. The Resources section after chapter 9 provides links to the Sustainable Sites Initiative, the International Living Future Institute, and the Climate Positive Design Toolkit to help guide your selection of materials. See box 3.3 for a comparison of natural grass and synthetic turf in athletic fields.

Reclaimed materials are products, materials, or furnishings that were previously used and then reclaimed from the waste stream to be used again. While many materials can be reclaimed, prioritize those made from natural and nontoxic materials. Bricks, stone or concrete pavers, sheet metal, fencing, glass brick, bottles, jars, metal drums, washing machine tubs, iron bathtubs, and kitchen sinks have all become commonly used landscape materials.

Having local craftspeople and manufacturers make school furnish-

---

Box 3.3: Benefits of Natural Grass versus Synthetic Turf on Athletic Fields

NATURAL GRASS	SYNTHETIC TURF
Cooler temperatures	Increased temperatures
Reduced risk of dehydration and heat stroke; lower rate of injury, skin irritation, and air pollution	Increased risk of dehydration and heat stroke; higher rate of injury, skin irritation, and air pollution
No introduced chemicals	Harmful chemicals in infill and synthetic grass
Allows for infiltration of water and reduced runoff	Runoff of these pollutants is harmful to nearby plants, aquatic life, and waterways
Direct Financial Cost	**Direct Financial Cost**
$160,000 installation and more maintenance	$275,000 installation and less maintenance

---

Source: Council for Watershed Health, "Comparison of Natural Turf to Synthetic Turf," https://www .watershedhealth.org/single-post/2019/11/08/SummerScienceFriday-Artificial-Turf-vs-Natural-Turf.

---

ings and materials benefits the community in several ways: the majority of the cost goes to local owners and employees, whose incomes are usually spent within the community and who likely have a vested interest in the school and its neighborhood. This type of school-business partnership can lead to innovative solutions and programs, as in the example that follows.

Ideally, we work toward regenerative materials and processes. This means the waste from one material or process becomes food for another material or another life cycle. Trees work this way. The fallen fruit and leaves from a tree break down to become new soil, which supports the seeds of the fallen fruits, which grow into new trees bearing more fruit. Students at Tohono O'Odham Community College in southeastern Arizona worked with environmental chemistry researcher David Stone on testing a concrete substitute that absorbs carbon dioxide. Ferrock turns waste steel dust and glass bottles collected from dump sites into a material that can be used for paving or in buildings. This is a beautiful example of how schools and colleges can partner with researchers to disrupt the waste stream.

Larger-Scale Physical Changes
Design for Generations

Many of our school buildings are over one hundred years old. They may have been added onto, retrofitted, updated, and improved. But the bones are still there. Some of our oldest classrooms are the best for mental health. Eagle Rock Elementary School's original 1920s building still stands. Its classrooms have tall ceilings and giant windows that take up most of one wall. Daylight streams in, and views of trees fill the rooms with green. Wooden floors, wood trim, and little coatrooms at the backs of classrooms absorb and interrupt sound to make a quiet learning environment. Because this building was designed before air-conditioning, it uses strategies that take advantage of natural daylight and the warming sun in winter and cooling breezes in the summer, fall, and spring. The design still stands the test of time. As you design a new classroom, building, or outdoor space, it is important to consider what changes may come—both planned and unplanned—and design as best you can to withstand them.

Designers often highlight flexibility to plan for change over time. This could mean large open spaces with systems to divide them into smaller places for more intimate uses. It could mean classroom walls that open up into an outdoor courtyard or garden. Or it could mean building structures that are easy to disassemble and put up somewhere else or to store until the next time they are used. Think about which school places and programs are essential to the community and how to keep them going through future disruptions. For an elementary school, for instance, how could we set up enough space for students to remain at a safe distance from one another and the teacher while allowing parents to keep working? At a larger scale, how could we ensure that students and communities have enough food, financial literacy, and other resources to survive during times of economic disruption?

As many communities around the country experience increasingly dangerous conditions related to climate change, we need to consider not only how a school site can be designed to improve physical, mental, and environmental health but also how the entire community can better prepare for health, climate, and economic emergencies. Chapter 4 discusses larger-scale approaches to address public health, equity, and climate resilience.

Inspire Awe

12. Design for Wonder, Beauty, and Awe

Our students need and deserve a world full of wonder and intrigue . . . a school site that engages their curiosity and sparks the imagination . . . a place where they want to be. Students need beauty, warmth, wonder, awe. These qualities help mental health and well-being. Awe makes us feel humble, small, and insignificant but in a good way that also makes us feel connected to the world around us.[21] Awe-provoking moments include seeing large vistas, seeing extraordinary architecture for the first time, viewing works of art that challenge the way we think of the world, and having new experiences that aren't yet integrated into our consciousness. Around the world, as students urge their communities to address ecological destruction, systemic racism, and the capitalist systems that thrive on both, schools provide an opportunity to explore and present new models of building, learning, and living. These new models can inspire students by giving them hope for a healthy and viable future.

Shifts in Thinking

Wonderful and awe-inspiring qualities tend to emerge when we listen to and engage the human and natural world with a hyperlocal focus. Similar to strategy 1, "Conduct an Inclusive Design Process," this act requires a shift in thinking. Instead of "designer as expert," design can be thought of as "designer as facilitator for human and natural processes." This approach can create places that blend culture, climate, human behavior, and habitat into rich and resonant solutions that respect and reflect it all. Wonder and awe don't rely on big money or big design moves. The opposite is probably truer. We can connect today's students with the cultural practices of the past that tended the natural world. This can transform a school community's view of their campus and the values and ecosystems that can be nurtured and grown by the school community itself.

Small-Scale Physical Changes

Schoolyards can be designed to attract wildlife almost effortlessly with the addition of a small habitat garden and a few trees. Many schoolchildren have nurtured silkworms or planted milkweed for monarch butterflies. It is nothing short of magical on planting days when winged creatures flit in minutes after native plants arrive on-site. It happens every time. Art and music ignite awe as well. We can usually find somewhere on even the most land-starved campus to carve out a place for a student-created sculpture garden or a space where wind chimes, natural drums, and other sound-making materials can invite interaction and awe.

Larger-Scale Physical Changes

We can expand the principles of designing with nature by researching and working with indigenous people to design food, irrigation, land management, and building systems that work with natural processes to bring the land alive. Artworks in the garden, sculpted trees or vines, living mazes, framed views, stoneworks, living ponds, and other elements of surprise or focus ground and absorb students in their environments. Aim for artful design. Imagine a school environment where every window, every walkway, every seat connects students to somewhere a little special. Dream of things that will captivate a child or tug at a teen's sense of self. Better yet, ask the students. What moments take them out of their worries and anxieties and bring them back into the world and their bodies? What moments spark their curiosity and imagination? These are the moments to aspire to in school design. Students who are inspired, awed, or simply comfortable are more likely to show up ready to learn. And during moments of stress or anxiety, these special places and moments become anchors to hold on to.

Special Considerations by Age

Students' mental health, physical health, and social and academic needs differ and evolve as they age. While students of all ages can benefit from homier indoor school environments and soft, cool, nature-filled grounds, there are special considerations for each school level when planning and designing for mental health. Some of these differences stem from the changes in educational and infrastructural needs between elementary, middle, and high school. High school campuses often include large fields and gymnasiums for competitive sports. Elementary schools more often include one large multipurpose field or blacktop yard. At the elementary school level, students typically spend recess outdoors in structured or unstructured play, while older students may have no formal break for recess and few opportunities for creative or unstructured play. The following are a few special considerations for each primary and secondary school level.

Elementary School

For elementary school children, nature play and unstructured time in green space develop social skills and support mental health, physical health, social skills, and academic success. Giving elementary school students time, space, and encouragement to engage in free and creative play outdoors will help establish healthy physical activity habits that will follow them into adulthood. School grounds with spaces of various sizes, shapes, and activity and noise levels will suit students of all ages, abilities, and frames of mind. Natural play spaces and outdoor classrooms made with natural materials, spread out across the entire campus, can provide places for teachers to teach outside and can entice children to visit different areas of the playground.

Predesigned and pre-engineered play structures are ubiquitous on elementary school grounds. But they can be problematic. Play structures offer a limited number of activities for a small number of children at a high cost. They are often made of plastic and placed on recycled rubber surfacing. Both of these materials are difficult to repair, and both can be unhealthy for children. Plastic and rubber composites get hot in the sun—so hot that they risk burning children's delicate skin. They also break down over time. Most school playgrounds drain directly into stormwater sewers or drainage ditches that lead to waterways. This means that as plastics and composite materials break down, they contribute toxins and plastics to the growing pollution problem in our waterways, rivers, and oceans. Recycled tire crumb rubber has become common in playground surfacing and as the bouncy base under artificial turf. Research shows it contains lead levels that are dangerous, especially for young children.[22] Because of heat and disrepair and for myriad other reasons, school playgrounds are often caution-taped off to prevent access. For all these reasons, it is worth rethinking the assumption that every schoolyard must have a play structure.

The best predesigned play experiences are made up of natural, nontoxic materials and offer replacement parts so that a school facilities team can do the repairs themselves. They are flexible or adaptable and ideally are manipulated or created by the children themselves. The US Environmental Protection Agency recommends sand, pea gravel, bark mulch or wood chips, and engineered wood fiber for natural playground surfacing that also absorbs the impact from falls (a health and safety requirement around play structures). The playground can use a variety of these materials as long as there is an accessible path of travel to each play area and equitable play opportunities for children of all abilities. If there are wild places already on the schoolground, they may need to be adapted only slightly to let children in to explore. Or, if your schoolground is completely devoid of nature, you might find an area where you can plant a few trees, spread a thick layer of mulch for digging, and introduce an array of loose natural materials such as tree stumps and logs, branches, pine cones, a sand area, or other natural materials available in your region. This is a relatively easy effort that can be organized and installed by community members. If asphalt has to be removed in order to do this, consult your district facilities team to make sure the proper soil tests and safety measures are in place.

Middle School

As middle schoolers gain autonomy, they are often stuck with little opportunity for free play and little freedom to test their independence in the confines of school. Yet middle schoolers as well as high school students and even adults benefit from unstructured and creative play. During this age of early adolescence and social development, students are especially in need of a strong sense of belonging and community. Look for the appearance of mental health issues, which often present themselves in middle school. Most after-school child care stops before seventh grade, leaving students who are transitioning from elementary school to middle school particularly vulnerable to isolation, boredom, and anxiety. In addition to the nature play suggestions for elementary school, the following strategies can support middle schoolers during this transitional stage:

• Create compelling and inviting places for middle schoolers to hang out after school, such as game areas, bouldering areas, make-it and fix-it spaces, music studios with DJ equipment, or outdoor amphitheaters. Work with local environment-, youth-, and community-based nonprofits to offer adolescent-friendly after-school programs.

- Design places and programs, with your middle school students, to host ceremonies for important life transitions. Robin Wall Kimmerer writes, "Ceremony is a vehicle for belonging . . . to a family, to a people, to the land. That is the power of ceremony. It marries the mundane to the sacred."[23] Unless they are star students, athletes, or musicians, students lack recognition for the important transition into adolescence. Not all students will get their driver's license, graduate from high school, or go to college. School communities could conduct a tree-planting ceremony when students enter middle school, perhaps giving each student a tree to nurture or each incoming cohort a grove to care for. Or a "Welcome to the Teens" day could acknowledge each student as he or she reaches the age of thirteen, fifteen, or another important transition year or stage.
- Find ways to gradually increase responsibility and freedom around campus and in the community.

High School

Teenage brains respond to stress with heightened anxiety, making it vital to create warm and comfortable places for them to restore calm and feel safe. Figure 3.16 graphs high school students' sense of safety compared with that of the adults in their lives. Teenagers also need more sleep than their younger and older counterparts. Remember that teenagers are still children, with developing brains. Develop school designs and programs that protect their youth, innocence, and safety. The following ideas can support high schoolers as they navigate the transition toward adulthood:

- Understand the heightened reactions of the teenage brain to stress and anxiety and the tendency to react to overwhelm with aggression.
- Provide manual arts, green jobs, and vocational training opportunities for students who learn or do better in an interactive environment.
- Break up large areas of athletic fields, lawn, paving, and parking with rows of trees, gardens, or both to create separation and shelter from the sun.
- Create calm, safe, and playful spaces for teenagers.

PERCEIVED SAFETY IN LAUSD HIGH SCHOOLS STUDENTS, PARENTS, AND STAFF

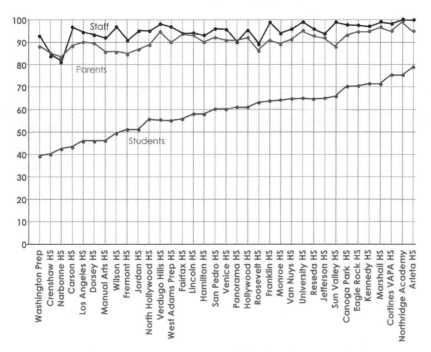

FIGURE 3.16: The annual Los Angeles Unified School District School Experience Survey asks students and staff how safe they feel in school and asks parents how safe they feel their children are in school. These graphs show a stark difference in perception of safety between high school students and the adults in their lives, for all schools.

The community-led, nature-based, student-centered design strategies included here reflect our innate need to connect with nature and one another. They come out of the community and resonate with each school's unique natural, social, and built conditions. These strategies do not represent all the opportunities to support students' mental health and well-being through design. They offer a starting point with solutions to common school conditions that work against mental health and well-being. The hope is that each school community and district will build on these ideas with site-specific design strategies to bring students joy, inspiration, mental health, physical health, optimism, and the promise of a healthy future.

CHAPTER 4

Leveraging Schools for Public Health, Equity, and Climate Resilience

Whether we plan to or not, the way we design schools erodes or supports public health, equity, and climate resilience. The connection between mental and physical health and unjust physical and social infrastructures is becoming more and more apparent every day. Decades of systemic environmental racism led to toxic environments, lack of public resources, and social and economic injustices in low-income and marginalized communities. These conditions lead to heightened stress, anxiety, and emotional overwhelm as well as poorer health and shortened lives. The recent coronavirus pandemic showed us just how fragile our economic system is. We need to proactively plan for the worst-case scenarios to ensure that historically underresourced communities have everything they need for mental health and well-being. Many schools already act as emergency shelters during hurricanes, heat waves, fires, winter storms, and power outages. They can be designed with mental health in mind to amplify this role to improve public health, equity, and climate resilience.

School district decision makers who want to help students and school communities thrive may be up against impossible budget shortfalls, the directive to protect student safety, and concerns over lawsuits should anything go wrong if they try something new. School districts serve the public. The broader school community can help by voicing their wishes for community-led, nature-based school design to support mental health and the many other associated social, physical, ecological, and academic benefits. Because public school districts control what happens on large areas of land spread across metropolitan areas, cities such as Boston, New York, and Los Angeles see and leverage public school design as a means to improve public health, equity through racial and environmental justice, and climate resilience.

The cumulative impacts of school sites would be difficult to overstate. School sites make up enormous areas of land. The country's one hundred largest school districts serve nearly one-quarter of our country's students in approximately sixteen thousand schools.[1] Added up, transforming public school environments can contribute greatly to quality of life. As mega-landowners and public institutions dedicated to our youth, school districts have a vested interest in working with local school communities to plan a just and equitable future in terms of economic status, race, gender, ability, and health. Access to housing, healthy food, health services, transportation, and social support systems can improve the mental health, safety, and well-being of students, teachers, and their families. All of these issues directly impact schools because all of these issues directly impact students. School districts can partner with government agencies and nonprofit organizations to build restorative school and community environments that surround students with a culture of care. Inclusive, interdisciplinary, and transparent planning and design processes can lead to holistic plans and policies that benefit the larger school district area and population.

As 2020 painfully illuminated, we don't know what tomorrow might look like. The COVID-19 pandemic and uprisings for racial justice added weight to the urgency of planning for equity and climate action. School closures in the face of social distancing impacted student and family mental health, food security, learning continuity, and the ability of teachers and parents of young children to work. This leaves us with serious questions about how school communities of the future should look and function. The pandemic showed us that many people can work effectively from home, but only if they have non-service-related jobs, internet access, and adequate space for privacy and productivity. We faced the inconceivable reality of schools shutting for months, putting many parents in the impossible situation of trying to earn money without the support of school or child care. We discovered that we need local urban agriculture and locally made goods in a crisis. The likelihood of prolonged future pandemics is yet another opportunity for systemic racism to unevenly burden marginalized communities. Schools and other properties owned by school districts can be thoughtfully and collaboratively redesigned to support the health and well-being of our least advantaged students and communities during periods of social distancing and at all other times, too. We have an opportunity to radically rethink public education as an equitable, resourcefull, and restorative justice system. Following are ten district-wide planning strategies that support public health, equity, and climate resilience—each of which is vital to student and community mental health.

Public Health

1. Treat Mental Health Upstream as a Community Condition

"The biggest gaps and opportunities for serving mental health are upstream," public health expert Manal Aboelata told me. "Supporting mental health could (and should) happen in the planning and design realm."[2] Unlike the public health profession, which has its roots in planning, the mental health profession began as a way to treat individuals once they have already developed issues or symptoms. Prevention Institute reframes trauma and mental health to break through the stigma and start treating mental health as the community condition that it is. The institute outlines a number of community strategies to address the social and economic factors that can influence health and well-being,[3] as shown in figure 4.1. Shifting our mindset to see mental health as deeply connected to the physical and social environments we inhabit can help us identify larger planning-scale opportunities that can support mental health as well as the site-scale design opportunities. Once we understand the research presented in chapter 2 connecting the mind, body, and environment, we can see how mental health planning falls into the realms of housing, urban forestry, air quality, transportation, parks and recreation, jobs training, and education as well as public health and social services. City and county planning agencies can help support students holistically by engaging school districts in regional watershed management plans and planning that promotes health and welfare as well as sustainability.

MENTAL HEALTH: A PATH FORWARD

Social networks & trust
Willingness to act for the
common good
Norms & culture that support
health and safety

Quality & affordable housing
Perceptions of safety
Safe parks and open spaces
Arts & cultural expression
Available safe,
healthy products

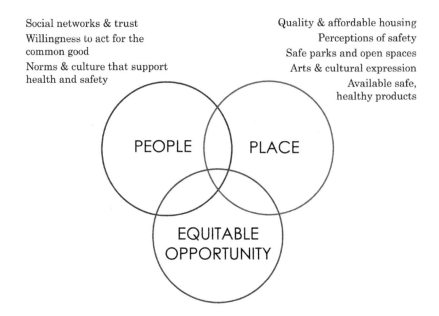

PEOPLE   PLACE

EQUITABLE
OPPORTUNITY

Living wages & local wealth
Quality education

FIGURE 4.1: Prevention Institute's framework for resilient, thriving communities. The framework treats mental health as a community condition and shifts from a downstream model of treating individuals' mental health (and all the inequities that implies) to an upstream model of improving mental health through supportive community systems. Adapted from Rachel A. Davis, MSW, Howard Pinderhughes, PhD, and Myesha Williams, MSW, "Adverse Community Experiences and Resilience: A Framework for Addressing and Preventing Community Trauma" (Oakland, CA: Prevention Institute, February 2016).

2. Develop School Gardens and Parks for Community Health Benefits

A growing number of doctors, mental health practitioners, and practices are tapping into the healing power of nature through park prescriptions, or Park Rx.[4] These programs connect health-care providers with local parks administrators to encourage people to get outside. The compelling mental health and financial benefits of connecting people to nature prompted the United Kingdom to provide a number of programs, including therapeutic gardening and farming and two innovative programs by Natural England: a nature conservation program to immerse people in nature, and Outdoors for All, which strives to increase access to nature for all ages, abilities, cultures, and economic statuses. The physical and mental health benefits of regular time spent outdoors in nature save money, too. In addition to the many social and community benefits found in the previous chapter, research connects access to nature with reduced allergies, reduced depression, higher activity level, healthier body composition, and lower blood pressure in pregnant women.[5] Lower stress and improved health mean less medication, fewer doctor and emergency room visits, and less pressure on our overtaxed health-care systems. More and more, public health agencies partner with park agencies, nonprofit park developers, and school districts to provide equitable access to high-quality parks for everyone. Because too many city neighborhoods have no parks, school districts can write policies and create processes to permit and encourage parks and recreation departments and nonprofit parks developers to create green spaces on school grounds to benefit students and the whole community.

3. Build Food Security for Schools and Communities with Urban Agriculture

In 2018, an average of nearly thirty million students ate school lunch at one hundred thousand schools and institutions each day. Over twenty million of those lunches were free. And schools and institutions served breakfast to nearly fifteen million students each day, including almost twelve million at no cost.[6]

Outsourced school lunch programs deliver ready-made meals wrapped in an enormous amount of single-use plastic packaging. Heroic efforts to meet high nutrition standards on measly budgets don't guarantee that students are eating nutritious food. Mandates to provide students with a certain number of fruit and vegetable servings, for instance, lead to a massive waste of food, along with the plastic wrapping it comes in. A recent two-year study found that an average of only 60 percent of food served during lunch was actually eaten, and that preparing and serving healthier food for school lunches could reduce food waste and increase the amount of nutrition students would receive.[7] Engaging students in where and how their food is grown increases ecological literacy and sets up healthy habits that can last their lifetimes.

Urban neighborhoods are ripe with opportunities to start community gardens, grocery co-ops, and other strategies to provide fresh, nutritious foods. Wisconsin's Fifth Season Cooperative launched with a mission "to produce, process, and market healthy, local foods in our region by supporting the values of environmental, social, and economic fairness for all." The benefits are endless. Not only does a local or community-supported agriculture system provide stable jobs; it also gives the community a chance to take over vacant lots to grow healthy, culturally important foods. School sites and urban lots are ideal places to rebuild soil health and grow fresh, nutritious, local food—especially in neighborhoods without access to grocery stores.

Unlike the common community garden model in the United States, in which people rent individual plots to plant, maintain, and harvest food for themselves, more communal and community-building gardens and food forests are growing in popularity. The City of Milwaukee Health Department launched a mentorship program for Black youth that began with neighborhood cleanup and evolved into building a community garden. The program and garden transformed the neighborhood and caused a significant drop in violence within three years.[8] Similar efforts have strengthened community ties in Flint, Michigan; Urbana, Illinois; and Philadelphia, Pennsylvania. The effects of community gardens mirror the results of other public gardens or plazas. They invite people to gather outdoors, bringing neighbors together to share space and get to know one another. This strengthens social ties and has strong effects on individuals, especially young people.

Perennial food-bearing shrubs and fruit and nut trees can provide long-term, low-maintenance food security. Many individuals, communities, and small agricultural operations are creating food forests, layering fruit or nut trees with understory berries or other edible perennials. This creates a longer-term, less maintenance-intensive food ecosystem to accompany annual crops such as lettuces, tomatoes, beans, and squash. Japanese engineer turned natural farmer Masanobu Fukuoka inspired generations with nature-based "lazy" farming practices that get more yield for less effort with *The One-Straw Revolution: An Introduction to Natural Farming.*

Equity

4. Prioritize Environmental and Racial Justice in District-wide Planning

The Health Effects Institute reported that unhealthy traffic emissions impact people up to 300 to 500 meters (984 to 1,640 feet) away from major roads. Public health departments recommend keeping schools and housing at least 500 feet from freeways; some suggest 1,000 feet minimum. Schools and parks within 1,500 feet of a freeway should be designed so that outdoor activity centers are located as far as possible from the freeway. Many metropolitan regions transitioned from trolley and train tracks connecting cities and outlying neighborhoods to major roads and freeways after World War II. It took less than twenty years to completely dismantle Los Angeles's 1,400-mile system of Red Cars. In hindsight, the electric-run systems look like an ideal replacement for the traffic-choked, emission-spewing freeways of today. The assumption that planning must revolve around existing highways is outdated and unjust. Some cities are removing underused stretches of highway and highways that cut through urban neighborhoods. This can especially benefit highway-adjacent school neighborhoods by improving air quality, reducing noise pollution, improving walkability, and re-knitting fractured communities. Planning studies of highways destroyed intentionally or by nature show a decrease in traffic congestion.[9]

Syracuse, New York, is joining the ranks of cities demolishing the highways that disrupted communities. When it was built in the 1950s, Interstate 81 displaced residents in the historically African American 15th Ward neighborhood.[10] A walkable, bicycle-friendly business district is the favored design to replace the nearly one and one-half miles of I-81 running through the neighborhood, where 40 percent of the community lives below the poverty level. Moving People Transportation Coalition volunteer leader Peter Sarver said, "It's part of a larger reframing of our community in terms of where people live and how they get to school and work and everything else."[11]

Tearing down the highway that destroyed 75 percent of the homes of Black Syracuse residents isn't enough to count as racial justice. The New York Civil Liberties Union, founded to fight the I-81 construction in 1951, is now working with the community to advocate for equitable construction. This could include protecting residents' health from construction pollution to working with the construction industry to hire and train Black and minority workers so they will benefit from the jobs created.[12]

"There is a cosmic reset on how we work and how we live," said architect Gabrielle Bullock, the second Black woman to graduate from Rhode Island School of Design's architecture program and director of global diversity for Perkins&Will. "Race is probably the most difficult problem to tackle. I see it as now or never."[13] In order to be effective, she urged us to evolve from destructive cultural blindness to cultural competency. Whether you're a designer, teacher, administrator, or student, understanding and working toward justice will increase equity as well as a sense of belonging. School districts have a vested interest in reducing air and noise pollution near schools to improve students' academic success as well as their mental and physical health. Inviting students and school communities to participate in all types of planning activities, and supporting them in doing so, can improve students' sense of belonging and investment in their school and neighborhood, educate students about historical injustices, and demonstrate the opportunity to create positive change through planning. All of these outcomes will benefit students and school communities while helping school districts address and correct historical inequities.

5. Link School Policy with Affordable Housing

A national study of school policy and housing policy released in 2019 found that one of the biggest obstacles to high-quality public education is housing.[14] Generations of inequitable financial and planning policies destroyed marginalized neighborhoods and led to widening resource and health disparities. That same study added affordable housing into the mix of services community schools can address, in response to a growing and urgent awareness of increasing numbers of people suffering from homelessness.[15] Disinvestment, poorly planned schools, and inadequate school funding need to be corrected at a bigger scale than the school site. In too many cities, rising rents have left students homeless and pushed teachers and school staff farther and farther away from work. We need affordable housing spread throughout cities, in neighborhoods at all socioeconomic levels, so students can access the schools that best serve them. Land use plans, general plans, and neighborhood-specific plans set the policies that guide future development. School communities and school districts can work with city and county planning departments to develop plans and policies for housing, transportation, and school assignment to amplify the positive impacts of community schools.

6. Create Schools as Community Centers

The community school model is gaining traction as a strategy to improve equity. The idea is to plan health and social services, family support, and community engagement around the school as the community center. This central resource hub works with families and community organizations as partners to support students holistically. The National Education Association describes six pillars or principles of community schools that shape the planning and design of a school and its surrounding neighborhood. They are as follows:[16]

- Strong and proven curriculum, including culturally relevant materials that address students' learning needs and expand their experience. Curriculum is supported by before- and after-school enrichment activities and job training programs.
- High-quality teaching, with a focus on collaborative teaching and student-focused learning, rather than testing, to meet students' needs.
- Inclusive leadership: shared leadership responsibility among educators, community school coordinators, the principal, and a community school committee of families, community partners, youth, school staff, and others.
- Positive behavior practices: positive relationships and interactions, with a focus on restorative rather than punitive discipline. Practices of peer mediation, community service, and post-conflict resolution.
- Family and community partnerships: including families, caregivers, and community members in ongoing roles in decision making, governance, and advocacy.
- Community support services: services that support the whole child, such as meals, health care, mental health counseling, and other wraparound services.

The benefits of working with students and communities to support and plan for their schools and surrounding neighborhoods are immediate and deep. Detroit Future City (DFC) developed a curriculum to incorporate community development into Michigan's high school and Common Core curriculums. The curriculum supports project-based learning by building partnerships between students and community organizations. Students at Edwin Denby High School partnered with Impact Detroit and Life Remodeled to organize a week-long stewardship blitz that collected contributions of time and money from over 250 organizations and businesses.[17] The project deepened students' under-standing and ownership of community organizing and city planning processes. Part of the effort involved partnering with the Detroit Community Design Center to develop community-led designs for Skinner Playfield, located across the street from Denby High School, and a Safe Routes to School plan. Over the course of a week, students and community members conducted major repairs on eighty students' homes, installed new basketball courts at Skinner Playfield, painted murals on community buildings, cleared overgrown shrubs from 303 blocks, boarded up 362 vacant homes, and installed wayfinding artwork and planter boxes marking the new Safe Routes to Denby Schools.

Community-driven design expert Barbara Brown Wilson wrote that the Denby community design practices "allowed for residents to enter into the project in a low-stakes, high-enjoyment manner. When desired, trauma could be processed and ideas could be generated."[18]

Schools are important yet underutilized emergency centers. They are spread throughout cities, convenient to most neighborhoods. They have bathrooms and water. They have classrooms for medium-sized gatherings and gymnasiums or auditoriums for larger events. Some schools still have full kitchens and cafeterias. And middle and high schools typically have locker rooms with showers. School grounds have the potential to act as mul-tifunctional landscapes to provide shade and shelter, to harvest rainwater and renewable energy, to grow and harvest food and building materials, and to become centers for community education, job training, and resources.

7. Replace School Policing with Restorative Justice

"Restorative justice is a justice that heals," Fania Davis said.[19] The current criminal justice system—beginning in school—punishes people who cause harm by taking away their freedom, their relationships, and their ability to support themselves or their families. This causes enormous harm to the individuals and their families, without repairing the initial harm. Davis founded Restorative Justice for Oakland Youth (RJOY) to promote the principles of healing justice in schools, the juvenile justice system, and communities. Within a few years, the effort had become so successful that the Oakland Unified School District replaced punitive discipline policies with restorative justice. Following Oakland's lead, school districts across the nation have replaced suspending and expelling students—which harm their chances of finishing high school—with community circles and repairing relational damages. While school policing is a programmatic policy, I include it here because it makes such an enormous impact on whether students feel safe and valued in their schools and communities. Student organizers across the country called for removing school police long before the recent nationwide calls to defund police.

Police are often present even in schools practicing restorative justice. Police presence creates an atmosphere counterproductive to learning. Two-thirds of high school students attend schools with one or more police officers. A study by the American Civil Liberties Union (ACLU) found that 1.7 million students go to schools with no counselors but with police presence. "There is no evidence that increased police presence in schools improves school safety," the report stated. "Indeed, in many cases, it causes harm."[20] Whether a school or community is policed or given the resources that prevent crime—such as affordable housing, access to food, job opportunities, mental health services, affordable child care, and high-quality education—determines the quality of life of students and community members and sets the mood for the physical landscapes we inhabit.

Architect Deanna Van Buren conceived of designing spaces specifically for restorative justice after hearing Fania Davis and her sister Angela Davis speak in the mid-2000s.[21] "I wanted to figure out how I could support the rise of [restorative justice] with design," Van Buren told me. She founded the nonprofit design and development organization Designing Justice + Designing Spaces (DJDS). Since then, she has designed nature-filled spaces across the country that are conducive to meaningful conversations and relationship building.

The deaths of Eric Garner, Michael Brown, and Ezell Ford—all unarmed men killed by police—sparked the Black Lives Matter movement and shed new public light on the inequities of America's policing and prison system. Oakland held a 2014 convening to imagine an alternative justice system, beginning with city resources. Deanna Van Buren, with Tessa Finlev of the Institute for the Future, documented the outcomes in an Oakland mapping project. The project included a conceptual infrastructure map highlighting a series of large Restorative Justice Centers supported by a network of smaller hubs to provide micro-local services in schools, recreation centers, living rooms, and parks. More recently, DJDS worked with community organizers in Atlanta, Georgia, to reimagine the downtown jail as a Center for Equity after Mayor Keisha Lance Bottoms closed it. The jail population shrank drastically after the cash bail system ended, since many people spent days or weeks in jail simply because they couldn't afford bail. This policy and a couple of others reduced the use of the jail until often only 0.25 percent of the beds were occupied.[22]

Plenty of communities and schools are proving that community-led, nature-based planning strategies make neighborhoods safer, even in terms of gun violence. Cities such as Chicago, Philadelphia, and Milwaukee are cleaning up vacant lots, planting trees and gardens, and employing young people who might otherwise get involved in negative activities.[23]

Reggie Moore, Milwaukee's director of violence prevention, said, "When you look at the areas that have the highest rates of gun violence, these are also the areas that have the highest rates of incarceration and the highest rates of poverty. Understanding the causes of trauma and the pain in that individual's life that may be a shooter is [paramount] . . . we must address it on the front end, so we don't have to address it on the back end." One successful program began simply by paying young men twenty dollars to help clean up their neighborhood. As they cleaned up, older men mentored them to give them life skills and a sense of worth. Over time, the community cleanup became a community garden. The neighborhood transformed.

"Within the first three years, violence in that block dropped significantly," Moore said. "It started with 100 young men who needed to be shown love and connection, no organization, no funding, just time. It really is an example of what a community should be." School districts can emulate this model by training teachers and staff in supportive restorative justice methods; by hiring community members as neighborhood mentors to foster life skills and a sense of belonging in middle school and high school students; and by creating district-wide policies on designing places and processes for restorative justice to happen. Investing first in building community resources and restorative environments and programs—instead of policing—will reduce the need for intervention in the long run.

Climate Resilience

8. Connect Schools through Multiple-Benefit Green Infrastructure Networks

In the past fifty years, the number of students walking or bicycling to school dropped from nearly 50 percent to just 13 percent, while students riding in a family car rose from 12 percent to 45 percent, even for distances well under a mile.[24] This shift in transportation to and from school means an increase in air pollution from auto emissions and a drop in physical activity for students. Both outcomes impact students' ability to learn. Young people living in dense city neighborhoods must navigate fierce traffic, chaotic intersections, bumpy sidewalks, unpredictable bus schedules, and sometimes the potential for violence on their way to and from school. Building on the community center and restorative justice approaches discussed earlier, school districts can improve students' feelings of safety in school by helping them get to and from school safely. Schools and districts can partner with nearby business owners, public agencies, nonprofit organizations, and neighbors. Efforts might include mapping the safest routes from residences to and from school.

Once routes are mapped, community members, business owners, street vendors, and the school community can be asked to activate the routes, providing eyes on the street while students are moving between school and home. "Walking school buses" can take pressure off parents for younger students and help older students group up on their way to school and home again. This is a system that expands on the presence of crossing guards at most elementary schools. School administrators can help teenagers and working parents by organizing a community-wide walking group in which older community members, grandparents, or business owners escort students on their way to and from school. The time spent walking can double as a time to mentor students on life skills, share job application tips, and check in about their school and social successes and struggles.

Creating safe pathways that also filter air and water pollution can triple the benefits of supporting mental health. Planners call streets designed for everyone (pedestrians and bicycles in addition to car drivers) "complete streets" and call streets designed to absorb and clean stormwater with trees and planting strips "green streets." Walking through nature or along tree-shaded streets helps students who struggle with attention deficit hyperactivity disorder to do better in school. A study found that students diagnosed with ADHD concentrated significantly better after a twenty-minute walk in a city park than after walking for twenty minutes through a downtown area or a neighborhood. The researchers suggested that "doses of nature might serve as a safe, inexpensive, widely accessible new tool in the tool kit for managing ADHD symptoms."[25] Connecting greener schools to residential neighborhoods with safe routes through parklike spaces, or sidewalks protected from streets by dense planting and tree canopy, will better prepare students to learn when they get to school and create safer pathways as well. Streets lined with trees slow down drivers and provide spots of shady comfort for people of all ages. Across the United States, the Safe Routes to School National Partnership provides resources, policy guidelines, and funding support to communities planning safer school connections.[26] Transportation agencies tackling historical inequities in planning bus and train routes and schedules can engage school communities to create transportation plans that fit students, parents, and the diverse needs of residents and provide routes and schedules that serve them. Good public transit can do more than improve the ability of students and community members to get to school and work and run errands. It can also reduce stress, reduce isolation, and help people save money on transportation. Current practices to reduce or make free transit fares for students can go a long way to alleviate both air pollution and mobility hardship.

9. Provide Nature-Based Job Training for School Employees, Youth, and Community Members

Some of the most important gaps in education are in preparing students to work in green careers and training school employees to manage nature-based systems on school sites. Public schools have an important history of serving as vocational training centers. During the Great Depression, schools engaged students and families in growing food on school sites as part of the Victory Garden movement and provided vocational training on-site throughout World War II.[27] Many of those programs remained in place for decades, and a few still function. Over the past decade, there have been many conversations around green jobs training, with far too little emphasis on implementing and managing nature-based systems. Green infrastructure training programs can hire and train youth, school employees, and other community members to build and care for local green infrastructure networks. While much green jobs focus has been placed on installing solar power, there are opportunities to use schools as sites to train people and create jobs in collecting and reusing rainwater and gray water; planning, planting, and managing urban forests; urban agriculture; and regenerative, habitat-friendly gardening. The Los Angeles–based nonprofit Council for Watershed Health partners with state and regional water agencies and local public school districts to provide technical training in regenerative landscape maintenance practices on school sites and in other public areas (see the discussion of Daniel Webster Middle School in chapter 7).

Another opportunity lies in engaging students and planners with local industrial landowners and business owners. As cities address climate resilience, industrial landowners and business owners are often forgotten in the participatory process. This is problematic for a few reasons. Industrial land uses often lie adjacent to rivers and waterfronts, the low-lying areas most at risk for sea-level rise. Industries employ people. And local industries provide local goods and services as well as a local tax base but can also produce high levels of pollution. Over ten years of Los Angeles River planning, a fifty-acre riverfront industrial area at the confluence of the Verdugo Wash and the Los Angeles River was depicted in various levels of transformation, including as a wetland park. Yet the landowners and business owners had not been engaged in dialogue about the future of their enterprises. In 2017, The Trust for Public Land (TPL) in Los Angeles received a Brownfields Area-Wide Planning Program grant from the US Environmental Protection Agency (EPA) to use an equitable and inclusive engagement process and develop an environmental jobs center model. TPL conducted a participatory community engagement process for the fifty-acre study that resulted in a series of planning and policy scenarios and recommendations to support the area's transition toward green infrastructure, green industry, and green jobs. With a growing interest in local manufacturing and urban agriculture, and a need for high-paying jobs in historically underresourced neighborhoods, this is a model worth repeating.

School districts and their large numbers of students and families can influence planning decisions and benefit neighborhoods in need of jobs, manufacturing, fresh food, and other resources.

10. Amplify Community-Led, Nature-Based Solutions for Climate Resilience

As cities and neighborhoods craft resilience and emergency plans, schools and their connections to surrounding neighborhoods should play a starring role. The community-led, nature-based design strategies in chapter 3 can be scaled up across neighborhoods and school districts to benefit entire communities.

Communities where people know and are connected to one another and can rely on each other during times of crisis have strong social capital. Our neighborhoods need community centers for heat waves, intense weather, earthquakes, power outages, pandemics, and other unforeseen emergencies. We also need to help older adults and teenagers build relationships in their communities to strengthen social ties and social capital, which will build community resilience in times of crisis. We can do this through design.[28] Creating attractive, welcoming places where people can hang out and linger (without the need to buy something) can build relationships between people and foster an attachment to their environment in neighborhoods, commercial centers, and schools. Strong relationships with our neighbors and the places we live help us feel connected and whole, which is essential to mental health. Integrating students and older members of the community into school and community planning processes can foster important informal relationships that will boost social capital in both age groups. As schools improve their physical characteristics to support mental health, the benefits will likely ripple out into the community by way of healthier, more engaged students, neighbors taking pride and ownership in their new community schools, and stability as increasingly invested teachers and principals stay longer at their schools.

The same community-led, nature-based strategies that support mental health and safety on a school site can support social and climate resilience, especially when they extend throughout the community. As cities grow, they replace forests, woods, and other ecosystems with building and paving materials that absorb the sun's heat. This creates "islands" of hotter temperatures in metropolitan areas as compared with the suburbs and rural lands around them. A growing library of environmental research shows that high temperatures and too much sun exposure put students at risk for heat-related illness, decrease their ability to learn, and increase mental health issues.[29] Climate-resilient systems work with natural processes instead of against them to minimize the amount of energy, water, and other resources needed to function while reducing the urban heat island effect and managing stormwater to reduce flood risk and increase local groundwater supplies. Design with nature at the community scale cleans the air, water, and soil; absorbs rainwater; cools urban areas; and provides food for wildlife and people, which in turn supports physical health, mental health, public health, and academic outcomes. Nature-based design strategies should consider human health and well-being as well as ecological health and financial security. The cumulative environmental, health, social, and economic benefits of nature-based planning increases overall resilience—the ability of a community or system to withstand or recover from disruption—as well as public health and equity.

CHAPTER 5

How to Communicate for the Best Chance at Change

Finding empathetic allies is essential to change minds and systems toward nurturing school environments. Ours is a campaign to shift the perceptions, priorities, and practices formed over more than a century of industrialized school design. This is not easy. First, we need to identify the issues that different school community groups care about most. Then we need to find a common language to move forward. Most people making decisions that affect students' mental health and well-being don't think the physical design of a school falls within their responsibility or ability to change. Teachers educate students within the strict confines of standardized curriculums and testing and limited resources. Many have little energy or time to think about teaching anywhere other than in the traditional classroom. Parents are overwhelmed enough without adding mental health advocacy, curriculum, school design, or administrative bureaucracy to their priorities and to-do lists. Government agencies and school administrators and facilities teams' primary aims are to make school campuses safe for students, easy and inexpensive to maintain, and free from cause for a potential lawsuit. The responsibility of managing public funds and expectations makes it difficult for them to agree to new systems or environments. School architects, landscape architects, interior designers, and engineers are usually not educated on how design affects trauma, stress, anxiety, and other mental health conditions. And the students—the only ones who know the way their school spaces make them feel and act—are voiceless in most school planning and design processes.

Sometimes the biggest obstacle to change is the language we use to communicate. Teachers talk about teaching the Common Core learning standards, preparing students with twenty-first-century skills, and the importance of having a growth mindset instead of a fixed mindset. School district facilities teams talk about MOUs (memorandums of understanding), architectural code requirements, liability, and operations and maintenance. Mental health professionals talk about adverse childhood experiences (ACEs), trauma-informed education methods, emotional dysregulation and reregulation. Environmental and community organizations use participatory planning and budgeting methods to identify community-based projects that strive for inclusion, equity, and justice. Architects, landscape architects, and engineers talk about scale, form and performance, urbanism, and functionality. Over this is a wash of terms such as "green," "sustainable," and "resilient" that can be difficult to pin down, depending on who is talking. What does it all mean? It is no wonder that parents and students feel disconnected from and unwelcomed into conversations about school planning and design.

We can learn and practice respectful, supportive, and open communication strategies that invite all parties to say what they think, feel, and know. One of the most important and effective approaches is to remember that we all come to every conversation with a lifetime of experiences behind us. Try to understand how your experiences might charge conversations with emotion, and then remember that the best way to have a respectful, meaningful conversation is to put the yesterdays aside and try to focus on your goals for today's dialogue.[1] We need to understand one another so we can work together to create change. The following words, concepts, and ideas can help almost anyone be more effective as they approach the key decision makers in school design.

Engaging Students

We start with students not because they are decision makers—sadly, they aren't—but because they are the inspiration and the instigation behind this movement. They hold untapped power to sway decision makers. And more than ever, they seek action on climate change, school safety, and environmental and social justice. Young people know what they need and want. They know which places on their school campuses they like and don't like and which places feel good and not so good. Current students have the deepest experiences on school sites. And future students will be most affected by changing school conditions, even during construction. This generation of students will be our next teachers, designers, politicians, and decision makers. We need to listen to them, respect them, and better serve them.

School eco-clubs, student leadership or government groups, and athletic teams are good places to start when looking for ways to engage students' energy in remaking their school environments. Students can also engage older people, especially those who may be isolated and in need of a social network, to serve their local schools. Nonprofit organizations and design professionals can offer to give presentations, participate in career days, or host field trips for elementary schools or upper-grade science classes. As more schools move toward project-based and experiential learning methods, it may become easier for students to lead actions that shape their environments. Today's students want to know that their school leaders care about their safety, their future, and the health of the environment. Students who are introduced to the concepts of restorative justice and trauma-informed education have shown greater resilience, academic success, and sense of community.[2] In order to best engage and involve students in changing their campus environment, we also need to engage teachers. It is crucial to understand and appreciate the inherent risks and responsibilities when working with minors and proceed with sensitivity and care. Before engaging with students, consult the school principal, school district, and/or local college or university for strategies to protect students' rights, well-being, and privacy during participatory planning and design processes.

Engaging students in school design that honors and regenerates ecological and social health can help them feel hopeful for their own future as well as the planet's. Many students look for opportunities to serve their schools and communities. Some are required to do so. Planning and participating in school cleanups, tree planting, and design strategy and implementation projects can help students and the community. School leaders are understandably wary of those who swoop in to offer help, often to serve their own goals, and then abandon the school once funds are gone or their goal is met. Make sure any invitation to organize programs, events, or planning and design processes is done with long-term student benefit in mind.

Teaching Educators

The evidence shows that students behave better and learn more in welcoming, comfortable, and restful school environments. Yet teachers aren't trained how to set up calm classrooms or how to teach outside. Education expert Taylor Allbright told me that not only is there little to no discussion of the physical teaching environment; there also is a disconnect between school facilities policies and whether educators use them as intended.[3] So even when schools provide outdoor classrooms or experiential learning environments, there is little support or training to help teachers shift their teaching approach.

Support teachers by understanding and aligning your design goals to the school's curriculum requirements and the teaching approach of the school and individual teachers.[4] If you can, join the classrooms of a few different teachers to think through how design could support their efforts. For outdoor learning environments, provide a teacher's guide, incorporating all the ways the environment can support the curriculum through different subjects and grade levels.

Eagle Rock Elementary School principal Stephanie Leach talked of the teaching time gained after the new living schoolyard opened. Teachers no longer had to calm down students and ask for their attention after recess. Once the playground provided a variety of places to play and run and tumble and jump, the students got their energy out and came to class ready to learn. Start conversations with teachers by sharing information on how students can benefit from softer, more homelike classrooms; views of trees and gardens; and experiential outdoor learning. Connect teachers with other teachers who have experienced the transformation for themselves. Share stories from other schools where habitat gardens raised students' science scores and nature play improved students' attitudes in the classrooms. Principal support is vital to get projects approved and done. If your school principal agrees to support students' mental health through design, you're halfway there. If not, help your teachers by finding a principal who can share success stories with your principal.

There are programs designed for intensive teacher or principal training on teaching with nature-based school design—such as Green Schoolyards America's Principals' Institute—but training can also be done in short two- or three-hour segments at a nearby school or park.[5] The Children & Nature

Network's Jaime Zaplatosch recommends the simple but important step of helping teachers take what they are already teaching to the outdoors. Understand that this feels daunting at first. For nonteachers, imagine the overwhelm of trying to manage thirty children or adolescents inside a classroom. And now, take that image outside. Teachers benefit from concrete demonstrations on how to manage students in outdoor classrooms and other experiential settings. This can be integrated into overall classroom management classes. Teacher development can happen at school in two or three hours and can be integrated into field trips to local natural areas or outdoor learning landscapes. Give a tour of a living schoolyard, learning garden, or natural area, model how to engage students in a typical lesson, and then ask the teachers, "What did you teach last week that could have been taught outside?"

The growing attention on adverse childhood experiences such as trauma, poverty, and bullying is not framed in relationship to school design. Helping teachers understand the impacts of trauma and other adverse childhood experiences through the mind-body-environment relationship can give them a better understanding of the power of design to support mental health and well-being.

Supporting Parents: The Experts on Their Own Children

There is perhaps nothing more overwhelming to parents than trying to make decisions about their children's well-being. One of those decisions is where their children go to school—if they even have options. Some parents' sole concern is how safe a school is. Others sort through available science, arts, and music classes, electives, advanced placement availability, college acceptance rates, and test scores. Parents without options—or the time or resources to find them—worry about school and community climate and safety and how to help their child navigate the right path to a positive future. To add to the weight, vocabulary around classes, curriculums, and special educational needs changes constantly. There seems to be a secret club for parents who magically know what questions to ask on behalf of their children. In most states, *anyone* can request that a student be screened for alternative education programs, including the student, parent, teacher, or a community member. Parents can also request that their child be evaluated for special education programs or classes to help children with learning differences or disabilities. If a student is eligible, the parents will meet with an education team to create an Individualized Education Program (IEP). Parents have the final say on what the IEP includes. The 1975 Individuals with Disabilities Education Act (IDEA) guarantees all students the right to a *free and appropriate* public education.[6]

More and more neuroscience and education research connects positive learning outcomes and mental health to calming and experiential learning environments—qualities that some schools have and others don't. Parents can use this research to educate principals, school boards and administrators, city agencies, and other decision makers about the opportunity to design schools to better support all students. Our focus should be on how to design schools where every child, no matter his or her learning style, thrives.

Empathizing with Administrators

School district administrators oversee the management and budgets of school improvements. They deal with policy regulations, complaints, and legal issues. District representatives are responsible for the health and welfare of students, teachers, and the entire school community. Administrators, as well as teachers and principals, experience the endless stream of new parents coming into schools and classrooms with new ideas and suggestions year after year. Administrators (and teachers and principals) are the ones who have to pick up the projects' and programs' remains when those parents' children grow up and they no longer have personal ties to the school. Administrators answer to the community, to state and federal regulators, and to the media when issues arise with budgets, student performance, or emergency situations. It is no wonder they can be hesitant when approving changes to school buildings and sites. The best strategy for gaining approvals from district administrators and school principals is to understand their concerns and work with them. Assume the best intentions. We have more success if we approach even the toughest administrator with an attitude of "How can we help you make this school better for everyone?"

First, acknowledge the likelihood that there are things your school administrators know that you might not. In addition to state building codes, there are specific requirements for schools set by the school district. Research the codes that apply to your school, and ask the district's facilities or design department for the most recent building codes and design guidelines. You can advocate for improvements only if you understand the requirements and opportunities specific to your school district. For instance, the director of architectural and engineering services for the Los Angeles Unified School District (LAUSD), Christos Chrysiliou, has to balance any increase in trees and gardens in schoolyards with the district's required minimum area of "open play space" for physical education.

"This is where we have to work with our curriculum folks, because of how we define 'structured, active play,'" Chrysiliou told me. "The state doesn't define play space. But PE could come in there and say, 'We have to run five physical education classes during the day with two hundred students on the field at once.'"

Possible partners to help you communicate with school district decision makers are principals, who often have a big say in what happens in their schools; outdoor education directors (both within and outside the district); school site maintenance directors or teams; security teams; and parent and community groups. Share research and case studies, grounding your ideas in scientific evidence. Take district and school decision makers and others on field trips to see programs and schools similar to your proposal.

One of the biggest obstacles to getting approval for natural materials or living systems is the perception that they require more maintenance. Chronically cash-poor school facilities departments prefer materials that don't grow, don't age, and don't break. You can do your school a favor by figuring out how to care for living schoolyards and other indoor and outdoor school improvements as you design them. Indoor and outdoor furniture, painted surfaces, window treatments, and other nonliving materials may be relatively easy to win approval for. When proposing living and evolving or changing systems—such as plants, trees, hedges, new grass fields, rainwater tanks, rain gardens, biofiltration planting areas, vines, food gardens, and green walls—expect some pushback. This doesn't mean you won't get approval. But it does mean you will need to have a plan for who will take care of these systems and how that care will be funded. Look to student clubs or classes to see whether you can harness student energy and tie maintenance to health, science, horticulture, or other classes. When you tie living systems or new classrooms or gardens to education, you open up the possibility of tying maintenance funds to general funding streams. Most states now measure attendance as key to student success, and many tie school budgets to attendance. This means you can get administrators' attention by talking about the connection between school design and attendance.[7]

Educating Designers about Mental Health

Because architectural design and landscape architectural design are such broad fields, it is not unusual for school designers to be unaware of the decades of research connecting mental health to design. One of the biggest opportunities to support students' mental health and well-being lies in helping designers understand the impacts of design decisions. District administrators, counselors, special education teachers, trauma experts, and community members can help educate the design team about the specific needs of the students and school community. This could mean sharing articles, books, podcasts, or other media with the design team about the mind-body-environment connection. It could mean conversations and presentations about students' specific mental health needs and how design can support them. At the very least, getting people from different disciplines and perspectives into the same room is a big step forward.

The Cal Poly Pomona Department of Landscape Architecture, Prevention Institute, and a dozen regional nonprofits sponsored the first Designing Schools for Mental Health Workshop in Los Angeles in 2018. The goal was to bring together school designers, administrators, and educators with public health and mental health professionals, environmental organizations, and local agencies to share the research and identify actions to move forward. Professor William C. Sullivan shared his research findings on access to nature and mental health and well-being. Sharon Danks presented insights from the Green Schoolyards America and International School Grounds Alliance advocacy networks. Professor Marcella Raney summarized the results of her Eagle Rock Elementary School living schoolyard before-and-after study on students' behavior and physical activity. LAUSD's director of student mental health and director of asset management and the founder of the Los Angeles Trust for Children's Health presented their work in building twelve community Wellness Centers at LAUSD high schools. After a morning of research and case studies, an afternoon workshop grouped people from diverse professions to brainstorm obstacles, strategies, and actions to support students' mental health through school design. That one workshop led to the following:

- relationships being built between design professionals, nonprofits, and community members seeking better school environments;
- a leading architecture firm launching an initiative to design schools that do more to support students' mental health and well-being;
- guest experts speaking to LAUSD facilities architects about the physical activity and mental health benefits of living schoolyards;
- a presentation to the Los Angeles County Office of Education on designing schools to support mental health and well-being; and
- nearly one hundred participants gaining a better understanding of the importance of school environments on mental health, and actions they can take to initiate change.

Sometimes creating change starts with bringing the right people together into the conversation. Identify the local, regional, and farther afield voices that can help you educate design professionals. Invite them to organize or participate in a workshop designed to create change.

Partnering with Government Agencies

School districts in the United States are largely planned and funded locally. There is tremendous opportunity to engage city and county planning, transportation, land use, public health, watershed health, and other agencies to partner in improving schools and communities. There are many reasons why this can be good for a particular school or neighborhood as well as for larger local and regional planning efforts. These agencies have budgets that can fund projects that serve multiple purposes. Funds earmarked for climate resilience, transportation or stormwater infrastructure, public health, environmental justice, or watershed health can fund school improvements that will also support mental health and well-being. Cities, counties, and states have a vested interest in managing urban runoff, reducing the heat island effect, and improving pedestrian safety. So proposing school sites as places to improve government agency goals to treat stormwater, plant trees, and increase the safety of students on their way to and from school can open the conversation.

Questioning the Status Quo

The foregoing conversation strategies have been well received at schools around the United States. It may be worth asking yourself and your school community some bigger questions related to mental health and safety. The questions and topics that follow challenge assumptions about school environments today. The same topics that may be taken for granted in some school communities may be controversial in others. The following can help a school community shake up preconceived notions about the built environment and invite deeper conversations around designing schools that heal.

What Makes a School Safe?

"As the old saying goes, when you're a hammer, everything looks like a nail," Allan Mangold told me. As a security engineer, Mangold works with school districts and design teams on school safety. We had just finished a workshop at HMC Architects to develop softer, student-centered school design strategies. I asked him why so many schools use such severe security methods, contradicting what all the research shows actually works.

"The physical security realm is dominated by former military and law enforcement, and the methodologies used reflect that background and experience. School safety and security is undergoing a profound transformation, and we need to recognize that trying to shoehorn standards and guidelines more appropriate to the anti-terrorism and Force Protection environment is not going to be effective and will most likely be counterproductive." Mangold advocates against the toughening approach that many school security teams are taking and toward the community-led, empathetic design approach used by Svigals + Partners.

"We use the Sandy Hook redesign quite a bit to make the point that guns, guards, and gates are not the way forward . . . they actually do more psychological damage than good," Mangold said. His team developed a "Facilities Master Planning 101" presentation to educate decision makers about simple, cost-effective changes they can make at schools to improve safety without creating a sense of being jailed. It includes a simplified approach to modernization: enhanced lighting; better doors (just commercial grade—not, he stresses, the superexpensive defense-rated ones); planted fence lines to prevent people from jumping up and over. Cost-effective and simple enhancements will do more than one might think. Mangold advises against closed-circuit cameras, which help only after something has happened, and toward a holistic approach to design that includes everyone in the conversation.

The redesign of a school is a time to reflect deeply on the school's purpose, its approach, and how it fits into the lives of its students and the larger community. The National Education Association (NEA)—the voice of education professionals in the United States—states in its core values, "All students have the human and civil right to a quality public education that develops their potential, independence, and character." It is our responsibility as designers, educators, and school community members to make decisions that support this right.

Often, landscape architects and public agencies invoke the principles of crime prevention through environmental design (CPTED) for reducing crime. In practice, CPTED became shorthand for maintaining visibility through and into an area—a way for police representatives and parks agencies to request or require the ability to see everything going on in a neighborhood. Its application and effectiveness are controversial and should be regarded with skepticism by designers, community members, school and parks administrators, and others prioritizing the safety and well-being of a neighborhood. Ray Jeffery, who coined the term "crime prevention through environmental design," called for an interdisciplinary, holistic approach to addressing the many environmental factors contributing to crime—including social relationships and the impacts of pollution.[8]

William C. Sullivan and his colleagues studied Chicago's public housing neighborhoods, infamous for widespread fear and violence. "Within these neighborhoods, there were pockets that promoted not only a sense of safety, but also actual safety," Sullivan wrote. "One thing these pockets shared was a characteristic of the landscape that drew neighbors together, and in doing so, helped strengthen social ties that in turn, created safer places. This landscape feature was the presence of natural elements such as a few trees and some grass."[9]

Parks as Schools and Schools as Parks

Even before the coronavirus pandemic, schools and communities were rethinking where and how children go to school. Charter schools pop up in former offices, retail spaces, and warehouses without an outside place to play. School districts with growing populations struggle to keep outdoor space in the face of more temporary classrooms. People of all ages spend more and more time in front of computer screens, phones, and other digital devices instead of outdoors and interacting with other people. And yet we know students do better with plenty of access to nature—Vitamin N, as Richard Louv calls it—and strong relationships with community. In response to this, a growing number of parents have found ways to let their children learn outside. Forest schools, outside schools, and unschooling are all methods of taking students out of the classroom and letting them learn from nature and natural processes. Child-led learning often happens in home-based programs and progressive schools. Why can't public schools follow a nature-based, child-led curriculum, too?

Many park equity organizations work to open up school grounds as low-hanging fruit in providing people with access to green spaces. Inviting the community into school grounds for play space, park activities, and meeting rooms in the evenings and on weekends creates a sense of belonging for the entire neighborhood. Nonprofit environmental and social justice groups see school campuses as a chance to bring in nature's services to green and cool the grounds, support academics, increase habitat, improve social cohesion, and boost mental and physical health.

As so many people have experienced during social distancing, there is a lack of park space in many of our poorest neighborhoods. Opening school campuses to the community can improve access to nature and help students, their families, and the community feel a sense of ownership of and responsibility toward the schools. In park-poor communities, schools provide places to play, gather, and hold community events where there might be no room or budget for a park. This includes partnerships between city parks departments and school districts to keep school sites open later at night and on weekends. They can also work to create shady, nature-filled outdoor classrooms to allow schools to stay open during times of social distancing. Four environmental and outdoor education organizations partnered to create the National COVID-19 Outdoor Learning Initiative to propose engaging schoolgrounds and parks as cost-effective resources for mental, physical, and academic well-being as schools reopen. Outdoor spaces on school grounds and in parks can immediately address the most urgent conditions threatened by social distancing, including exacerbated education inequities, disrupted learning, and increased social isolation, trauma, and stress. See box 5.1 for the informational summary that went out to schools to share resources developed by the initiative.

Continued on page 118

Box 5.1: National COVID-19 Outdoor Learning Initiative

The following is a proposal by the National COVID-19 Outdoor Learning Initiative to engage school grounds and parks as strategic, cost-effective tools for improving academic, mental, and physical well-being as schools reopen.

Background

Schools across the United States will use distance learning through the end of [the 2020] school year due to the COVID-19 pandemic. Although it is not clear what the next semester will look like, there is an urgent need to reimagine Pre-K–12 schools in order to safely reopen school campuses.

Since social distancing will be required far into the future, pending adequate testing and a widely available vaccine, students must spread out beyond the traditional four walls of the classroom. While staggering students' schedules and continuing distance learning will likely be elements of the new normal, these options place additional stress on caregivers' capacity to work and may not be enough by themselves. Many school buildings were already at capacity before this crisis, and the costs to adapt building infrastructure to accommodate COVID-19 safety measures are also well beyond schools' budgets.

Expanding the classroom into outdoor spaces both on and off school grounds will address academic, health, and economic needs. Studies show that spending time outdoors is critical to student academic, physical, and mental well-being. Outdoor environments typically have better air quality than indoor spaces, and "environmental conditions, such as wind and sunlight, may reduce the amount of virus present on a surface and the length of time the virus can stay viable."* Outdoor classrooms are one of the most cost-effective ways to increase school capacity. If schools are able to safely accommodate more children by going outside, there will be less disruption in the lives of students and families.

Existing Conditions

The following conditions are threatened by COVID-19 and can be addressed by using outdoor spaces:

Box 5.1: Continued on next page

Box 5.1: Continued

Equity. This health crisis is exacerbating existing inequalities across America. There are vast disparities in students' access to online learning, adequate food, stable housing, medical care, and access to nature.

Learning. Despite best efforts by school districts to provide distance learning, students are experiencing significant academic disruptions and loss.

Mental Health. This crisis is causing substantial adverse experiences for children and adults. Students will return to school with a mental health burden caused by social isolation, uncertainty, trauma, and stress.

Physical Health. Most children and youth are spending their time indoors on electronic devices. It is likely that many will return to school at a reduced fitness level. Some may also have suffered from COVID-19.

Economic Health. Our country's economic strength and security are threatened when much of the workforce stays home and businesses close. Many school and childcare programs that allow parents to return to work are closed.

Education Workforce. The nonformal education sector is facing large-scale job loss. If these skilled, professional outdoor educators, naturalists, and museum staff leave the field, schools will lose vital academic program partners.

Vision
Engage school grounds and parks as strategic, cost-effective tools for improving academic, mental, and physical well-being as schools reopen with required social distancing measures in place.

Use and Expand Outdoor Learning Opportunities. Provide simple outdoor classroom spaces on school grounds and in local parks to accommodate a portion (10%–50%) of the students or classes at each school. Use these outdoor environments to provide options for social distancing and take the burden off indoor spaces.

Related infrastructure needs will include:

- Basic seating—log rounds, straw bales, picnic tables
- Outdoor teaching supplies—clipboards, whiteboards
- Shade—tree canopy, shade umbrellas, tents

- Storage—supply sheds
- Accessibility—ADA-compliant paths and bathrooms

Other needs:

- Professional development—help teachers and aides to increase comfort teaching outside
- Temporary personnel—to achieve smaller groupings of students, include nonformal educators via partner organizations, out of work due to COVID-19
- Labor—to create outdoor learning spaces
- Transportation—to ensure equity for schools that do not have outdoor space on-site or nearby

Outdoor Spaces Are Therapeutic. Students and staff may return to school with stress and trauma associated with isolation, uncertainty, and illness. To ease the burden, nature-rich outdoor areas identified and developed on or near each campus can provide quiet, reflective spaces to unwind and relax.

Collaborate to Rethink Physical Activity. Many PE and recess activities require physical proximity and shared equipment. They will need to be reconfigured to accommodate social distancing guidelines, including moving from indoor gyms and crowded blacktop to nontraditional outdoor spaces, on and off campus. Social distancing during physical activity could be improved by:

- Limiting the number of children playing together, and assigning students to consistent cohorts
- Engaging smaller groups of children in nontraditional activities to develop strength, balance, and other skills without play structures or shared equipment
- Increasing gardening and creative activities with natural materials (e.g., art projects, imaginative play)

Box 5.1: Continued on next page

Box 5.1: Continued

Collaborate with Before- and After-School Programs. Many families need before- and after-school child-care programs to be able to go to work. These programs will also require new social distancing measures. To address this issue, they could expand their footprint to use additional outdoor spaces on campus and in nearby parks. They will also likely need additional staff.

Act Now

This pandemic has completely changed how people interact with one another and the surrounding environment. As communities emerge from shelter-in-place, nature-rich outdoor spaces on school grounds and in local parks present a cost-effective opportunity to improve health, heal our collective trauma, and support students, families, and the economy.

Source: National COVID-19 Outdoor Learning Initiative, "Outdoor Spaces Are Essential Assets for School Districts' Covid-19 Response across the USA," 2020, http://www.greenschoolyards.org/covid-learn-outside. Reprinted by permission of Green Schoolyards America.

*National Academies of Sciences, Engineering, and Medicine, "Based on Science: How Long Does Coronavirus Live on Surfaces?," https://bit.ly/NASEM_COVID.

Broadening Equity and Environmental Justice

Another conversation worth starting with your school community is about environmental justice. What does environmental justice mean to your community? At a minimum, it usually aims to even out the resources directed toward different neighborhoods or communities of a particular region, with a focus on correcting past injustices. For example, the practice of insurance companies redlining marginalized and low-income neighborhoods in the 1940s resulted in those neighborhoods losing generations of potential investments, equity, and income because of lending practices that allowed investment only in "green" neighborhoods. Working toward environmental and social justice could mean investing to bring those neighborhoods to a similar standard of environmental health as other neighborhoods in the region. Chapter 4 introduced how some communities improve and strengthen neighborhoods while trying not to price people out of them.

Many school communities work to provide support and safe space for LGBTQ+ students, students experiencing homelessness, Dreamers, immigrants, and students who will be the first in their families to go to college. An individual educator, school, or school district can improve students' feelings of belonging, inclusion, and value in school and in the world by teaching them about relevant people, places, communities, histories, and plans.

Another view of environmental justice questions our right as humans to displace other species. Anthony Tróchez, PhD, expands the concept of environmental justice to include animal and plant communities. "In a social justice context, the curriculum in your history class erases your own history," he told me. "You see that same lack of existence in the environment. For every house, every hotel, every built environment, there are displaced animals, fungi, trees," Tróchez said. Until we recognize and acknowledge what we are doing to our fellow species, we can't repair and restore our communities and ecosystems. And that, he said, is his goal.

"As destructive as we can be, we can also be restorative," he said. Despite actions that suggest otherwise, we depend on plants and trees and animals for the air we breathe, the water we drink, and the food we eat. We cannot live without trees and plants creating oxygen, animals pollinating our food crops, and microorganisms cleaning our water and soil. Our lives depend on the health of all of the species on the planet, human and nonhuman. And we've been doing a terrible job taking care of both. Our young people see this and feel this. They need the promise of a better future.

Physical Education, Athletics, and Mental Health

Around 7 percent of high school athletes in the United States go on to play a varsity college sport, and the odds that a high school athlete will play professionally are less than 1 percent.[10] The average professional sports career lasts five years. Yet most public elementary, middle school, and high school campuses devote significant land area and time to organized sports. This approach is unique to the United States. Other developed countries, especially those excelling in education, don't emphasize sports in school. They emphasize academics. With growing concerns about traumatic brain injury and the relatively small likelihood of a sports career, it is worth exploring whether competitive sports improve or reduce students' mental health and safety. As with all strategies, the answers will differ in each school community.

Traumatic brain injury (TBI), or chronic traumatic encephalopathy (CTE), in athletes causes a variety of mental health issues, including loss of brain function, aggression, violence, suicide, and changes in personality. A growing number of athletes are raising concerns over the safety of sports such as football, wrestling, and soccer. There are myriad ways to support physical health and mental health while also improving a school site's ecological health. The research presented in the first two chapters suggests that nature play and green areas increase vigorous physical activity as well as creative and cooperative play, especially in groups that don't participate in competitive play. This is an important consideration. A number of school districts are turning to artificial turf playing fields as a maintenance solution, despite growing concerns about infection, high costs, and potential toxic exposures to the rubber fill. Watershed health experts add to the debate with concerns about the massive concrete pans beneath the fields and plastic waste entering waterways. If our goal is to boost physical health across all school populations, why not provide a variety of settings that invite different kinds of activities while regenerating ecological health? We can redefine physical education and athletics to include activities that promote physical health *and* brain health, vigorous activity *and* ecological awareness. Small and large natural areas, woods, and forests can host walking, running, Frisbee golf, tree climbing, and ropes courses. As interest in bouldering and rock climbing soars, campuses are building climbing walls. We could bring natural boulders and climbing walls to school grounds.

A major obstacle to increasing access to nature in schoolyards is not how physical education is defined but how it is practiced. The Centers for Disease Control and Prevention defines physical education as "a K–12 academic subject that provides standards-based curricula and instruction" and that is "designed to develop the knowledge and behaviors for physical activity, physical fitness, and motor skills in students." This appears to be a reasonably broad definition.

According to the Society of Health and Physical Educators, a well-designed physical education program "meets the needs of all students;

keeps students active for most of physical education class time; teaches self-management; emphasizes knowledge and skills for a lifetime of physical activity; and is an enjoyable experience for all students."[11]

Many physical education programs, however, provide outdated and narrow sets of skills that don't appeal to or serve all students. If the intent is to prepare students today for a healthy lifestyle, physical education standards aren't doing that. I asked physical education expert Marcella Raney what she thought physical education *should* look like. She answered, "First of all, the standards have to change. PE is currently based on having all students achieve a certain threshold. We're ignoring developmental change. We're not reporting how students change over time. And we're only measuring in fifth, seventh, and ninth grades . . . why not earlier?"

Raney went on: "Are we successfully encouraging students to adopt an active lifestyle? Our current system doesn't do that." In fact, because physical education is so focused on competitive sports and calisthenics, many students opt out if given a chance. When schools and districts offer a choice between physical education and health classes, more girls choose health than physical education. This matters because the physical activity habits we establish at a young age follow us through our lifetime.

Today's physical education classes, especially in elementary and middle schools, are often taught by teachers trained to teach language arts, science, or other academic subjects. On the other hand, in high school, athletic coaches are often asked to teach academic subjects they aren't experts in. We can't inspire students to strive for healthy lifestyles without physical and mental health experts teaching them.

Other activities such as digging, climbing trees and rocks, gardening, walking, and forest bathing—immersing oneself in the atmosphere of trees—bring us closer to the earth while strengthening our bodies and minds. Some schools bring in yoga, meditation, and other mindfulness techniques. Dance and movement practices can be done in almost any setting, through trees or other objects. Other schools engage students in the care of their environment, activating their bodies and ethics in sweeping, mopping, raking, washing, cooking, and growing. Caring for the school environment and the people within it can be a powerful way to strengthen students' sense of belonging and responsibility to the community as well as their bodies and minds. If the point is to teach them to be healthy and active, Raney summed it up best: "Couldn't we teach them what's fun and have them figure it out?"

We need to start framing school design as a "both/and" proposal. It isn't this *or* that: mental health *or* academics, nature play *or* physical education, living schoolyards *or* lower maintenance costs. Healthy school environments can include all of these things when designed with the entire school community using a holistic, integrated, nature-based design approach. Supportive school environments will not just help students feel safer and interact better with their peers, teachers, and school communities . . . they will also support the learning they are in school to do. Students learn more in safe, quiet, restorative environments. Adding nature and natural systems to school campuses can give students living laboratories to explore and learn the life sciences, the laws of physics, the aesthetic beauty of nature, ethnobotany, and plant science in an experiential setting. Putting hands on natural materials both is restful and awakens the mind in ways that reading words on paper cannot. Design to support mental health can also heal the environment and work toward social and environmental justice. Our success in designing and funding schools to support students' mental health and well-being will depend on how we talk about it and who we include. The next chapter presents information to clear another big hurdle: paying for school improvements.

CHAPTER 6

Money Doesn't Grow on Trees . . . or Does It?

Once all the decision makers agree on the benefits of designing schools that heal—and sometimes long before—the next question is "How will we pay for it?" Public schools receive more funds than any other infrastructure system in the United States besides transportation. And yet funding is a perpetual challenge for most school districts, especially those in working-class and poor neighborhoods. A 2016 report estimated an $8 billion shortfall on public school facilities spending for maintenance and operations and a $38 billion shortfall for capital construction. Overall, that represents a $46 billion shortage of the spending schools need in order to keep up with maintenance, repairs, and new schools.[1] That equals 32 percent of what schools in the United States currently spend on facilities. The level of disrepair our schools have fallen into is overwhelming, inequitable, and sad. While some students attend new, healthy schools with modern technology, many others suffer in outdated and toxic buildings without clean drinking water or modern learning facilities. The quality of school facilities depends almost entirely on zip code. It is difficult to say whether and how education funding might change to prioritize public health, equity, and resilience in the near future. Equitable and generous school funding is a long overdue way to support our children, our communities, and our planet.

Public education is arguably the most important resource we can give our country's future. Yet the system relies mostly on local budgets. Currently, only 9 percent of school funding comes from the federal government. Each school district, county, and state has its own method of approving and paying for school buildings and programs. The processes guiding school design, approvals, funding, and construction are vague and hard to understand. Buried within those complex processes are strategies to fund mental health—most often as part of special education programs or programs designed to identify students needing counseling. We need a clear way forward through the chaos of planning and funding school facilities in general and environments that support mental health in particular.[2] Healthy, well-designed schools improve student success, teacher satisfaction, and community connectedness and resilience.

Public education and public health professionals advocate for more federal funding. The vast majority of Americans agree. In a recent survey, 72 percent of adults responded that school infrastructure spending was an extremely or very important priority.[3] Until that happens, however, we need strategic and creative ways to pay for schools that heal. This chapter sheds a little light on school budgets and funding sources.

Types of Costs

Understanding the categories of funding is essential to looking for and requesting funding. Most places we look for money for school improvements have limits on the types of projects they can support. Some funding sources will pay only for capital projects. Others will pay only for programs. Understanding these limits and shaping your plan and priorities around them can help open funding from sources that otherwise would be unavailable.

Capital Costs

Capital costs cover the construction or major renovation of new buildings or schoolyards. Think of these as one-time costs that cover construction. This category is divided into hard costs, directly related to construction, and soft costs, or indirect costs. The materials and labor needed to actually build the school are considered hard costs. These are the concrete costs of purchasing and putting together the materials to create real educational spaces. Architectural, landscape architectural, and engineering fees; permits; and taxes are considered indirect or soft costs. These are the costs related to planning and designing the school before construction starts. This includes the money used to pay for architects, landscape architects, and engineers to design the school; money to buy permits from the city planning agencies to allow site improvements to be made; and any taxes or other fees required to allow construction to start. Both soft costs and hard costs are included in the overall capital costs associated with making a new school or renovating an existing school. Capital costs include everything up until the day the renovation or new construction is complete and the school opens.

Maintenance and Operations Costs

The ongoing costs of taking care of school buildings and grounds, repairing things as they break, and performing general upkeep fall under the maintenance and operations funding category. This type of funding is crucial to the success of any project, especially for living landscapes and systems, which require some regular maintenance. Daily cleaning and maintenance of classrooms, administration offices, cafeterias, and other building-related spaces are covered by general school funds. Even landscapes that are designed with natural systems and trees and plants that are native or adapted to the place they are planted need some consistent care. The trees, plants, and organisms that keep soil healthy in living schoolyards grow and change from season to season and over time. Covering the costs of ongoing care and maintenance of living schoolyards is one of the biggest challenges to getting a school or district to agree to them. While these living systems are vital to the health and well-being of students, the community, and the planet, they aren't directly associated with school curriculums—at least not yet. So they are treated as an excess maintenance cost instead of an essential asset. One issue with this perception is that many budgeted and grant funding sources limit spending to capital improvements. If a living schoolyard or an outdoor classroom is tied to an academic curriculum, the maintenance costs may be included in the school's general budget, in the same category of maintenance related to classroom instruction and upkeep.

Program Costs

While capital costs cover building and grounds construction, and maintenance and operations costs cover anything related to maintaining those buildings and grounds, program costs pay for things related to special events or educational activities that supplement the required school curriculum. So while regular classes would be part of the general instruction budget, program costs might include music, arts, or gardening programs not covered in the state's general education requirements. After-school care, mentoring, tutoring, and jobs training could all fall into the program costs category, which fall under support services. These are things often decided on and covered by parent groups and special fundraising efforts school by school, and they generally refer to school-related activities that aren't required by the state or school district. See figure 6.1 for a breakdown of school funding sources and spending categories.

The Triple Bottom Line

We can understand the true costs and value of designing schools to support mental health and well-being only if we begin measuring and documenting the true and full costs and benefits of our efforts. Nature-based, community-led design strategies rely on qualities that can be difficult to quantify as far as financial costs or a return on investment. These types of school improvements don't just cost money. They have numerous benefits related to human and ecological health and productivity as well. The triple bottom line measures the social and environmental impacts of a plan or development—not just the economic return on investment. A recent study on urban forests in five United States cities found that every $1.00 spent on planting and maintaining trees returned between $1.37 and $3.09 per year in human, environmental, or economic benefits.[4]

Nature-based design strategies provide us with vital ecosystem services—those services provided by natural systems that directly and indirectly contribute to human health and well-being. These services are organized into four categories: supporting services, necessary to produce all other ecosystem services; provisioning services, which provide products such as food and water; regulating services, which regulate ecosystem processes such as carbon sequestration; and cultural services, which describe the physical and mental health benefits we receive through access to nature (see box 6.1, page 129).

US SCHOOL FUNDING
SOURCES & SPENDING CATEGORIES

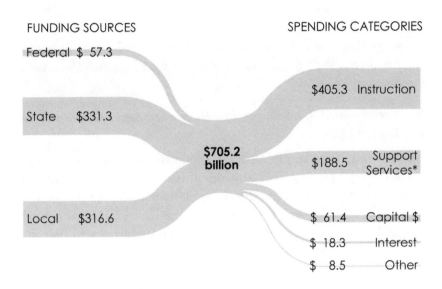

FUNDING SOURCES

Federal $ 57.3

State $331.3

Local $316.6

$705.2 billion

SPENDING CATEGORIES

$405.3 Instruction

$188.5 Support Services*

$ 61.4 Capital $

$ 18.3 Interest

$ 8.5 Other

*includes student support services, O&M of plant, student transportation, general administration, school administration, and other support services

FIGURE 6.1: The vast majority of primary and secondary school funding in the United States comes from state and local sources, with an average of just over 8 percent of schools' funds coming from the federal government. Most of the school budget—more than 90 percent—goes toward instruction and support services, such as teacher salaries, guidance counselors, psychology services, speech and audiology services, student health, school libraries, and materials and classroom supplies, including textbooks. Sources: United States Census, "Annual Survey of School System Finances," 2018, accessed September 8, 2020, https://www.census.gov/programs-surveys/school-finances.html; Institute of Progressive Education and Learning, "A Look at a School District Budget," n.d., accessed September 8, 2020, http://institute-of-progressive -education-and-learning.org/k-12-education/k-12-adminisrtation/a-look-at -a-school-district-budget/.

Approaches to Funding School Design to Support Mental Health and Well-being

Given the budget shortfalls and strict parameters around school funding, it is important to be creative and proactive when seeking funds for school improvements—especially those to support mental health and well-being. The following strategies might open doors or minds in order to secure the financial support students and communities need and deserve.

Use Nature-Based, Community-Led Design Strategies: Cost-Effective and Longer-Lived

We frequently mistake the costlier solution for the best solution. But research on the measured performance of school improvements related to mental and physical health shows us that sometimes the best solution is the less expensive one. Engineered, off-the-shelf play structures are incredibly expensive and take up a lot of playground space. They are often underlaid with expensive rubberized surfacing that is supposed to cushion a child's fall. But that surface melts and stiffens in excessive heat and can cause more broken bones and injuries than playground mulch.[5] On the other hand, a mulched and wooded area with a few rope swings, boulders, and logs donated by an arborist or a tree service is affordable or even free. This type of area offers students of all ages enough opportunities for physical challenge and creative play to keep them engaged and active for years to come, and it can be designed to manage stormwater and increase habitat, too. The most expensive part of such an area is likely the cost to remove asphalt or concrete, if needed, and to test and treat soil if any newly uncovered soil tests positive for dangerous substances.

Another example compares affordable nature-based surface runoff management strategies with engineered filtration systems requiring big excavations or grading. While most states now require schools and cities to clean and absorb urban runoff before it enters creeks and rivers, there is often a choice between nature-based and engineered strategies. The engineered strategies tend to be underground, be hidden from students and the community, and require cost-prohibitive grading and excavation. Nature-

Continued on page 130

Box 6.1: Ecosystem Services from the Sustainable Sites Initiative

The Sustainable Sites Initiative is a partnership of the American Society of Landscape Architects, the Lady Bird Johnson Wildflower Center, and the United States Botanic Garden in conjunction with a diverse group of stakeholder organizations to establish and encourage sustainable practices in landscape design, construction, operations, and maintenance.

The services people enjoy from healthy ecosystems are the unobtrusive foundation of daily life. Trees help regulate local climate by providing shade and acting as windbreaks. Through evaporation, transpiration, and the uptake and storage of carbon, plants moderate the climate of the world and provide a breathable atmosphere. Thousands of different pollinator species visit their respective flowers and promote the growth of myriad plants and crops. Healthy wetlands protect us from floods and help to improve water quality. Soils and vegetation purify stormwater seeping through to groundwater and underground aquifers. Ecosystem services such as these occur at a variety of scales, in habitats ranging from equatorial rain forests to urban parks. Yet because these services occur largely in the background, governments and businesses don't include them in their conventional cost accounting. In fact, people often underestimate or simply ignore these benefits and services when making land use decisions—only to realize later how difficult, expensive, and sometimes impossible it is to replicate ecosystem services once they are lost. The Sustainable Sites Initiative is dedicated to fostering a transformation in land development and management practices that will bring the essential importance of ecosystem services to the forefront. For purposes of the initiative, land practices are defined as sustainable if they enable natural and built systems to work together to "meet the needs of the present without compromising the ability of future generations to meet their own needs."*

Ecosystem Services

Ecosystem services are goods and services of direct or indirect benefit to humans that are produced by ecosystem processes that involve the interactions of living elements, such as vegetation and soil organisms, and non-living elements, such as bedrock, water, and air. Researchers have come up

Box 6.1: Continued on next page

with a number of lists of these benefits, each with slightly different wording and some lists slightly longer than others. The members of the Sustainable Sites Initiative's committees and staff have reviewed and consolidated the research into the following list of ecosystem services that a sustainable site can strive to protect or regenerate through sustainable land development and management practices.

Global climate regulation: Maintaining a balance of atmospheric gases at historical levels, ensuring breathable air, and sequestering greenhouse gases

Local climate regulation: Regulating local temperature, precipitation, and humidity through shading, evapotranspiration, and windbreaks

Air and water cleansing: Removing and reducing pollutants in air and water

Water supply retention: Storing and providing water within watersheds and aquifers

Erosion and sediment control: Retaining soil within an ecosystem, preventing damage from erosion and siltation

Hazard mitigation: Reducing vulnerability to damage from flooding, storm surge, wildfire, and drought

based strategies can be low-budget, relying on inexpensive gravel, plants, and trees, and can offer students living laboratories to learn from as well as the restorative experience of witnessing nature at work. Big impacts can be made through a series of small, incremental improvements in phases.

Tie the Improvement to the Curriculum

With limited maintenance budgets and personnel, districts often worry about how they will manage and take care of school improvements, especially living landscapes. Districts such as the Los Angeles Unified School District recommend connecting outdoor classrooms, learning gardens, and other living schoolyard improvements to the curriculum. This ensures a route to care—even if that route is the students, teachers, and school volunteers doing the maintenance.

Children & Nature Network's Jaime Zaplatosch points to a shift that

Pollination: Providing pollinator species for the reproduction of crops and other plants

Habitat functions: Providing refuge and reproduction habitat to plants and animals, thereby contributing to the conservation of biological and genetic diversity and evolutionary processes

Waste decomposition and treatment: Breaking down waste and cycling nutrients

Human health and well-being: Enhancing physical, mental, and social well-being as a result of interaction with nature

Food and renewable nonfood products: Producing food, fuel, energy, medicine, or other products for human use

Cultural benefits: Enhancing cultural, educational, aesthetic, and spiritual experiences as a result of interaction with nature

Source: Sustainable Sites Initiative, *Sustainable Sites Initiative: Guidelines and Performance Benchmarks, 2009,* https://digital.library.unt.edu/ark:/67531/metadc31157/m2/1/high_res_d/Guidelines%2and%20Performance%20Benchmarks_2009.pdf.

*This definition of sustainability is from *Our Common Future,* the 1987 report prepared by the United Nations World Commission on Environment and Development, chaired by Gro Harlem Brundtland, then prime minister of Norway. The report is often referred to as the Brundtland Report.

needs to happen in order to help fund living schoolyards, outdoor classrooms, and makerspaces as well as other natural systems that may require special care over the long term. If a facilities or management team defines these spaces as separate from the learning environment, they will be reduced to an optional and troublesome space to maintain. If they are treated as extensions of the classroom, they will become open to capital funds supporting the curriculum. The key to this approach is to understand that we don't need to develop new curriculums. Instead, help and support teachers to think about what they are already teaching and how they could teach it outside in a learning garden, an outdoor classroom, or another experiential setting. Connecting school gardens, play areas, and outdoor classrooms to the curriculum unlocks funding and teacher involvement. In order to gain teacher support, however, teachers need to be involved in discussions of goals and school design from the onset.

Find Where Small Investments Can Gain Meaningful Results

Often the most meaningful impacts can be achieved with less disruptive changes. It is a little counterintuitive until you think of the processes that drive economic markets and that what is often best for our students and ourselves is less expensive in the short and long terms. While working in design firms, I saw constant requests from manufacturers to let them bring in their newest materials and products, and often lunch, to show us the latest and greatest trends in landscape furniture and equipment. Many of those products were made or mined on other continents, and rarely were the ingredients or processes used to make them available or easy to find. They were expensive, too. In nature-based design, we can look to local ecology and cultural history to see how people built and lived off regional materials. We can use the soil excavated to create biofiltration areas to make rammed earth walls or mud bricks. We can reuse and repurpose old materials and furniture that would otherwise be thrown out—such as clothes, bedspreads, newspapers, cardboard—to make insulation, curtains, rag rugs, stuffed cushions, seat walls, papier-mâché furniture, or art pieces. Instead of spending money to buy expensive products from far away, we can hire local craftspeople and artists to make things with local or reclaimed materials. This means the funds will stay in and support the local economy. Reclaimed concrete walkways used in chunks as flagstone-like paving or stacked into walls has become so commonplace, it has a name: urbanite. In taking this approach, we support the local economy, save school resources, and avoid the environmental and human health costs of shipping and any unknown toxins that might be in the products' manufacturing process.

Demonstrate to Seniors and Other Voters How Local Tax Increases for Schools Will Benefit Them

Local school funds are voted on by the local population, in the form of tax increases and school bonds. When school districts lose the trust of their communities, and when schools fail to serve the larger population, people don't vote for tax increases or bonds. The staggering number of communities that don't vote for property tax increases for school improvements is evidence of our public school system's failure to ignite the spirit of generosity and hope in our students and communities. Before we can expect bonds and property tax measures to pass, we must show people the potential for public schools to provide a better quality of life for students, parents, and neighbors. Including seniors in the planning and design process can help them understand how improvements benefit the entire community, including themselves.

Think of New Ways to Apply School District Funds for Holistic, Multilayered Benefits

Tying the school environment to students' mental health, physical health, and academic success provides an avenue to funding that is earmarked for those very things. School improvements that support the curriculum can be maintained by general operating funds. And school districts have budgets for maintenance and operations that include large periodic expenses such as repairing asphalt pavement, repairing plumbing and mechanical systems, and painting. These budgets can be put toward changes in those systems that accomplish more than the original, single-purpose systems did. Examples include painting student-led murals on exterior walls and pavement; removing 25 to 50 percent of the asphalt before repairing, to be replaced with plants, trees, outdoor classrooms, or learning gardens; updating mechanical and plumbing systems to include local rain harvesting; and other strategies to gain autonomy and resilience.

Mental health funding could support students who wouldn't otherwise be treated by providing a positive school climate safety net beneath all students, teachers, and school community members. Estimates predict that only one out of five students who need help with mental health will receive treatment. The rest struggle without diagnosis or help. Providing mentally healthy school environments can help those students and may help to reduce or avoid issues developing in others.

Physical health funding can be leveraged for projects that get more students to behave in physically and mentally healthy ways. What if designers looked to the research on what helps girls and middle schoolers to be active, and created walking trails through trees and soft surfaces with natural features to run around and jump off, making a natural obstacle course of sorts that could reveal natural systems for science education while also serving to boost student activity levels and prosocial behaviors? This type of space could be funded through mental health funds, physical education funds, stormwater management funds, and experiential learning funds.

The Los Angeles Unified School District commits a portion of funds dedicated to every asphalt repair project toward replacing a portion of the asphalt with trees and natural stormwater management areas. The Los Angeles Beautification Team and the Los Angeles Conservation Corps leverage funding for stormwater management and jobs training to hire youth to plant trees and install and maintain native gardens. A great example to emulate is an action call, "Funding Trees for Health," put together by The Nature Conservancy, The Trust for Public Land, and Analysis Group (see figure 6.2). The document identifies the compelling benefits and barriers to growing and caring for urban forests. With a collection of research and case studies, the partnership outlines common funding mechanisms and proposes a new funding stream from health-care providers based on urban forests' known health benefits.

Blended Funding

How we talk about and define school improvements influences the type of funding that can support them. For instance, California and most states tie school funding to enrollment and attendance numbers. Many school districts spend a good chunk of money trying to boost attendance by telling students and their parents not to miss school. Research connects green views and access to nature in work environments with fewer sick days, higher job satisfaction, and more productivity. The same should be true for students in better-designed schools with more access to nature: if improving a school environment leads to greater student well-being and increases attendance rates, that school should gain additional funds to help offset the costs of the improvements. Understanding the district and state mechanisms of funding school construction and operations will help unearth opportunities to pay for projects that will support mental health and well-being. It can also reveal potential economic benefits of designing for mental health that can change funding policies. School improvement projects that support mental health and well-being can be planned and framed in a lot of ways. The multidimensional benefits of mentally healthy design open up a lot of different funding possibilities. School communities that want to increase students' contact with nature, for instance, can look for district, state, or federal grants or funds aimed at climate resilience, habitat restoration, or natural stormwater management.

HOLISTIC SCHOOL FUNDING FOR PREVENTIVE HEALTH

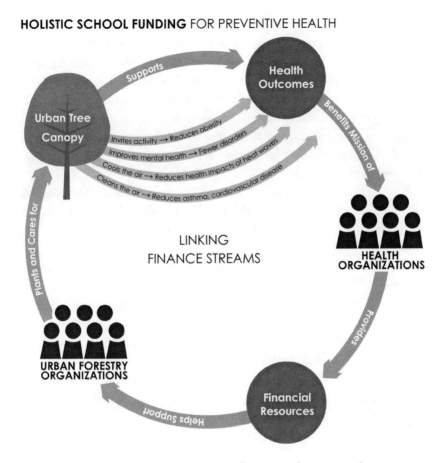

FIGURE 6.2: This conceptual diagram illustrates the potential connection between funding streams to acknowledge the impact that spending to increase and care for the urban tree canopy has on improving public health. Source: Adapted from The Nature Conservancy, The Trust for Public Land, and Analysis Group, "Funding Trees for Health: Finance and Policy to Enable Tree Planting for Public Health," September 23, 2017, https://www.nature.org/en-us/what-we-do/our-insights/perspectives/funding-trees-for-health/.

One potential method of covering school improvement costs could include job training programs that allow students to install school landscapes and green infrastructure systems. Other methods could be to look for grants and nonprofit organizations working to support public health, renewable energy, stormwater management, carbon sequestration, environmental education, social and environmental justice, and/or habitat improvement. With any of those potential funding sources, remember that tying the improvements to educational goals and mandatory programs could allow the maintenance and operations to be covered by the school's general budget.

More and more, local, state, and federal decision makers are understanding the opportunities for multiple-benefit nature-based infrastructures to provide overlapping resources at lower costs. As this understanding begins to find its way into budget language, funding streams are likely to become more inclusive and flexible.

A prime example could be the Sunrise Movement's Green New Deal. A ten-year plan on the scale of Franklin Delano Roosevelt's New Deal, the Green New Deal has five primary goals:

1. Achieve net-zero greenhouse gas emissions through a fair and just transition for all communities and workers.
2. Create millions of good, high-wage jobs and ensure prosperity and economic security for all people of the United States.
3. Invest in the infrastructure and industry of the United States to sustainably meet the challenges of the twenty-first century.
4. Secure clean air and water, climate and community resilience, healthy food, access to nature, and a sustainable environment for all.
5. Promote justice and equity by stopping current, preventing future, and repairing historical oppression of frontline and vulnerable communities.

Future Funding Sources

To help identify funds for mental health, the national Center for Health and Health Care in Schools put together "A Guide to Federal Education Programs That Can Fund K–12 Universal Prevention and Social and Emotional Learning Activities."[6] The guide includes a description of school improvement programs that could be funded:

Social-emotional and community-oriented services that may be offered to students in a school implementing a turnaround model may include, but are not limited to: (a) safety programs; (b) community stability programs that reduce the mobility rate [the number of new student enrollments and withdrawals during the school year divided by the total enrollment of students on the first day of school] of students in the school; or (c) family and community engagement programs that support a range of activities designed to build the capacity of parents and school staff to work together to improve student academic achievement, such as a family literacy program for parents who need to improve their literacy skills in order to support their children's learning.

While not mentioned directly, physical school improvements can support each of these programs. As advocates, we can request the use of mental health and socio-emotional learning funds to improve the environmental and built conditions of schools that affect all who attend and work there.[7]

Re-Build America's School Infrastructure Coalition is a nonpartisan coalition of organizations including the Center for Cities + Schools and the 21st Century School Fund, which partnered in 2016 to advocate for schools to be included in a federal infrastructure bill. Thinking of schools as infrastructure aligns with using them as Federal Emergency Management Agency (FEMA) emergency centers and preparing our next generation of thinkers and employees in all fields, especially green infrastructure. Once a school community understands the breadth and depth of opportunities opened in the spirit of designing schools that heal, it becomes difficult to deny the potential for schools as infrastructure.

Evidence shows that nature-based, community-led school design improves students' mental and physical health and promotes positive behavior and academic success. Therefore, funding schools that heal sets up students for healthier, higher-quality lives. Students attending supportive, mentally healthy schools will be mentally and physically healthier, more likely to attend college, and less likely to engage in crime or self-destructive behavior or need state or federal assistance. With heightened awareness of the potential disruption due to pandemic disease, designs that address disease prevention, foster immune system health, and support social distancing are likely to receive priority funding in the near future, if they are not already doing so. We could divert a portion of any one of the large funding streams dedicated to anti-truancy, juvenile justice, law enforcement, crime prevention, or public health toward schools. Designing and building schools that heal can benefit each individual student and society as a whole. The environmental, social, and economic gains will be both immediate and long-lasting.

CHAPTER 7

Ten Schools to Inspire and Guide You

School decision makers want to know that a proposed change will work before they approve any improvement. One of the best ways to understand and communicate the potential for school design with mental health in mind is through built examples. This chapter shares ten schools with designs and programs in place that successfully support mental health and well-being. The following schools exist in a variety of contexts, from densely populated cities with people from many cultures and socioeconomic backgrounds to neighborhoods with less diversity or density. Examples are shown in cities, in suburbs, and in more rural and agricultural areas. The schools are located throughout the United States and in England, Germany, and Japan. They range in scope from program interventions to small and large renovations to a new building and grounds. These examples, and those spread throughout the previous chapters, represent just a fraction of the broad range of possibilities and opportunities to nurture a sense of belonging, create nature-filled environments, and inspire awe. The best examples will come in the future as more of us begin practicing school design with mental health in mind. All students everywhere can benefit

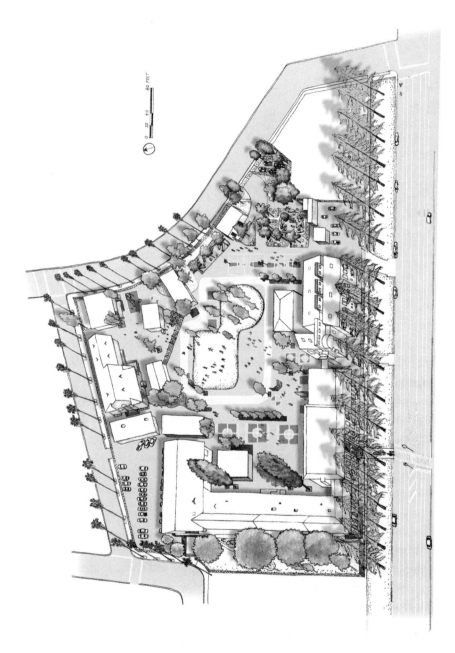

FIGURE 7.1A: Eagle Rock Elementary School. Drawing by Adrian Chi Tenney.

Eagle Rock Elementary School

2057 Fair Park Avenue

Los Angeles, CA 90041

Grades pre-K–6; ages 4–12

Built: 1920s; addition: 1990s; schoolyard redesign: 2017

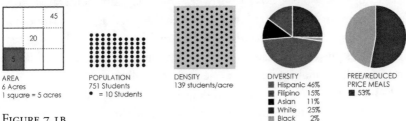

AREA	POPULATION	DENSITY	DIVERSITY	FREE/REDUCED
6 Acres	751 Students	139 students/acre	■ Hispanic 46%	PRICE MEALS
1 square = 5 acres	● = 10 Students		■ Filipino 15%	■ 53%
			■ Asian 11%	
			■ White 25%	

FIGURE 7.1B
■ Black 2%

Living Schoolyard funding: California Department of Resources
Proposition 84 Stormwater Grant ($349,000)

Eagle Rock Elementary School is a public elementary school in Northeast Los Angeles. Founded in 1910, Eagle Rock was its own city for a mere ten years. It sits in its own small valley surrounded by hills. As with many smaller cities in the area, Eagle Rock became an annex to the growing city of Los Angeles in order to have access to its water and energy infrastructures. California State Route 134 and California State Route 2 now define the northern and western edges of the community. Pasadena lies to the east. And to the south is Highland Park—a hotbed of gentrification protests over flipped houses, new businesses, and low-rent apartments being converted into high-rent luxury lofts. The community is part of the Los Angeles Unified School District (LAUSD), the second-largest school district in the country. Over half of its students qualify for free or reduced-cost meals. This makes it a Title I school eligible for federal funds to help schools with large numbers of low-income students meet educational goals. Once marketed as a haven for White families escaping the city, it is now one of Los Angeles's most diverse neighborhoods. Nearly 80 percent of the students are Hispanic or Filipino.[1] Eagle Rock Elementary has so far maintained its cultural and socioeconomic diversity despite its adjacency to Highland Park. The school benefits from its cultural and socioeconomic diversity. The rising rents and home prices of Eagle Rock could endanger affordability and diversity. Two new affordable housing developments along the main boulevard might help.

This was my children's school, and it had a lot of things going for it. An elegant and welcoming entry in a 1920s historic building was approached along a wide, grassy parkway shaded by hundred-year-old deodar cedars. The school sits a block away from where the two main boulevards cross. Once routes for Red Car trolleys that served the Los Angeles metropolitan region, they are now major automobile thoroughfares—too wide, too fast, and not designed for pedestrian safety. Many students walking or biking to and from the school cross at least one of these six-lane roads.

On my children's first day of school, we stood, stunned, staring at the bleak asphalt yard inside the school walls. It felt so different from the grassy yards the kids and I knew in all our previous schools. Four years later, I taught a landscape architecture studio that partnered with my son's class to redesign the playground. This inclusive design process engaged second and third graders in reimagining what their school could be. My students taught them watershed health concepts through a mapping exercise requested by their teacher to meet a curriculum requirement. The Cal Poly Pomona students worked with the Eagle Rock Valley Historical Society and local ecological artist Jane Tsong to understand the historical water and settlement patterns, which suggested that Eagle Rock Elementary sat close to or over an old stream corridor. This helped explain the basement flooding during heavy rains. Then they developed concept designs based on their work with the elementary students. A couple of years later, a group of parents applied for and won a California Proposition 84 Stormwater Grant to improve the site.

Environmental nonprofit Los Angeles Beautification Team hired landscape architecture firm Studio-MLA to manage the design and implementation of the living schoolyard. In one of those small-world moments, I worked there at that time and got to design and manage the project. The process benefited from my existing relationship with the community and commitment to the school. The PTA president at the time, Occidental College economics professor Bevin Ashenmiller, engaged her colleague, Occidental College behavior researcher Marcella Raney, to study the school. Raney and her students observed which playground areas were well used and which weren't. These observations were critical for the design. The places that invited a lot of physical activity were kept as they were. The underused places—such as the enormous and exposed center of the play-ground—were where we focused our changes.

The final design replaced 21,000 square feet of asphalt with soil and mulch, native plants, permeable surfaces, and grass. Twenty-four new shade trees increased the tree canopy to provide protection from the sun and provide green views from classroom windows. A new learning garden (see figure 7.1c)— its small hills planted with fragrant California native sages, buckwheat, and grasses—provides a sense of "being away," essential to reducing stress.[2] Stumps and logs, placed just far enough apart to invite students to leap from one to another to another, double as an outdoor classroom. The underused middle of the playground became a grassy kickball field and tree-covered park space. The logs and grass and boulders spread throughout provide plenty of places for students to sit, rest, walk, and lie down. Two rows of trees standing in long, shallow trenches covered in mulch intercept rainwater as it runs down the play-ground to the storm drain. These tree planters and the large grassy play field work with nature to allow rain to recharge the groundwater basin and clean the runoff instead of allowing pollution through the drain and into the Los Angeles River. The design broke up the large expanse of asphalt to create smaller, shadier play spaces and includes native trees and plants, boulders, logs and stumps, and mulch areas. The design supports the health of all species—human and oth-erwise. Trees and plants selected from the local plant communities need little irrigation or maintenance and provide vital habitat for birds, butterflies, insects, and soil biota. LAUSD policy dictates organic management and maintenance practices to protect students from chemical exposure.

Before the playground improvements, Principal Stephanie Leach worked with teachers and playground monitors to remove any playground rules limiting students' choice of activity and play area. Allowing free play was essential for Raney to measure the impact of the physical changes on students' behavior. Buchanan Street Elementary School, two miles away in Highland Park, served as the study's control school. The most popular recess activities before creation of the living schoolyard included handball, kickball, tetherball, and four square. After the playground became a living schoolyard, the most popular activities were tag and chasing, gymnastics (handstands and cartwheels), climbing, jumping, and making up games.

"Handball was one of the most popular activities before the greening," Raney told me. "But not after.

"After greening, the kids who were already active didn't change their activity," she said. "That's fine." But the number of kids who were not doing anything at recess fell dramatically.

"At the beginning, nearly 55 percent of all students were sedentary or standing. Then, when we greened, now 46 percent were sedentary," Raney said. "Thirty to forty new students were now active who before didn't move at recess." And even those who were not active chose to sit or lie down in the learning garden or on the lawn, where they were immersed in the nurturing qualities of nature. Though the improvements included dozens of stumps and logs that were sanded and finished to lie flat on the ground and minimize splinters, tippy and odd-shaped stumps prove to be kids' favorites. A selection of stumps, some split in half, invite students to test their balancing skills by rocking back and forth on one end or by placing their feet on the flat side of a half stump, rocking with the round side against the ground.

The most popular places for students to play on the greener schoolyard were the stumps, logs, and mulch areas (see figure 7.1d). These types of play settings, made with natural materials and loose parts, encourage creative play and cooperative social play. With the emphasis on socio-emotional learning in schools, providing play opportunities that support this is no small matter. It worked. Among Raney's findings was a 50 percent decrease in antisocial behaviors after the schoolyard improvements were made.[3]

Eagle Rock Elementary was honored with a US Department of Education Green Ribbon Schools Award for its innovations to improve human and environmental health and education. The awards honor pre-K through twelfth-grade schools that reduce environmental impact and costs, improve health and wellness, and educate students about the environment and sustainability. Eagle Rock Elementary's living schoolyard helps cool and clean the air, absorbs and cleans stormwater runoff, provides wildlife habitat, and sequesters carbon in addition to supporting students' health and well-being. The planting design plans for the future, too. The need for shade was immediate and urgent. Riparian tree species were planted in the lawn and rain strips. But the learning garden revolved around the oaks that grow slightly higher in the natural ecosystem, and they grow very slowly. Fast-growing, shorter-lived *Tipuana tipu* trees, planted between the oaks,

FIGURE 7.1C: The learning garden was designed with teaching, discovery, and play in mind. A small hill planted with fragrant California sage, buckwheat, and deer grass separates the garden from the main play space, giving a sense of being away. Photo by Edmund Barr.

FIGURE 7.1D: When class isn't in session, students can leap from stump to stump to log or play in innumerable ways in the mulch and with loose logs, sticks, bark, and fallen leaves.

FIGURE 7.1E: A student walks past one of the tree rows breaking up the large playground into smaller, more student-scaled spaces. The tree rows are placed perpendicular to the slight slope of the asphalt, allowing them to intercept rainwater as it runs through the campus. This gives trees ample water during rainy season, allowing them to establish deep roots that help them survive the long dry season.

provide quick shade while the oaks grow in, and they can be cut and used for more seating once the oaks start providing real shade.

After just three years of growth, the trees provided shady play places throughout the yard. The rows of trees on each end of the playground divide the main play area and create roomlike places where students can experience feeling apart from others (see figure 7.1e).

Principal Leach said that teachers came to her after the living schoolyard was finished, saying their students came back to class after recess ready to learn, without needing to be redirected as usual. They've gained time to teach. The week after the living schoolyard opened, she told me she took one of her students with autism spectrum disorder out to the learning garden while he was acting out. She said that upon sitting on one of the logs, he immediately and visibly calmed down, looked around, and declared this was *his* classroom.

Three years later, when I revisited the school, Principal Leach told me, "A parent thanked me this morning for the sense of community in this school. The greening built that and sustains it because it's a living thing."

Kesennuma Shiritsu Omose Primary School

58 Matsuzakishimoakada

Kesennuma, Miyagi 988-0133

Japan

Ages 6–12

Built: 1984

AREA	POPULATION	DENSITY	DIVERSITY	FREE/REDUCED
5 Acres	252 Students	50 students/acre		PRICE MEALS
1 square = 5 acres	● = 10 Students		Unavailable	Unavailable

FIGURE 7.2A

Kesennuma, Japan, is a port city dating back to the twelfth century. It served as a post station and gold-mining town on the eastern end of Japan's Golden Route. The community's historic structures were meticulously rebuilt after a fire devastated them in 1929. It has since become a city supported by fishing tuna, swordfish, shark, and mackerel and raising oysters. Then, in 2011, one of the largest earthquakes in recorded history shook the ocean floor and released a devastating tsunami. The wave swept homes and buildings off their foundations and lifted cars and ships onto rooftops and hills. Its retreat left Kesennuma covered with splintered buildings, cars, boats, and ships. The destruction sparked one of the biggest fires in Japan's history, destroying anything left of the city. Of the nearly twenty thousand who lost their lives that day, over half came from Miyagi prefecture.[4]

Omose Primary School is located two-thirds of a mile from Kesennuma Bay and just one-tenth of a mile from the Omose River. The school has offered strong programs in environmental education and sustainable development since 2004 as part of an international movement for Education for Sustainable Development (ESD) initiated by Japan in 2002.[5] The tsunami spared Omose Primary School but flooded areas

FIGURE 7.2B: Students play in the main play area of Kesennuma Shiritsu Omose Primary School. The schoolyard is kept free of structures in case the space is needed to build temporary shelter from disasters. Photo courtesy of Omose Primary School, Mr. Taniyama, Principal.

as close as one thousand feet from the school. Much of the Kesennuma Bay shoreline, including that closest to Omose School, has been armored by seawalls. Three miles to the south, the ruins of Koyo High School stand as a memorial where the bay meets the Pacific Ocean, telling the story of the earthquake's aftermath. Curated exhibits accompany classrooms still cluttered with the debris and crushed cars that the tsunami left behind. Japan has a tradition of disaster education as a strategy to prevent future loss. Stone slabs dot the country's northeastern coast, marking the highest reaches of tsunamis as far back as six hundred or more years. In Kesennuma, a tsunami stone reads: "Always be prepared for unexpected tsunamis. Choose life over your possessions and valuables."[6] Survivors of the 1960 tsunami expressed regret that they hadn't done more to educate younger generations about the need to get to higher ground after an earthquake. Many of those lost had gone back to their homes.[7]

Even before the Great East Japan Earthquake in 2011, Omose School focused on teaching students resilience through environmental education for healing the mind and body.[8] The tsunami caused enormous damage to the coast of the Omasegawa estuary and the Ozaki area, destroying the learning field the school depended on. Mitsunari Terada of the International School Grounds Alliance shared the school's approach to supporting students' mental health and resilience through environmental awareness. Omose School demonstrates sustainable development principles in its local community by linking learning with local nature, culture, and community. This includes place-based education to teach marine biology and disaster prevention. On the school site, students helped transform part of the schoolyard into a biotope (see figure 7.2c). Nearby, students partnered with the community to create Omose Fureai Farm. Farther out, students work along the Omasegawa River and the Kennesuma Bay seashore (see figure 7.2d). The community and local environment both play essential roles in the school. In the field of the Omase River that flows near the school, students conduct biological surveys with university researchers and water quality surveys with local river protection organizations.

On the edge of the large playground, the schoolyard hosts its own biotope. Principal Tomohiro Taniyama noted that the biotope was named by the children and serves as their playground. The south side of the school is edged by a sloped terrace left by a former rice paddy. Spring water comes out of the sloped wall. When Principal Taniyama arrived in 2018, he looked into the ditch at the base of the wall and saw a dragonfly larva and a giant worm living in it. The biotope had a perfect environment. About a decade before, teachers had noticed the same thing and created a small pond. It had since been buried in earth and sand and transitioned to a wetland. The Mamose Elementary School Biotope Review Committee convened with school staff, community leaders, and university fish researchers to discuss the opportunity to create a new pond that could be used for life sciences, science, and comprehensive learning. With help from the Japan Ecosystem Association and Parent-Teacher Association (PTA) leaders, the pond was excavated to a depth that would allow fish to survive over winters (60 to 80 centimeters, or roughly 2 to 2.5 feet).

FIGURE 7.2C: Students explore a pond on the Omose School site that was created by digging out an area around a natural spring. The students have spawned and hatched fish for their pond as a science class project, and they monitor insects and other visitors to their Omose Pond. Photo courtesy of Omose Primary School, Mr. Taniyama, Principal.

Next to the biotope, the PTA installed two grass yards, a compost area, and flower beds with sunflowers. Principal Taniyama wrote, "I wanted to make it a biotope that would be familiar to children, so when I asked children for a nickname, they decided that it was an 'omotope' because it was 'Omose's biotope.' In addition, the pond itself is called 'Omosae Pond' with an interesting pond with various creatures and Omose."

Principal Taniyama said it is now difficult to get close to the sea because seawalls and disaster prevention parks have been built along the shore. The seawalls are controversial. Fishermen, environmental researchers, and community members argue that they separate people from the sea and prevent a deeper understanding of the ecosystem and long-term planning that will protect people from disaster in the long run.[9] As an ESD leader school, Omose School contributes practical research and works to disseminate information and exchange between schools. Omose School teacher and

FIGURE 7.2D: Omose School students interact with and learn from their natural environment. The school is one of twenty-four Education for Sustainable Development schools in Japan selected as an Asia/Pacific Cultural Center for UNESCO (ACCU). Environmental education is used as a way to prepare students for disasters such as the Great East Japan Earthquake and tsunami and to support students' mental health after such traumas. Photo courtesy of Omose Primary School, Mr. Taniyama, Principal.

environmental conservation expert Masahito Abe advocates for a holistic approach to disaster preparation based on the importance of environmental education and community involvement. "The basis of disaster preparation is a relationship with the community and its knowledge about the region: the natural environment and local facilities and resources," Abe wrote a couple years after the tsunami. His article in *Academic Trends* included a number of suggestions to help school communities recover from and plan for future disaster:

1. Disaster victims need time to recover from the trauma of disaster. Some tend to avoid the place or memory of trauma. Understanding response to trauma coupled with the use of nontechnical language and images will make discussion more productive.
2. Help residents learn about the area's nature, history, culture, geology, characteristics, future use, and planning processes to help them imagine the future of their area.
3. Coordinate a comprehensive urban planning conversation to help residents understand and engage in a holistic perspective.
4. The eroded topography and a newly formed estuary from the tsunami presented an opportunity to educate about disaster prevention and preparation and environmental resources. Help locals and decision makers understand the potential value of remnant and new ecologies for raising awareness or economic value through tourism.
5. The coast environment is a national asset. Include people in project talks with a viewpoint beyond the local.
6. Children learn and cultivate adaptation skills through nature play. The natural environment is worth preserving for the next generation, where children can learn about the local ecosystem as well as develop collaboration, creativity, and social skills.
7. Invite open discussions that cross gender and age.
8. Find a facilitator with the ability to engage locals and officials in meaningful discussions.[10]

After the tsunami, the students designed, planned, and constructed a playground with the help of a local organization. The student-led and student-built project brought all generations together to create a communal play place. Grandparents set up a fire and cooking pots in an impromptu picnic area as children of all ages worked with hand tools and moved wood and materials. The playground itself was relatively simple. A freestanding wooden structure featured a playhouse below and a ladder up to a platform with a chalkboard and wooden slide. The process leading up to it was everything it could be: collaborative, informative, community-building, and inspiring. Omose Primary School prioritizes students' mental health by including them in the design and planning of their school and neighborhood environments, by teaching them the patterns and processes of nature—especially the destructive ones—and by engaging them in planning for their future. Students and teachers care for their buildings and grounds, increasing the sense of ownership and long-term maintenance of the school. The emphasis on community collaboration and environmental education is a model any school in any location can replicate. The school's impact was recognized from 2016 to 2018 by the Asia/Pacific Cultural Center for UNESCO (ACCU), which selected it as one of twenty-four sustainable schools nationwide.

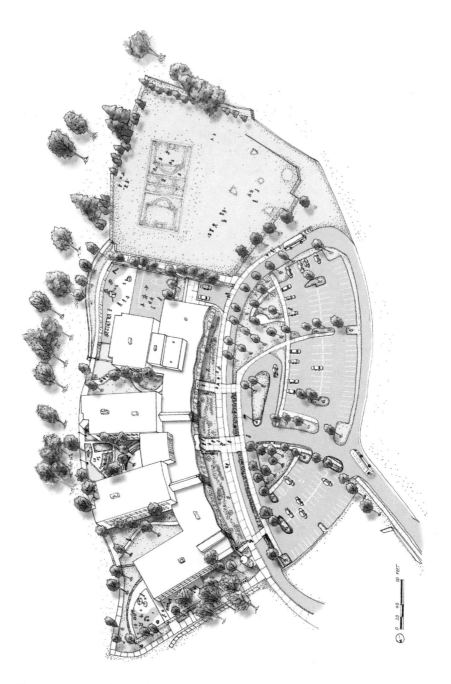

FIGURE 7.3A: Sandy Hook Elementary School. Drawing by Adrian Chi Tenney

Sandy Hook Elementary School

12 Dickinson Drive

Newtown, CT 06482

Grades K–4

Built: 2016

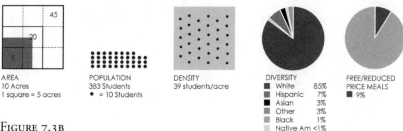

AREA
10 Acres
1 square = 5 acres

POPULATION
383 Students
● = 10 Students

DENSITY
39 students/acre

DIVERSITY
■ White   85%
■ Hispanic   7%
■ Asian   3%
■ Other   3%
■ Black   1%
▨ Native Am <1%

FREE/REDUCED
PRICE MEALS
■ 9%

FIGURE 7.3B

New construction funding: $50 million out of a $2.2 billion district-wide school bond for renovation

Until 2012, Newtown, Connecticut, was barely known outside of the nearly thirty thousand people who lived there. Originally called Quanneapague by the Pohtatuck people who farmed and fished along the Housatonic River, the little sandy bend in the river is now called Sandy Hook.[11] This small village housed a few thousand from the early 1700s until after World War II. The population then grew steadily to its current number of around 11,250. The rural residential neighborhood was favored for its scenic qualities, good schools, and horse culture. Since December 14, 2012, Newtown, home to Sandy Hook Elementary School, has been known around the world as the site of one of the deadliest school shootings in American history. Twenty children and six adults died at the school that day.

After the tragedy, the Newtown School District shuffled scheduled district-wide renovations to rebuild Sandy Hook Elementary School first.[12] The surviving students, teachers, staff, and their families and the community needed a new space to help them heal and move forward. Architect Barry Svigals and his firm facilitated the design process with a focus on deeply engaging the community. They selected fifty community advisors to drive design decisions. "The opportunity was clear—that they needed to be able to reset emotionally. We started with what they loved about their community, a remembering and a re-visioning of what their community could be." Six workshops engaged the advisors in developing a design concept for the new school.

In the years after the Sandy Hook school shooting, schools and districts around the country hardened their perimeters, adding automatic gates, security cameras, and guards to watch the building. It is poignant to see that Sandy Hook Elementary School took a different approach. The community wanted a school that symbolized an embrace.[13]

The design accomplished this feeling of welcome while being secure in a few ways. The first was the community-driven process. The security and safety team acted as advisors along with parents, teachers, mental health professionals, public health experts, social workers, students, and the design team. This interdisciplinary group represented the interests of the entire community and fostered a holistic view of safety and wellness. The team wanted the school to be secure, but not at the cost of feeling safe. Since no other school had been designed specifically with this in mind, there was no comparable research to guide the design. Instead, they looked to the research on human behavior and feelings of safety. The design is welcoming and warm and connects the school community to the healing qualities of nature.

The building reaches out to the community in a broad curve like two arms outstretched. A new parking area guides school buses to a drop-off at the front, with visitor parking separated from staff parking. Three bridges lead people across a sunken swale with boulders and plants. The swale captures rainwater runoff from the parking lot and roof and acts as a beautiful natural defense mechanism. Administrative offices inhabit the front wall, allowing staff to see who is visiting and approaching as they cross the bridges. The artful design, created in close collaboration with the students, is whimsical as well, creating hidden surprises to be discovered throughout the day. The classrooms extend out from the back of the curved building, in four branches reaching back toward the trees. Three courtyards between the branches host amphitheaters and trees, giving students vibrant green views from every classroom and community space. At the ends of the branches sit cozy treehouse spaces, with soft furniture and carpet inviting students to sit and rest amid the trees. A central shared space opens two stories to the

FIGURE 7.3C: Sandy Hook Elementary School presents a warm, inviting entry. The design places offices along the front of the building so that approaching visitors can be seen by school staff. A shallow swale cleans stormwater that drains from the parking lot and doubles as a separation from the sidewalk and the school building as a natural security feature. Image: Robert Benson Photography.

ceiling, with stained glass panels adorning a back wall completely made of glass (see figure 7.3d). Morning sunlight streams through those windows, throwing blocks of glowing yellow and red onto the furniture and floors. Flocks of birds adorn the walls, lifting in flight toward the sky in hope.

The original school building was essentially a square structure with a square courtyard. The community wanted to keep the feeling of the courtyard, but they needed new places to enter, congregate, park, and inhabit in order to move forward.[14] The architects sited the building close to the woods and wetlands that edge the school property. The location and layout of the school give every classroom views of trees, and every office has views of the front entrances.

"Connections between the interior and exterior are really important," Svigals + Partners architect Julia McFadden told me over the phone. "The building's orientation and massing and connection to the natural surroundings were all a part of the design." Biophilic design was a central principle.

FIGURE 7.3D: Light streams into the atrium through stained glass windows in Sandy Hook Elementary School's central community space. Image: Robert Benson Photography.

The school not only looks out into woods but also is full of natural materials and references to nature. Trees and gardens are always within sight of students, teachers, and staff.

A series of retaining walls, fences, and gates deter visitors from accessing the back of the school but also blend into the surrounding environment. All of these details were intentionally designed to help the school feel safe and be safe . . . to feel welcoming and warm in order to nurture a sense of belonging. Rather than adopting the hardened edges that schools across the country applied after the tragedy, Sandy Hook Elementary School became a model for healing.

ASCEND School

3709 East 12th Street

Oakland, CA 94601

Grades TK (transitional kindergarten)–8

Built: 2005

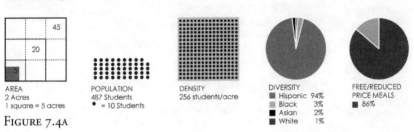

AREA	POPULATION	DENSITY
2 Acres	487 Students	256 students/acre
1 square = 5 acres	● = 10 Students	

DIVERSITY
■ Hispanic 94%
▨ Black 3%
■ Asian 2%
■ White 1%

FREE/REDUCED
PRICE MEALS
■ 86%

FIGURE 7.4A

ASCEND School serves Oakland's Fruitvale neighborhood, on the east shore of San Francisco Bay. California's East Bay region has seen dramatic transitions in ownership, population, culture, and urbanization since Spanish missionaries colonized the Ohlone people's land in the late eighteenth century.[15] Oakland became a city in 1852, just after the United States and the Mexican Republic signed the Treaty of Guadalupe Hidalgo. Over the next fifty years, the city established itself as an urban center, with its Long Wharf, the Central Pacific Railroad, and the founding of the University of California. One of the oldest Chinatowns in the United States is in Oakland; it was established during the California gold rush of 1849. After the Great San Francisco Earthquake struck in 1906, Oakland doubled in size as people left San Francisco to settle across the bay. The population growth led to the city annexing Fruitvale along with surrounding neighborhoods such as Melrose, Elmhurst, and much of the area to the south. Soon after, industry took advantage of Oakland's waterfront and railroad access. The port expanded, and warehouses and automobile assembly plants came. Oakland came to be called the "Detroit of the West."[16]

In the 1940s, a massive migration of Black people out of the Jim Crow South settled in Oakland. Wartime jobs at the Oakland Army Base and nearby Richmond shipyards led to the construction of thousands of temporary housing structures in both cities.[17] These areas remain home to the biggest Black populations in the Bay Area to this day. The loss of industry

FIGURE 7.4B: ASCEND School sits almost against the elevated tracks of the Bay Area Rapid Transit (BART) light-rail A-Line. Image: Google Earth.

after the war meant people lost their jobs . . . and then their homes. After Oakland's industrial peak during World War II, a number of planning practices forced marginalized communities into unstable living situations. Freeway construction meant demolition of more homes in largely minority neighborhoods.[18] Between 1980 and 2000, Oakland was the epicenter of the crack cocaine epidemic and the mass incarcerations that followed.[19] Its disproportionate impacts on Black and Brown communities are well documented. Economic downturns and the Great Recession further harmed the community. In the thirty years leading up to 2010, Oakland's Black population decreased by nearly 20 percent.[20] Since then, the second dot-com boom brought a slew of high-tech, highly paid employees to the Bay Area. Home prices and rents skyrocketed. Any family that lost a home during the mortgage crisis was essentially priced out of the area.

FIGURE 7.4C: ASCEND School welcomes students, parents, and visitors into a cozy entry that feels more like someone's home than part of a school. Image: Barry Svigals.

Just down the street from the Fruitvale BART (Bay Area Rapid Transit) station sits ASCEND School, tucked against the elevated light-rail tracks (see figure 7.4b). ASCEND was one of the first schools to open after the Oakland Board of Education passed its New Small Autonomous Schools Policy in 2000. It was an effort to address the inequities between the Oakland Hills area and the lower-income neighborhoods in Oakland's flatlands. In elementary schools built to hold 500 students, the median student population in Oakland Hills elementary schools was 315, compared with 815 in flatlands elementary schools.[21] Some schools had as many as 1,400 students crammed into facilities meant for one-third of that number. Year-round, multitrack schedules were adopted in an attempt to alleviate the crowding in Oakland and elsewhere. But student performance suffered severely. ASCEND, which stands for "A School Cultivating Excellence, Nurturing Diversity" was to accept students from two overcrowded neighborhood elementary schools. The school was proposed, organized, and designed by teachers and parents from nearby overcrowded schools who wanted to create a different, more nurturing model of a school.

The founders wanted a school where parents were partners in their children's education and where communication between the school and par-

FIGURE 7.4D: Stanford design school students partnered with ASCEND middle school students to make their school environment safer. The student partners engaged in activities to get to know one another and build trust. Image by Patrick Beaudouin.

ents would be supportive instead of humiliating.[22] Their goals were to build a welcoming school where students would learn a love for learning and be taught with a variety of culturally relevant, student-centered approaches. The initial years were spent in a not-so-great building under the BART train tracks. Acoustics were so bad that teachers had to pause every four to ten minutes as the trains passed overhead. After a bumpy beginning, they worked out the system. The new school building was built in 2005. Students did well there in comparison with their home schools.[23] When ASCEND School opened in 2001, its students represented the diversity of Fruitvale—Black, Hispanic, and Asian. Today, in part because of a shift from a school-centered student selection process to a district-wide lottery process, nearly all of its students are Hispanic.[24]

Upon entering an unassuming building, students and visitors are welcomed by a two-story entry hall flooded with natural light and a collection of couches and chairs. Twinkle lights hang from above. This living room–like environment comes complete with framed student art above the bookcases of a free library (see figure 7.4c). Parents sit here while they wait for their children at the end of the day. Despite the school's small size on a

FIGURE 7.4E: ASCEND students proposed solutions for areas around campus that could benefit from an improved sense of safety, such as the restrooms. Image by Patrick Beaudouin.

tight city lot, homey details appear throughout. A play area is made as cozy as possible with a thick planting of trees and shrubs along the fence line at a corner intersection. A little vegetable garden is tucked out in back under the BART tracks. The inside rooms are painted in warm or calming colors. The mood matches the intent of the founders: supportive, welcoming, culturally relevant, student centered. It is no surprise, then, that the school leadership would engage its students in making more improvements.

In 2019, Assistant Principal Jeff Embleton invited Stanford Design School K–12 director Sam Seidel to partner with ASCEND middle schoolers in exploring ways to create a safer school environment. Embleton had participated in a Stanford School Retool program five years before. He suggested a course in which Stanford University and ASCEND students could learn side by side.[25] Seidel invited architect Barry Svigals—the same architect who led the Sandy Hook Elementary School redesign—to coteach the course, which became "Safe by Design: From Fear to Joy in Learning Environments." An interdisciplinary team of Stanford graduate students designed and led participatory workshops with ASCEND students (see figures 7.4d and 7.4e). Students discussed how different areas on campus

---

Box 7.1: ASCEND Middle School Students' Wishes

ASCEND middle schoolers requested the following features for their campus through a series of workshops facilitated by Stanford Design School graduates.

What Students Want on Their Middle School Campus

Sunken living room, all classrooms outside, sparkling water fountain, libraries in every nook, massive tree houses, live celebrity concerts, more garbage cans w/liners, look into clever outdoor garbage designs, grow up the game in the schoolyard, Babylonian hanging gardens, video game station, make a roller rink, roller coaster, zip line into school, tree house, tennis court, have the students build the tree house, parent snack rotation, swimming pool, hot tub, life-size chess/checkers, bring your plant + add your name to the arch, pick your own fruit, student gardeners, mirrors, self-portrait wall, mural, litter competition, carts for basketballs and soccer, free dress passes, beanbag toss, games cart, mosaic, hanging gardens, time machine, trampoline, chefs, unlimited snack bars, repaint the chairs, banners, snacks on table, snack shop, photo booth, lending library, forest-trail/hiking, roller coaster, students' pictures or drawings, water slide, climbing wall, activity

Restrooms

Student bathroom monitors, mirrors so that people can see bathroom entrances, holograms of celebrities monitoring

Functionality: Screens from floor to ceiling, making walls/doors bigger, clean the bathroom, hand dryers, lights in stalls, fix sinks, having paper towels and soap, feminine products, toilet paper, cleaning the mirrors, ceilings

Decorations: Paint the walls, paint the stall doors, vans decorated bathroom, signs with upcoming school events, TVs with music videos on loop, student-run playlists, music, musical performers/DJ

#1 Understairs Area

Beanbags, relaxing place, table, pillows, books, murals on sidewall, lighting, glass panel, lighting, skylight, big window

#2 Stairs

Colors! Light and colors, colors and words, pictures of students/teachers, paintings (walls and ceilings), plants, railing, decorative steps, happy steps, footprints, music studio, sound, dance step

Parking Lot

Use of space: Crew garden visits, Let eighth graders go outside, needle abatement

Garden: Plant jasmine, bright + light, flowers

Gate: Put camera on both gates, lock the gate sometimes, block visibility of needles (?), basketball hoop at closed gate, parking attendant, "safety" patrol @ drop-off

Art: Murals on BART pillars, murals on the fence, blocking acoustic barrier for BART, make a garden, more gardens, vegetation + sculptures on BART pillars

Traffic: Build on elevated parking level, no traffic at all, have pedestrian zone only, vertical garage, shuttle service from school to outside pickup, speed bumps

The students' requests provide a window into both the conditions students everywhere endure and the (mostly) humble wishes middle schoolers make. Aside from the size of a roller coaster and structural engineering it would require, most of the ideas are feasible in the scope of supporting students' mental health and well-being.

made them feel, and they brainstormed ways they might improve them to create a safer, more welcoming school environment (see box 7.1).

ASCEND illustrates the potential for shifts in thinking and small-scale physical changes to create a safe, supportive, and nurturing environment. The school founders' focus on students' mental health and well-being shows in the nurturing nature of its student-centered approach, the welcoming design of the entry hall, and the student-led design process most recently initiated by the assistant principal to help students feel safer and more welcome. The school is missing what most schools are missing—nature-filled spaces. The students' small-scale suggestions, such as providing sanitary supplies in the bathrooms and creating a cozy calm space under the stairs, could be done overnight. Their larger-scale suggestions—all classrooms outside, an acoustic barrier for BART, massive tree houses, more gardens, sparkling water fountains, hanging gardens, and pick-your-own fruit—illustrate just how well students know what their minds and bodies need.

FIGURE 7.5A: Daniel Webster Middle School. Drawing by Adrian Chi Tenney.

Daniel Webster Middle School

11330 Graham Place

Los Angeles, CA 90064

Grades 6–8

Built: 1954; campus stormwater improvements: 2020

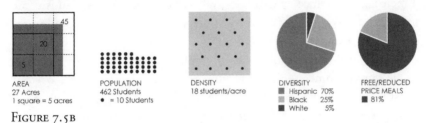

AREA	POPULATION	DENSITY	DIVERSITY	FREE/REDUCED
27 Acres	462 Students	18 students/acre	■ Hispanic 70%	PRICE MEALS
1 square = 5 acres	● = 10 Students		▦ Black 25%	■ 81%
			■ White 5%	

FIGURE 7.5B

Stormwater funding: $1 million from the California State Water Board's
$30 million Drought Response Outreach Program for Schools (DROPS)

Daniel Webster Middle School was designed and built during an era
when the public education system had become adept at responding to the
urgent needs of its communities and country. Through the Great Depression and World War II, public schools became resource centers for students and adults, providing food gardens, vocational training, and social
science curriculums to promote the discussion and understanding of
complex societal issues.[26] At a national level, design strategies supported
these programs as well as a move toward progressive, student-centered
education standards. A national standard for school design promoted
strong indoor-outdoor relationships, generous outdoor space, sheltered
corridors, and a unified campus design.[27] Schools were designed and built
at a domestic, human scale—usually one story for elementary schools and
one or two stories for middle and high schools. After the tuberculosis and
Spanish flu pandemics, there was a strong focus on designing the most
healthy and efficient schools possible. Considerations included building
siting, window size and location, and cross-ventilation.[28] Designs were
informal, with classroom buildings often arranged in clusters or fingers
with parklike spaces in between. Into the late 1940s and the 1950s, as
the student population exploded with baby boomers, as much attention

was paid to efficient, modular design as to the human-centered qualities of a residential scale, with north-facing walls or windows to invite in indirect natural light and excellent acoustic ceiling design. Slightly sloped roofs with deep eaves shaded south-facing windows from direct sunlight. Transom windows at the tops of walls opened to let heat escape and ventilate the room. Building sections and details were designed at four-foot increments, a strategy that takes advantage of common building material dimensions to reduce construction waste. For instance, wall studs come in eight-, twelve-, and sixteen-foot intervals. Drywall and windows are standard at a width of four feet.

Daniel Webster Middle School, built in 1954 in a sea of small single-family homes, epitomizes this era. Bars of two, three, or four classrooms are arranged like branches off a central green tree trunk. Arcade-covered walks shade the southern facades, where the classroom entrances are. A continuous band of double-hung windows makes up about 70 percent of the north classroom walls.[29] The Auditorium, Health & Counseling, Library, and Cafeteria buildings present the school to the community with a variety of building heights and types. Names of the other building names on the original campus map speak to the design and curriculum values of the era when the school was built: Social Living & Oral Arts, Industrial Arts, Art Science & Ceramics, Art Science & Drafting, Instrumental Music, Clothing Building, Sanitary Building, Home Economics, and Typing. The southeast corner next to the Gymnasium is the Agriculture Building, accompanied by the Lath House, Greenhouse, and Garden Tool Shed.

Ten years after the school was built, two of Los Angeles's most heavily used freeways—Interstate 10 and Interstate 405—were constructed, intersecting within a few hundred feet of the school. The elevated interchange ramps connecting them provide a constant visual and audible backdrop within the school.

In 2015, Webster was one of five LAUSD schools to participate in the California State Water Board's Drought Response Outreach Program for Schools (DROPS). The program funded projects to reduce stormwater pollution, increase the amount of rainwater recharging the aquifers, and provide multiple adjacent benefits. The grant required community outreach and environmental education to increase student and public understanding of opportunities to conserve and protect California's water resources. LAUSD selected Webster and the other four schools in part because they were in need of asphalt repair, and thus the district could save material and time costs by replacing some of the asphalt with trees and plants, and because they were spread geographically throughout the district.

LAUSD partnered with three local nonprofit organizations—the Council for Watershed Health, TreePeople, and the Los Angeles Audubon Society—to amplify the benefits of the stormwater improvements. Each of these organizations came with decades of experience in engaging with communities and in conducting environmental education. And they understood the unique ecological and policy context of the Los Angeles Basin, making them supportive and effective partners. In addition to working with the school community, the Council for Watershed Health monitors the stormwater management features to measure their benefits over time.

The Council for Watershed Health led the DROPS project's technical support by helping school administrators understand the technical requirements and benefits of low-impact and nature-based design strategies for stormwater management, and they will finish the project by monitoring and reporting the measured benefits of each school. Webster students visited the nearby Ballona Wetlands for a deep dive into the natural ecologies that have been all but erased from the Los Angeles landscape. TreePeople established an EcoClub on the school site to engage students in action-based projects focused on the stormwater improvements. To facilitate those projects, the Los Angeles Audubon Society demonstrated to teachers how to use the new habitat and rain gardens to support learning and integrate those lessons into the curriculum.

The design concept created by landscape architecture firm Studio-MLA focused on revealing the path and treatment of urban runoff on campus where students could see it and benefit from it. The entry garden became a California garden featuring native flowering plants and trees that thrive on little or no irrigation. As parents and children enter the school, they will see, smell, and hear the rich scents of California plants and the birds and insects they invite to the schoolgrounds. Each courtyard between classroom build-

FIGURE 7.5C: The DROPS design improved the campus landscape where students could most benefit. Courtyards between classroom buildings were turned into rain gardens to collect and absorb rainwater from the roof through downspouts. Inset shows before. Image courtesy of Studio-MLA and LAUSD.

ings became a rain garden. Downspouts from the covered walkways drain into the rain garden, allowing deep winter watering of California-friendly shade trees to encourage deep roots that will help them survive the summer dry season. As they mature, the trees will provide green garden views from classroom windows. And a soggy swath of the multipurpose field became a wide sunken garden where native plants provide habitat for birds and insects and filter any contaminants carried in as rainwater washes off the campus buildings and pavement. Educational signs teach and remind students about the benefits of healthy soils, water conservation, and habitat gardens, including water conservation, water supply augmentation, energy savings, increased awareness of water resource sustainability, and reduced dry weather runoff.

The support of the school principal is essential for the wholesale success of a campus improvement. When principals and teachers

FIGURE 7.5D: A soggy area along the field's edge became a wide and shallow swale full of habitat-friendly trees, grasses, and flowering perennials. Inset shows before. Image courtesy of Studio-MLA and LAUSD.

who were instrumental in bringing changes leave a school site, those changes may be undervalued, underutilized, or simply not understood. This was a challenge at Webster, which gained a new principal halfway through the project. Similar challenges can happen over time when architects and decision makers move on or retire. Eileen Alduenda of the Council for Watershed Health told me that the current challenge was the coronavirus pandemic, which forced the school to close before the project partners could see the new campus improvements in action with students.

Alduenda's team created an ArcGIS StoryMap that provides a virtual tour of Webster with links to the community presentation and maintenance guidelines as well as project impact. The council measured pollutant loads in stormwater runoff before and after the campus improvements were made. It found that the new design reduced total

FIGURE 7.5E: Small square tree planters in the lunch area were connected by cutting out the asphalt between them to create biofiltration areas to collect and clean stormwater from the surrounding pavement. A new seat wall includes small cutouts along the bottom to allow rainwater to flow into the planting. Image courtesy of Studio-MLA and LAUSD.

suspended solids, total nitrogen, cadmium, copper, lead, and zinc by at least 40 percent.[30]

School closures because of the pandemic raised an opportunity for schools such as Webster. A recent historic resources survey report noted the school as "an excellent, intact example of a postwar indoor-outdoor educational facility in Los Angeles," apart from added security grills and some windows—notably many of the clerestory windows, which are vital for fresh air circulation—having been filled in.[31]

The many schools built during the progressive and post–World War II school-building boom could be studied for ways to retrofit them to match their original intent. Windows and sliding doors or walls that were removed or covered during school renovations can be restored or reinstalled to recreate the natural ventilation strategies they were designed for. The deep overhangs along walkways and courtyards between classroom buildings are ready-made to become outdoor learning spaces. Like those at Webster, the agricultural buildings and gardens that proliferated during the school Victory Garden movement could be used to propagate shade trees as well as to grow food, eventually shading more places where outdoor classes could be held. The lessons from the Daniel Webster Middle School transformation are worth revisiting for ideas about new jobs training, local agriculture, and vocational education as well as improving flood control and climate resilience.

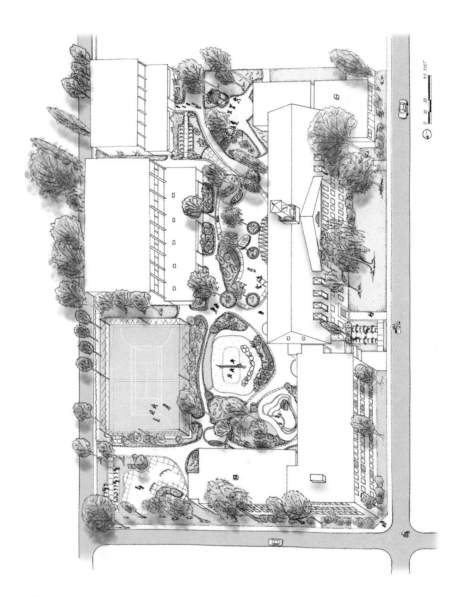

FIGURE 7.6A: B. Traven Community School. Drawing by Adrian Chi Tenney.

B. Traven Community School

Recklinghauser Weg 26

13583 Berlin-Spandau

Germany

Grades 7–13; ages 12–18

Original building: 1940s; addition: 1970s; schoolyard redesign: 2010

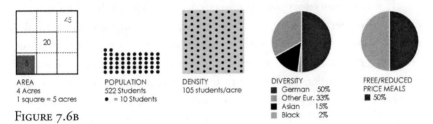

AREA	POPULATION	DENSITY	DIVERSITY	FREE/REDUCED
4 Acres	522 Students	105 students/acre	■ German 50%	PRICE MEALS
1 square = 5 acres	● = 10 Students		■ Other Eur. 33%	■ 50%
			■ Asian 15%	
			■ Black 2%	

FIGURE 7.6B

Schoolyard redesign funding: 687,000 euros ($841,000) in urban redevelopment funds

B. Traven Community School is a high school in the Spandau district of West Berlin. Once the industrial center of the German Reich, Spandau was known for machinery, machine guns, and transport equipment.[32] After World War II, this neighborhood was the westernmost district of West Berlin, in the British sector. It includes the confluence of the Spree and Havel Rivers and the Spandau Forest just north. The Spandau Prison held Nazi war criminals sentenced by the Allies until it was demolished in 1987, after Rudolf Hess, its last inmate, died.[33] The area is still largely industrial. Spandau is home to predominantly immigrant working-class families. The Falkenhagener Feld West settlement around B. Traven was built in the 1960s as the first large social housing development in West Berlin.[34] The region struggles with high community turnover as middle-class and higher-earning families leave the area and lower-income families move in. This high turnover is coupled with high unemployment and increasing segregation between German resettlers and Turkish-speaking families. Immigrants make up about 40 percent of the population.[35]

In the 2008–2009 school year, B. Traven joined the first group of Berlin schools to embrace the principles and practices of becoming a community school. This means the school acts as a community partner with parents, students, other schools, and community organizations in working toward the students' well-being. The school employs social workers to guide individual students as well as to mediate conflicts between students. Several programs are in place to reach out to students who miss school and to develop creative, strengths-based learning paths. Partners from the Berlin University of Applied Sciences work closely with counselors and teachers to introduce students to a wide variety of career and job paths.[36] The school building includes wood-, metal-, plastic-, and textile-processing studios and a modern teaching kitchen for vocational classes and professional orientations. The architectural design reflects the school's focus on supporting students' mental health and development. Several rooms are dedicated to social work; a game room provides table tennis and table games; and a cozy library, a meditation room, a tutoring room, and a cafeteria that opens onto the schoolyard provide a variety of places where students can go, whether they need quiet, calm, guidance, or company. Small teachers' lounges are spread throughout the school where teachers can rest, reduce their stress, get advice from peers, and generally feel supported—a crucial aspect of enabling them to assist students.

Ten years ago, B. Traven Community School took part in Berlin's Grün macht Schule program. Beginning in the early 1980s, this initiative, which roughly translates to "green makes school," aimed to develop and strengthen environmentally conscious behavior in children and adolescents. The Grün macht Schule initiative, which is run by the city, informs, advises, and guides schools in implementing schoolyard projects and participatory schoolyard planning. Its goal is to create student-friendly natural living spaces and ecological learning venues to prepare schoolyards for climate change.[37] Key to the initiative was the intention to reduce students' stress and improve behavior.[38] Teichmann landscape architects designed the new schoolyard with the active participation and cooperation of students, teachers, artists, and other community members.

B. Traven shares a city block with a primary school. The original building and its 1970s ell addition create two sides of the schoolyard. The gymnasium and a fenced-in multipurpose sports court border the opposite side. The fourth side opens into the primary school play space, expanding the visual size of the campus. The four-acre nature-filled campus design and participatory community-led design process reinforced the community school model.

I visited in September 2017, just before school began, as part of the International School Grounds Alliance biannual conference. From the moment it came into view as we walked from the train station, the school felt different from any other I had been to. Trees and vines created a soft welcome along the residential street where the entry stood. Small flowers and grasses sprouted between granite cobblestones and in the squares of open-grid pavers. The low fence acted more as a bike rack than a barrier. As we walked through the gate into the schoolyard, the fuzziness continued. Plants spilled over brick planter walls and onto walkways. Willows bent to the slightest breeze. Little green shoots and leaves sprouted between paving stones, cushioning the walkways under our feet. Unruly plant growth after a summer of little maintenance left a landscape full of blurred edges and boundaries. It felt wonderfully wild and alive.

Where most schools exemplify minimalism in materials and plant selection, this one presented an abundance of textures, materials, trees, plants, and sizes and shapes of spaces. The Grün macht Schule program has been driven in large part by a new Berlin policy requiring schools to capture and manage 100 percent of the rainwater that falls on-site. In the green schoolyards world, the Grün macht Schule program is frequently held up as one to aspire to.

The renovated schoolyard is teeming with life and rich with unique spaces and opportunities for discovery. Students' wishes for a sand volleyball court eventually won over the decision makers, despite its need for regular maintenance. Students have the option of enrolling in an afternoon volunteer program. Thirty-five different options include beach volleyball on the sand court and rock climbing in the gym as well as more common activities such as basketball, soccer, dance, music, and archery. The school and grounds provide a nurturing, nature-filled, and inspiring physical context that supports and strengthens B. Traven's community

FIGURE 7.6C: The B. Traven campus is characterized by permeable brick paving, layers of plants and trees, and plenty of places where students can sit alone or in small groups.

FIGURE 7.6D: A sunken amphitheater allows bigger outdoor events as well as smaller informal gatherings. It absorbs rainwater, and plants sprout through at the end of summer, when less maintenance occurs than during the school year.

FIGURE 7.6E: A sand volleyball court honors the students' wishes, despite its need for regular maintenance.

school model. It seems to be working. In a recent survey of teachers, parents, and students, a majority of teachers responded that they liked working at their school; most students said they knew who to contact if they had problems and needed help; and parents said they would send their children to the school again.[39]

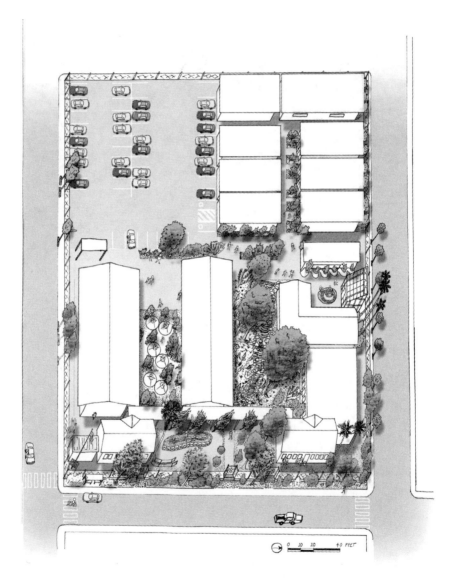

FIGURE 7.7A: Environmental Charter High School. Drawing by Adrian Chi Tenney.

Environmental Charter High School

16315 Grevillea Avenue

Lawndale, CA 90260

Grades 9–12

Built: 1929; modernization/school founded: 2010

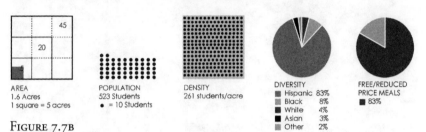

AREA	POPULATION
1.6 Acres	523 Students
1 square = 5 acres	● = 10 Students

DENSITY
261 students/acre

DIVERSITY
■ Hispanic 83%
■ Black   8%
■ White   4%
■ Asian   3%
■ Other   2%

FREE/REDUCED
PRICE MEALS
■ 83%

FIGURE 7.7B

Environmental Charter High School challenges many preconceived notions about what high school is. From the minute you step onto campus, you know that ECHS is something different.

The front gate opens into an entry garden with a stack of kidney-shaped platforms creating an informal amphitheater in the middle. Each platform was made from carefully placed pieces of broken concrete reclaimed from demolition on the school site. Like most schools, the whole school used to be concrete and asphalt. Now, it is covered with layers of dense vegetation. Shade trees tower above small fruit-bearing trees and shrubs. Vines adorn the perimeter fence. Ground cover plants vary between flowers, vegetables, and edible flowers.

You can see the original 1920s middle school campus through the plants and trees, a rich texture that is unusual for schools in the United States. Classrooms in the two main buildings faced each other beneath long covered walks over a central courtyard arroyo. Students transformed the courtyard, formerly a blacktop, to reveal the natural riparian systems that used to trace through Southern California. The arroyo collects and filters runoff from school roofs and paving during rains. During the dry season, a small fountain feeds the arroyo, and a pump at the low end recirculates the water back up to the top (see figure 7.7e).

In the lunch garden, umbrella-shaded tables share space with fruit trees,

Figure 7.7c: Students eat outside, surrounded by edible plants and trees such as the nasturtium at the bottom right and the citrus tree behind the tables. Signs placed next to fruit trees and vegetables invite students to pick a nutritional snack. A chicken wanders through the lunch area, sometimes accompanied by one or more bunnies.

perennial vegetables, and edible annuals. During our visit, one of those edibles is chayote, a fruit common to Mexico and Central America. "I try to grow things the students might be familiar with," says Eddie Cortes, the grounds manager.

"Here are our free vending machines," Cortes says at the garden café, which is packed full of small fruit trees. A sign invites students to pick a piece of fruit for a healthy snack. Nasturtiums grow low beneath the citrus trees. A chicken wanders freely around the tables, pecking at small grasses and weeds. Around the back is a small demonstration garden. A wall painted with a green scaly pattern snakes along the west edge. A small greenhouse stands against the fence, and a railing leads down two steps into a sunken circle with an iron maintenance cover at the center. We hear about the rainwater tank below the cover, capturing rain as it drains off the roof of the building next to it. The rainwater is then used to irrigate the fruit trees

FIGURE 7.7D: ECHS grounds manager Eddie Cortes stands in a small circular depression marking the location of an underground water storage tank. The hand pump allows students to fill watering cans with the collected rainwater to water fruits and vegetables growing in raised planters and around campus.

and vegetable gardens. A hand pump stands next to the sewer cap, inviting students to pump water from the rainwater tank and fill a watering can or bucket to give the nearby plants a drink. A bit of movement catches my peripheral vision, and I turn to see three bunnies bouncing along the quiet back wall of the school.

ECHS's unique flavor grew organically from its site and the people who made it. The campus character evolved and morphed—and continues to do so—with each new student group that comes through and graduates from the program. This was the intent of its founder, Alison Diaz.[40] She opened the school with a focus on connecting low-income students with the environment because they are disproportionately affected by industrial contamination and lack of access to parks and open space. The school doesn't just recycle and compost, though it does these things. ECHS tackles the environment through big, systems thinking.

FIGURE 7.7E: The Arroyo replaced a central asphalt courtyard with a recirculating stream to create a living laboratory for students to learn from and enjoy. Construction by La Loma Development.

FIGURE 7.7F: Environmental Charter High School's entry garden features shade trees, climate-appropriate plants, and a stacked-wall amphitheater made of broken concrete that was reclaimed from the site. Design and construction by La Loma Development.

Students designed the arroyo while learning about the natural eco-systems that used to inhabit the site. Students grow the food that supports their local organic meal program. Students run the on-campus bicycle repair shop that encourages students and staff to ride their bikes to school. Students take care of the chickens and rabbits and the closed-loop aquaponics system. Students also engage in an annual four-week "intersession" project with their community and local nonprofit organizations. Past topics included "How does gentrification affect education, business, housing + the environment in my community?"; "What does it take to make LA thrive?"; and "How does the minimal living movement affect our societies?"

"One of the questions students are asked during intersession is 'Why does my community need me?,'" school counselor Lacey Harris said.[41] "We help each student understand who they are and how they can make an impact within their community. Being able to apply the skills they're learning, whether it's just about knowing their self-worth and knowing that they're worthy of having a voice, they're worthy of speaking out even when they sometimes don't feel that way."

In support of its environmental mission, the school is known for its strong community partnerships, interdisciplinary approach, and dedication to preparing all its students for college. It works. *U.S. News & World Report* ranks Environmental Charter High School in the top 3 percent of public high schools in the United States. And 96 percent of ECHS graduates are admitted to a four-year college or university. That accomplishment is made more poignant knowing that 85 percent of graduates are the first in their families to go to college. ECHS students develop leadership skills while they are at school. Each year, students lead campus tours for up to three thousand visitors to share knowledge about the environment and sustainability.[42] Students organize and host an annual Earth Day educational fair for around one thousand local elementary students, leading lessons, demonstrations, art exhibits, and performances focused on environmental sustainability.

In 2012, the high school was in the very first cohort of schools given a US Department of Education Green Ribbon Schools Award for environmental and sustainable education. Today, there are four campuses united in their goal to reimagine public education for low-income communities of color. The school focuses on student-led, strengths-based education with community service at its heart. Each year, all high school students participate in a four-week community-based project in which they engage with the community and build an understanding of issues and opportunities related to environmental health and social justice. Although the school has no sports fields, it does offer sports.

José Guadalupe Gutierrez, a community organizer who attended Environmental Charter High School, told me about some of the partnerships that make the school so special. "We relied a lot on Lawndale [School District] having joint use agreements with local elementary and middle schools so that if we were training, we could go to Anderson Park at Will Rogers Middle School," Gutierrez said.[43] "There has to be a connection between the schools that don't have a field and the local districts and local parks organizations that have joint use agreements. That allows us to have these spaces without having a field in our own schools."

The partnerships extended beyond joint use agreements. Environmental organizations worked with students and communities to sponsor community-based, student-led learning. Gutierrez was introduced to planning, community organizing, and landscape architecture through an urban planning course taught by Viviana Franco, founder of the local nonprofit park developer From Lot to Spot. He kept in touch with her, and when he finished college she hired him as a community organizer.

ECHS works to build relationships between students and relationships between students and their school. Every year, students go camping or backpacking. The overnight trips immerse students in the natural world—a first for many of them—and build strong bonds among student cohorts. These relationships benefit students individually but also serve the school's long-term success. The deep connections built between students, the community, and the school don't disappear when students graduate. Gutierrez went back a few years ago to work with a horticulture class the school established to plant native plants. And he intends to keep going back, he said. "My hope is as I get older that I may be able to fund things that I'm interested in and passionate about, to be able to give back to the school in some form."

By creating a student-centered curriculum and approach intended to nurture a sense of belonging, create nature-filled spaces, and inspire awe in the natural world, Environmental Charter High School sets a compelling precedent. In a repurposed older school building, teachers and students work together to transform the school into a model exemplifying environmental sustainability, community partnership, and student ownership. The slow transformation allows thoughtful planning and design based on the students' lived experiences and careful observations over time while also giving them hands-on experience in changing their environment and community.

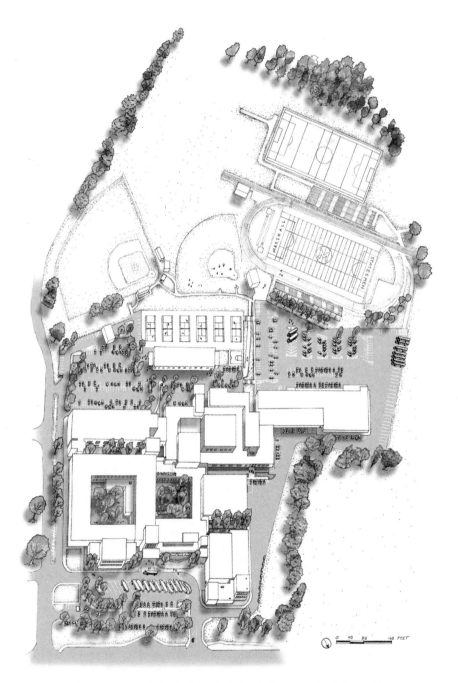

FIGURE 7.8A: George C. Marshall High School. Drawing by Adrian Chi Tenney.

George C. Marshall High School

7731 Leesburg Pike

Falls Church, VA 22043

Grades 9–12

Built: 1962; renovated: 2010–2014

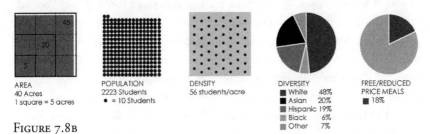

AREA	POPULATION	DENSITY	DIVERSITY	FREE/REDUCED
40 Acres	2223 Students	56 students/acre	■ White 48%	PRICE MEALS
1 square = 5 acres	● = 10 Students		■ Asian 20%	■ 18%
			■ Hispanic 19%	
			■ Black 6%	
			■ Other 7%	

FIGURE 7.8B

Funding: $60 million from a district-wide bond for facility renovations; student-raised funds for energy conservation (Get2Green program)

George C. Marshall High School opened in 1962, just one year after the Interstate 495 Beltway was built through Fairfax County, Virginia. The school sits in Falls Church, across the highway from Tyson's Corner—a scramble of big-box retail stores, corporate headquarters, automobile dealerships, and the usual restaurants, hotels, and gas stations that accompany highway interchanges. The Freddie Mac Corporate Headquarters is here, along with a slew of apartment and condominium complexes. Tiffany & Co. stands across the street from McDonald's. The Ritz-Carlton adorns one side of the Tysons Galleria mall, connected by a skywalk to Saks Fifth Avenue and Kate Spade. On the other side of Leesburg Pike you'll find TJ Maxx, Marshalls, and a Walmart Supercenter. This seems like an odd place for a high school, yet the site embodies so much American development history.

Marshall High lies less than ten miles from the White House. Fairfax County remained largely devoted to farming until the post–World War II development boom of the 1950s. Steady development occurred during the 1960s and 1970s. In the 1980s, the widening of Highway 267 into the Dulles Access Road catalyzed massive development in the triangular island between State Route 267, SR 7, and I-495. Its location close to the nation's capital means that many of the fourteen thousand people who live in Falls Church work in Washington, DC. Its position in a DC suburb helps it serve a broad diversity of students. It also spurs steady student population growth.

The school underwent a major renovation a decade ago to respond to two urgent issues. First, the student body had grown from 1,440 to 2,200 in less than ten years, overcrowding a campus built for 1,500.[44] Second, several stormwater quality laws and mandates, including the State of Virginia's Chesapeake Bay Initiatives and the federal Clean Water Act's requirements for the Municipal Separate Storm Sewer System (MS4) Permit, required the school district to capture and clean all rainwater that landed on school sites.[45] Marshall High leveraged the required stormwater treatment to create visible nature-based water and habitat systems throughout campus. These include bioretention ponds, stormwater filter boxes in the storm sewer catch basins, permeable pavement in the main entry parking area, and a green roof.

Marshall High is typical of big public high schools. Unlike B. Traven Community School and Environmental Charter High School, Marshall serves over 2,200 students. It's located in a large suburb of a large metropolitan area. It's a traditional public school—neither a charter school nor a magnet. Students may opt into an international baccalaureate program, or not. The high school's physical environment isn't extraordinary for a high school. But therein lies its power. It serves as a functional, positive example to large, risk-averse school districts. The original 1960s classroom buildings could be described as square donuts with courtyards in the middle. Classrooms open onto two sides of a main corridor running around the donut. Classroom walls opposite the doors are full of large windows that look out into garden courtyards or the tree-filled edge of campus, depending on which side of the corridor you're on (see figure 7.8). A small addition in the mid-1980s stayed true to the original concept. The 2011 renovation included a new entry, a new library, and renovated floors, windows, ventilation, and lighting. Energy efficiency was a central focus. The district installed "cool" coatings on the roofs to reduce the amount of the sun's heat they absorbed. Passive solar shading was added over windows. And other improvements included lighting with

FIGURE 7.8C: Samaha Architects designed the new two-story entry and the community-facing school library. Both stand above the 1960s building with window-filled walls. Design and image: Samaha Architects.

FIGURE 7.8D: Sunlight and views of trees fill the library. Soft surfaces such as carpet and upholstered furniture absorb sound and provide a comfortable seating and studying environment. Design and image: Samaha Architects.

motion and light sensors, a high-efficiency heating/cooling and ventilation system, and energy-efficient kitchen appliances.[46]

Two of the improvements include a grand entry lobby and a new library.
The new lobby feels more like a museum entrance than a high school
entrance. It's easy to find from the parking lot. The front doors are clear
glass set inside a clear glass wall. When you walk in, the front office is visible and brightly daylit behind clear glass doors. Inside, comfortable arm-
chairs arranged in clusters, complete with side tables, invite you to rest.
The library shares the same design strategy, with a two-story atrium full of
sunlight streaming through abundant glass. Carpet and upholstered chairs
invoke the feeling of a living room (see figures 7.8c and 7.8d). The library
doubles as a community room and a museum. The archives room holds
digitized *National Geographic* magazines dating from 1888. An important
added function is that students can use the daylit living room as space for
quiet time, too.[47] A new classroom building added twenty-two classrooms.
The additions were designed with a focus on organizing space according to
program. A 300,000-gallon underground storage tank captures and holds
rainwater under the practice field until it is needed to irrigate the athletic
fields. The school benefited from the timing of construction, in the early
2010s, as the Great Recession lowered both material and construction
costs. This helped the school upgrade to longer-lasting, more sustainable
materials, such as terrazzo tile floors, which have a hundred-year warranty,
instead of linoleum.

Around the time of the school renovation, Fairfax County Public
Schools hired Elaine Tholen as its first sustainability director. A trained
educator, she approached the design and management of school sites holistically, connecting the school's physical environment and its surrounding
natural resources to what happened in the classroom. Tholen began the
district's Get2Green program with a small group of principals who were
enthusiastic about sustainability. The district set aside $50,000 per year that
schools could apply for to improve sustainability. The projects were small,
$1,000–$3,000 each, and student driven. Kids often apply for the grants
and install the improvements themselves.[48] Over the years, the program
took off countywide, with bigger goals each year.

George C. Marshall High School earned the National Wildlife Federation Eco-School's highest honor in the Green Flag Award and won

FIGURE 7.8E: The renovation included improvements to meet new stormwater mandates as well as opportunities for experiential learning and student-led efforts. The main courtyard provides shade trees, a habitat pond, and seating. Classrooms on all four sides of the garden have views through generously sized windows.

FIGURE 7.8F: Curb cuts direct water from the back parking lot into a planted swale edging the football field that collects and absorbs stormwater runoff.

the Environmental Protection Agency's annual Battle of the Buildings competition for water. Both awards recognized the school's student-led environmental achievements, which included saving 16,000 gallons of water and almost 114,000 kilowatt-hours of electricity.[49] Students conduct energy audits and drive a lot of the suggestions for a more sustainable campus. During the high school renovation, it was the students who asked for a green roof and chose to locate it where it would be seen from a second-floor hallway. Students formed the Green Team and led the design and maintenance of the native species garden. Student eco-guides lead tours with VIP media, education, architecture, and environmental visitors.

Marshall High offers auto shop, cosmetology, culinary arts, and cybersecurity. Other high schools offer programs in nursing; heating, ventilating, and air-conditioning (HVAC); dental hygiene; and landscaping. Any students from the district can take any of these concentrations, with transportation provided. The environmental science classes take field trips to do field testing, spending five hours in the field conducting water quality tests. Before they go, they spend the first quarter learning how to test water quality and about the impacts of nitrites and other contaminants. The Fairfax County curriculum includes seventh-grade environmental and life sciences and ninth-grade biology focused on the environment. Elaine said that the National Wildlife Federation approached the district in search of ways to support more green jobs, maybe in renewable energy or LEED (Leadership in Energy and Environmental Design) certification.

I met with Elaine Tholen and Principal Jeff Litz at Marshall High to tour the school and interview them in late 2017.

"Generally anything environmental that people approach me with, I'm game," Litz said, "because it's an important part of the curriculum and an important part of being a human walking on this earth."

I asked him about students' mental health.

"In twenty-three years, I have seen a difference," Litz told me. "Mental health has become more of an issue, but I also think we are becoming more vigilant and aware. There is a standard ratio of counselors/psychologists to students now."

He actively checks in with students to see how they are doing. This contributes to students' sense of being cared for and valued and of belonging there.

"I am constantly asking our kids, 'How do you take care of yourself . . . what do you do for fun?,'" he said. "When they can't give me those answers . . ." he rattles off the school's resources. Marshall employs eight full-time counselors, a full-time psychologist, and a career center specialist. Each counselor works with 250 kids. They run depression screenings in the ninth and tenth grades. They train teachers to identify depression and symptoms through professional videos. In addition, they hold two mental health–related events per year. In the spring of 2020, it was yoga. He had therapy dogs in all the courtyards the day before my visit.

"I think many of our kids are overscheduled," Litz said. "I'd like to see some of our kids sit on a bench and meditate for a minute."

I asked, "Do you see the campus or landscape design playing a part in mental health?"

"I don't know that I do," he responded. "Certainly, the kids who take care of the landscape have an outlet. I know the kids who work with us are generally happy kids who enjoy what they're doing."

Tholen asked my question in a different way: "Do you notice a post-renovation difference?"

"Yes," he said. "Since the renovation, the students are proud academically and proud of their building."

Whether acknowledged or not, this is a characteristic of mental health. Pride reflects a sense of ownership and belonging that is vital to students' mental health and well-being. Marshall High boasts a welcoming entry and lobby with clear and logical organization. Students are engaged and screened to check their mindset and are provided with physical and programmatic resources to help reduce stress. Calming gardens and a quiet and cozy library provide respite. Most classrooms and the library and band room look out into trees and gardens, and the stormwater system is based on natural processes. Marshall High provides an example for larger schools of the potential for school-wide policies and programs that can build on a humane, well-organized, and well-designed campus environment to support students.

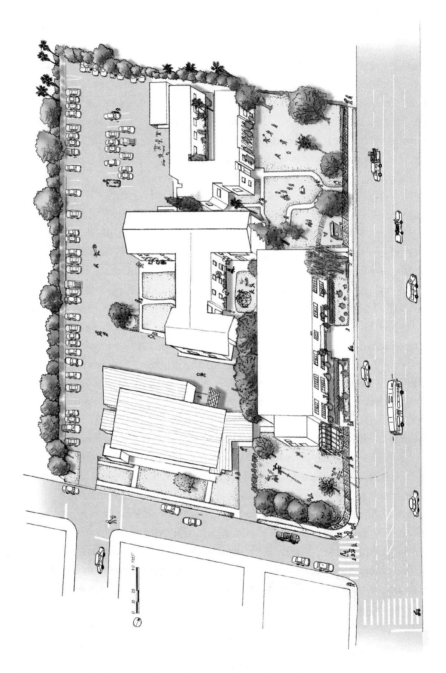

FIGURE 7.9A: Bridges Academy. Drawing by Adrian Chi Tenney.

Bridges Academy

3921 Laurel Canyon Boulevard

Studio City, CA 91604

Grades 4–12; approximate ages 9–18

Built: 1947; modernization/school founded: 1994

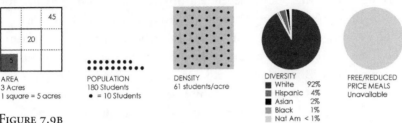

AREA	POPULATION	DENSITY	DIVERSITY	FREE/REDUCED
3 Acres	180 Students	61 students/acre	■ White 92%	PRICE MEALS
1 square = 5 acres	● = 10 Students		■ Hispanic 4%	Unavailable
			■ Asian 2%	
			■ Black 1%	
			■ Nat Am < 1%	

FIGURE 7.9B

Bridges Academy is one of a small number of schools devoted to "twice exceptional," or "2e," students. Twice exceptional students have high intellectual ability and also experience learning, executive functioning, production, or social challenges. If most students fall into a middle "norm" and can be taught through standardized materials (which is debatable), then twice exceptional students are those who perform above and below the norm at the same time.[50] This is sometimes described as asynchronous development, since the student's abilities develop at different rates. Their intellectual gifts might cover their special needs. These students and their families can struggle for years before understanding why. Schools often provide resources for academically advanced ("gifted") students and resources for students with learning differences. But these resources rarely overlap. Parents with twice exceptional children and teenagers are then left to choose between a program that challenges them academically but neglects their special needs, or a program that serves their learning differences but fails to challenge their strengths. These students likely feel out of place in traditional schools with no one really understanding their unique strengths and needs. They may act out in frustration or fail to follow directions. Parents probably have few good options nearby. And they can advocate for their twice exceptional child only if they know what twice exceptional is. Most teachers don't know that students can be high achievers and have learning differences. So unless parents have the financial resources to have their child thoroughly assessed, students can be set up for failure. The National Education Association estimates that 6 percent of students with disabilities may be twice exceptional.[51] The NEA also suggests we assume that every school has twice exceptional students. And yet only a tiny fraction of schools specifically serve twice exceptional students. Most of these are private.

Bridges Academy is an independent private school with programs for fourth- through twelfth-grade students. Over 90 percent of students are White. Eighty-eight percent are male. The school serves some students whose tuition is paid for by public school districts that cannot meet the students' needs. Bridges takes a student-centered, whole child approach that addresses the complex relationships between gifts and talents, socio-emotional profiles, family context, students' interests, developmental asynchrony, and learning differences.[52] Teachers treat students as individuals, working with their strengths instead of focusing on their differences. The small school site, the small student body, and several design considerations support student success and the Bridges approach.

The school site was first home to Corvallis High School, the San Fernando Valley's first Catholic high school, established in 1941.[53] The first classes were held in an old Spanish Revival house until the main academic building was constructed in the mid-1940s. A residence building for the nuns opened shortly after. Corvallis operated there until 1987, when it closed because of declining enrollment.[54] The OSULA Education Center for teaching English as a second language occupied the site briefly and made some changes to the buildings. Bridges Academy opened there in 1994. Along the main road, the 1940s facade is largely intact. Windows were replaced for efficiency but in the same dimensions and pattern. Even the way they open for ventilation (outward with a top hinge) is the same as originally designed. An addition holds an elevator shaft. The administration office is in a newer building closest to the parking area at the back of campus. It greets students and visitors with a carpeted waiting room furnished like a living room (see figure 7.9c). Built-in benches adorn the corridors of each academic building.

One of the first things you notice when visiting, especially when you are used to visiting public schools, is the shady, parklike setting (see figure

FIGURE 7.9C: A cozy waiting room outside of the Bridges Academy offices invites students, parents, and visitors to get comfortable.

7.9d). A skyful of tree branches shade two big common areas on each end of campus. Part lawn, part mulch, part garden, they offer cool and respite away from the hubbub of the central courtyard. The north lawn is enclosed enough to feel sheltered, despite the steady traffic noise. A loose green hedge dots the north and east sides. The middle and high school building defines the south side. And the old convent separates the lawn from the parking lot. The space feels like the big backyard of a grandmother's house—slightly worn and unkempt but also homey and welcoming. Half of the space is grass; the other is covered with mulch. Four chickens scratch around in the dirt around a chicken coop fenced into one mulched corner. Walking up to a low circular stone wall in the middle, I peer in and discover turtles. The south lawn has a similar scale and character, but its location at the corner makes it feel more open and a little exposed. There is a greenhouse near the building. The chain link has been screened with mesh to help reduce the visual distraction of cars driving by.

Picnic tables, umbrella tables, and benches spread around the grounds

FIGURE 7.9D: This invitation is present in classrooms, too, with carpeted corners and a variety of desk heights and chair types. The north lawn feels like a park with its mature shade trees and a row of hedges separating it from the adjacent property.

invite students, teachers, and visitors to sit in the sun or shade, depending on the weather. On my first visit to the school, I met with Director Carl Sabatino and parent advocate Amanda Millett. From the parklike setting to the daylit classrooms to the teaching approach to the service dogs accompanying teachers around campus, the school stood out. While the teaching philosophy and programs nurtured twice exceptional students, the physical character of the school grounds was in need of some improvements. Each year, the academy offers a series of enrichment classes for students to choose from. Our Cal Poly Pomona (CPP) landscape architecture graduate design studio partnered with a Bridges middle school enrichment class on sustainable campus design to reimagine their campus. CPP graduate students introduced Bridges seventh and eighth graders to the site analysis and design process, and Bridges seventh and eighth graders introduced CPP students to their campus and the main design issues (see chapter 3, box 3.1).

CPP students learned that the road noise was an issue, but even more distracting for students was the noise from the central courtyard. Younger students playing on the dome outside the high school classroom windows disrupted the studies of older students. Flooding impacted the campus in ways we never would have guessed by simply walking through the site. Bridges students told of splashing through the puddles and trying to dodge spouts of water gushing down from gutters that clogged and overflowed during heavy rains. Several students stood in the stairwell of the old building and described water pooling a couple feet deep in the bottom of the stairwell, which happened to house the elevator shaft— the only accessible route upstairs. Art teacher Caroline Maxwell, music teacher Dylan McKenzie, and architecture teacher Tyler Peck shared their own observations and their students' expertise. Bridges students made diagrams with the CPP students, and the CPP students sent out digital surveys to ask students and teachers what they liked most and least about the school grounds. Other questions included what activities they would like to do or teach outside and what would be their ideal outdoor environments. The student and teacher responses had quite a few overlaps. The most liked qualities of the Bridges campus were the trees, the north lawn, the general sense of open space, and the plants and animals. In addition, the students favored the dome. This was their play space, social space, resting space, and study space. Both students and teachers least liked the wood chips on the north lawn, the fake grass, and the bare dirt. For teachers, noise was a big issue, as was a lack of play areas. For students, rules were an additional issue, and for some, the dome. Teachers said they would like outdoor spaces for teaching, including physics, music, health, sports, and for the restorative mood enhancement. Students' ideal outdoor school environments included trees, grass, shade, and seating but also swings, tables, places for climbing and seating, flowers, "nice stuff," and quiet activities.

The CPP team explored design strategies to support mental health, with a specific focus on twice exceptional students. They shared their initial site analyses, survey results, and design concepts with the Bridges team and teachers just as the coronavirus began shutting down schools. Working collaboratively, CPP students created concepts that spoke to the specific ecological conditions of the site as well as students' mental health and well-being. The relationships they built with Bridges students, teachers, and staff gave them access to the vital information they needed to make meaningful design suggestions. Eighty-five of the 200 Bridges students and 46 teachers responded to the online survey. CPP MLA student Robert Douglass[55] captured some important design considerations for twice exceptional students with his concept of P.E.E.R.—provide places to Play, Express oneself, Experiment, Rest, and connect with others to create environments that foster physical, emotional, intellectual, and creative growth. Since this benefits all students, he said, "there's no good reason not to do it."

Redwood Park Academy

Wembley Grove, Cosham

Portsmouth, PO6 2RY

United Kingdom

Ages 11–16

Built: 1950s

AREA	POPULATION	DENSITY	DIVERSITY	FREE/REDUCED
5 Acres	141 Students	28 students/acre		PRICE MEALS
1 square = 5 acres	● = 10 Students		Unavailable	■ 58%

FIGURE 7.10A

Redwood Park Academy is one of four special schools in the United Kingdom's Solent Academies Trust. The trust is a public school district serving students with special needs in Portsmouth and Compton. Mary Rose
Academy is a special school for students aged two through nineteen who
have severe and complex learning difficulties often associated with physical disabilities, autism spectrum conditions, and medical conditions.
Cliffdale Primary Academy is a primary school for students aged two
through eleven, the majority with autism and severe learning difficulties.
The Littlegreen Academy serves students aged seven through seventeen
who have social, emotional, and mental health needs. Many also have a
range of additional needs, including autism, attention deficit hyperactivity disorder (ADHD), attachment disorder, anxiety, and speech and
language delays. Redwood Park Academy serves students with complex
learning difficulties sometimes accompanied by autism spectrum conditions; speech, language, and communication difficulties; and medical
conditions.

   I visited the Redwood Park Academy campus with Mary Jackson of
Learning through Landscapes (LtL), a UK organization dedicated to making lives better through connection to nature. LtL develops school grounds

FIGURE 7.10B: The entrance to Redwood Park Academy presents a friendly face to the community, even with gates that can secure the campus.

and trains teachers in taking their curriculums outdoors. We were there to learn what the school was doing to support students' mental health through outdoor learning. Our guide was Ed Bond, a former science teacher who leads all four Solent Academies Trust schools' horticulture programs. It is important to note that in addition to teaching science, Bond is an expert gardener. He took a break from teaching to participate in (and win!) the first season of BBC television's game series *The Big Allotment Challenge* in 2014. Upon returning, Bond joined the Solent Academies Trust to run the horticultural program. The curriculum looks different at each of the four schools. Mary Rose School, for instance, serves older students but has no outdoor space. Bond guides them in student-run businesses. The nursery program makes jams and jellies, runs a kitchen to cook meals for homeless individuals, and grows flowers and plants to sell. Redwood Park Academy had the ground space to spare.

Built in the 1950s to serve special needs students, the school is located in the 1930s Highbury Estate development in Cosham, Portsmouth, on the United Kingdom's south shore. It sits in a mixed socioeconomic neighborhood, with many of its residents working in the manufacturing, retail, health, service, and defense sectors. The school site covers five acres, bordered on its south side by the six-lane A27 highway on the north bank of Ports Creek. More than half of the site is a field, marked for soccer. The field is marshy much of the year owing to its location over a former creek. A thick edge of meandering pine trees between fifty and one hundred feet wide separates the highway from the school. The school buildings are located at the far north side of campus. The school includes an indoor swimming pool and the ubiquitous painted hard-surface sport courts.

We were there to visit the gardens, though. So, after catching up on the background over a cup of tea, we headed out to the first of two courtyard spaces. A greenhouse occupied the middle ground. It was January, with bare trees and shrubs standing stoically over planting beds, some of which were tucked under blankets or carpets for the winter. The others in this smaller space were neatly planted with winter annuals and perennials. An orderly line of concrete pavers led through a gravel mulch. The path led to a second space, which exploded with a sense of action. This larger courtyard was stuffed full of planter beds separated by narrow walks and surrounded by a collection of materials: string netting, plastic mesh, metal screens, twigs held together with twine, little woven walls of hazel switches (see figure 7.10c). Sticks stuck in the ground were topped by upside-down plastic bottles. Laminated signs poked up, printed with the words "Parsley," "Fennel," and "Parsnip," each accompanied by a drawing of the plant. In a mostly empty bed, "Lupine" poked up with a few small five-fingered tabletop-style leaves. Rust-colored chickens pecked in the dirt along the pathways and in the beds. A garden shed sat in the back beneath the branching black silhouette of a bare tree. A conglomeration of farm and repurposed objects were formally arranged in alignment with the beds and garden shed: a wire-and-plastic chicken coop, an old metal canoe, a wooden picnic table. A small structure made with wood posts and planks and topped with a warped piece of corrugated metal covered a dome of clay-covered bricks with an opening in the front. A sheet of paper, stapled to the front, read "Pizza Oven" and included a picture of a slightly more perfect version and a drawing of a pizza pie.

FIGURE 7.10C: The main garden area at Redwood Park Academy was built and is cared for by students.

It is hard to understand the impact of a school garden without seeing students use it or interviewing the teachers who guide them. Bond told us about a girl who a year ago wouldn't come outside. She had since started taking care of the hens.

"Now she sits on the ground with them while she gets the seed out," he said. "She has gained confidence with them. She's savvy with her own progress, saying, 'Look what I've done.' The students gain self-confidence and comfort by working in the garden. They have the ability to be independent in this space. They're caring for stuff and not being cared for. In a life full of short, targeted activities, they develop an awareness of different time scales. Worthwhile things aren't necessarily immediate."

Each class has a primary teacher who delivers the education. Bond is there two days a week, working with fourteen- to sixteen-year-old students for forty-minute sessions to support science. The value of the garden extends beyond the two days he works with the students there. It's an open, free, safe, quiet, calm space. Every student has free access

FIGURE 7.10D: Students gain a sense of freedom and autonomy in the garden—rare experiences for all students but especially for those with special needs. Image by Ed Bond.

during lunch and breaks. The chickens help draw the students outside, and other teachers take them out, too. It's in the middle of the school, so you cannot not see it over the course of the school day. Every piece of the gardens is made and cared for by students. The work and time in the garden benefits them all. They do an hour of hard gardening, and they get social time, and they get adult time, which is rare. For some, it becomes a livelihood. Those who are more physically able can go on to be gardeners and landscapers . . . or attend colleges with special needs programs. Bond told of one student who was always in the office until he braved coming outside. By the time he left school, he had won his Royal Horticultural Society "gardener of the year" award and was giving tours to visitors.

From the sound of it, these gardens are just the beginning. The students here grow flowers for the Mary Rose School prom. They use the pizza oven for special class meals. Bond led us around the playground and out past the marshy field. A small forest school, complete with a yurt and a newly planted orchard, was tucked behind a handwoven hazel fence occupying an odd-shaped corner jutting off the farthest reach of campus near the highway. He was preparing for four hundred saplings to come in March to create hedgerows. I never heard whether they were able to do that before the stay-at-home order. On the overall benefits of the garden, Bond was humble. He said the program highlights and supports everything else the school is doing to support students, which is already working really well. He had seen another school that started with horticulture but didn't get it right. Their evaluations suffered. This is an important point. It takes the right school, with the right supports, and the right instructor who understands the material as well as respects the students' unique individual needs. Both Bond and Jackson saw a growing need for programs for students with special needs. Across the city, special schools were seeing increased numbers of students diagnosed with special needs. The same is likely true in other parts of the world, too.

Asked what he'd want to be done differently, Bond responded simply, "I would want year-round access. And I'd want paths and raised beds instead of that mud."

CHAPTER 8
Conversations on Transformation by Design

School design is not a topic that begins and ends at the site boundary or with the principal architect or landscape architect. It affects students during the hours they are at school and permeates the rest of their lives. School environments shape the minds, bodies, achievements, and self-worth of students over their lifetimes. It is not the only thing that matters to children, teens, and their families. But it is a big thing.

School design is largely informed, intentionally or not, by how we (as community members, parents, educators, administrators, designers, and advocates for social and environmental justice) define school physically and philosophically. The public education system in the United States has changed very little over the past 150 years. Over the course of 2020, we saw both a massive closure of schools around the country and a global reckoning with systemic racism in our social and physical institutions, including education. The coronavirus revealed deep inequities in the impacts on those with and without resources. Schools and districts seem frozen in time. As they begin to consider and communicate strategies for reopening, it is clear that most are operating under the same pervasive and limited assumptions about what school should look like and act like as before the pandemic . . . only six feet distanced. If there is ever a time to completely reimagine school design, this is it.

Over the past five years, I've talked to and learned from so many school experts, community members, researchers, designers, and student advocates pushing at the boundaries of what school could be. Many of those voices are included in the previous chapters. Following are longer conversations intended to open doors to futures we might not yet imagine.

On the Past and Present of High School Horticulture

Willie Nakatani, former horticulture teacher; and Jeff Mailes, present horticulture teacher, Eagle Rock Junior/Senior High School, Los Angeles

Willie Nakatani taught horticulture for thirty-seven years at Eagle Rock Junior/ Senior High School in Los Angeles, beginning in 1967. Of forty-three LAUSD high schools at the time, twenty-five had fully operational horticulture programs, each run by two or three men. The number of high schools is at least double that now. After he retired seventeen years ago, the garden was managed by a well-meaning special education teacher. Now it is back in the hands of someone with the special horticulture knowledge needed for a healthy garden—Jeff Mailes—and his students. I met Willie Nakatani and Jeff Mailes in the horticulture classroom on the day LAUSD decided to close its schools because of the coronavirus. Nakatani was there to give a demonstration on using land surveying equipment. I interviewed him in the building he designed.

CL: What was it like when you started here?
Willie Nakatani: I started in the old 1920s building. We planned this building for horticulture. This wall is indoor siding from my old bungalow. There was a photo bungalow too. They tore that down. After the earthquake of '71 they phased out the old bungalows, which were better for earthquakes because they were made of wood. We had the old glass house where Eagle Rock is now. The lath house is the same. Where the plots are was the biggest open space. I had them [for the] junior high students. Each kid did spading and ridges and planting. We did floral arrangement in here.

CL: With flowers you grew?
WN: No, that would have only been enough for one class. I worked with the downtown floral people who saved broken heads and the stuff they knew they couldn't sell.

We planted all the trees, conifers and eucalyptus, on the hillside. And up above Eagle Rock Boulevard, we planted those too. Scott Wilson [founder of North East Trees, an environmental nonprofit] used to teach here and then he taught at Crenshaw, then at North Hollywood. I took over and we actually competed against one another at LA Beautiful. It was quite competitive.

Jeff Mailes: Willie has been coming to show me some pruning techniques for the black pine and the topiary letters.

WN: I like it to be curved. Plants do better with a curved edge.

CL: I understand there was a woodshop and a metal shop, too, back in those days when schools offered drafting and shop and home economics?

WN: Yep, we had everything. My last couple of years, we saw a lot of vocational programs closing. It happened very slowly, not overnight. We lost the teachers who had the least seniority but best programs. A lot of them went into private industry.

CL: And how did you get here, Jeff? What started you on this journey?

JM: I studied at UC Davis—that's where I caught the farming bug and where I got into outdoor education. It was through the Kids in the Garden program. We learned early education techniques. I fell in love with the idea of teaching kids about nature.

I taught high school one year, [then] stayed in Davis to start an edible landscape business. I had a colleague who was working in AmeriCorps at Luther Burbank High School in Sacramento, in the agriculture program. I helped with a couple lectures.

Then I did AmeriCorps at Portland Community College, teaching on a 3.5-acre farm with a huge worm composting area that used cafeteria food, closing the loop of food waste. Then I moved to LA and worked with a couple master gardeners . . . worked with EnrichLA . . . kept coming back to schools because gardens in schools have always been meaningful to me. That's how I met Phil Christ and Principal Mylene Keipp. Through EnrichLA.

I've always done part-time outdoor education either through horticulture or through landscape design. I got into farming because it was a good zombie apocalypse skill to have. I was thinking about dropping out of college. Growing my own food gave me a sense of security, and now I give that sense of security to my students.

WN: Well, you're doing a good job . . . they really look up to you.

On the Influence of Attending an Environmentally Focused High School

José Guadalupe Gutierrez, green space organizer and landscape architecture student, Los Angeles

CL: *What made you decide to attend Environmental Charter High School?*
José Guadalupe Gutierrez: At the time, my predetermined high school was Hawthorne High School. Back then, Hawthorne was known as a school with lots of gang violence and not the best curriculum. It was more my parents' decision to place me at ECHS—it just seemed like a calmer school.

CL: *What did you most appreciate about attending ECHS?*
JGG: Students were generally calm people—a huge difference from what we knew the local high schools were like. Through our annual trips we all got to bond as a class. Ninth graders went to Catalina. Tenth graders camped in Joshua Tree. Eleventh graders went backpacking in Sespe. I also really appreciated the funky teachers we had. Most of us recognized them as the Venice Beach hippie teachers—their vibe actually really made the environmental curriculum work. They came with a lot of ideas on sustainability, loved backpacking and teaching about plants and nature.

Later on in my time at ECHS, I grew to really like the campus—which was seemingly over summer turned into a riparian woodland. Where there was blacktop, suddenly there was a stream and sycamores. We had a really cool amphitheater made entirely of repurposed concrete.

CL: *What did you most appreciate about the school's physical environment?*
JGG: Lots of trees and native plants. I had a chance to plant a lot of them during my last two years at ECHS. It was so much nicer to have a tree to sit under instead of the really hot blacktop or having to hide in a class during lunch.

CL: *Was there anything you would have changed about the program or environment?*
JGG: Most of ECHS's cool environmental programs came after I left. In the last few years, kids have been able to do internships out in Montana, work on invasive plant control, travel the country with teachers, have botany experts teach about natives, take urban design classes.

CL: Do you think going to ECHS shaped your higher education and career path? If so, how?

JGG: Absolutely. It was in ECHS that I was introduced to park equity work in Los Angeles. Since then, I have worked as a park and community garden organizer and even opened a park in my hometown of Lawndale, where ECHS is located. I am also pursuing a master of landscape architecture degree because of my passion for parks, which I owe to my time at ECHS.

CL: If you could change public school education and/or environments overnight, what would you do?

JGG: I would invest in quality materials for students and more opportunities for kids to experience the outdoors like I did in ECHS. I would fund and develop culturally competent curriculum and teachers to support the educational development of Black and immigrant communities. I would tear out all the blacktop and install tons of trees and natural settings in all public schools. Also aim so that each school develops its own vibe and avoid all the schools looking the same. I would get rid of all the alarms that control the movement of kids in and out of school and adopt other practices of working with children so that they follow rules. Alarms are especially problematic in Black and immigrant communities, where they make it seem as if we're training the kids for prison.

On Juvenile Justice and How Schools Could Value Each Child's Unique Strengths

Lori A. Harris, attorney, juvenile justice defender, executive coach, Los Angeles

CL: Can you talk a little bit about how you got into working with youth? With teenagers?

Lori A. Harris: I'm the eldest in my family. My mom was very, very strict because she was very afraid. She didn't want anything bad to happen to us. But I was definitely the most challenging. And even as a kid, I had this understanding of adolescent brain development and I was like, you're just growing up. It's okay. You're okay, you're not a bad person. So I carried that with me. And when I went to law school, I wanted to just kind of reach out to kids and share that message. My first work in criminal defense was as a juvenile defender at a place called Kenyon Juvenile Justice Center. That was when I first had this introduction to how hard it is for young people and particularly for people who are economically challenged.

I remember a girl who [with] her friends went into J. C. Penney and stole matching pajamas. Did we really need to file a case on that? No. But we did. Or stealing another kid's skateboard. Or school fights. I think we should be able to do something other than file a case.

CL: If you could, overnight, design the school system of your dreams, what would that look like? It could be about the people, the physical design, anything.
LAH: I like the idea of not having borders. When I lived in Michigan, our house had the woods behind us, and there were no fences between any of the houses. So all our yards blended together, and they all converged around the woods. And it was beautiful. I would really love if we could have a sense of community in that way, where you had the woods. And I would love to have a system whereby there was diversity. Because everyone really does have something wonderful to contribute to every community, and this desire to drag people over to "This is the path—this is the best path . . . this is the only path"—stifles creativity and personal evolution, and so we never get to see how beautiful an academic community could be.

I would love to see a more nurturing environment and people playing with things and parents getting to explore different teaching styles and different learning styles and see which one works best for the family. It's not just the kid. When the kid is going through something, the whole family is going through something. You know, there's the Waldorf method and the Montessori method, and that's just the teeny tiny little bit I know. And those two methods seem to really emphasize "We're going to love on you" because we know that you're fundamentally great and our job is just to not f*ck it up.

CL: Wouldn't it be amazing to have a school where they thought all children were gifted?
LAH: Right! And it was their job to figure out what their gifts were.

On Design to Support Restorative Justice and Abolishing Prisons

Deanna Van Buren, architect, founder of Designing Justice + Designing Spaces, Oakland, California (from two interviews, conducted in 2018 and 2020)

CL: *Can you talk about how your approach to design relates to mental health?*
Deanna Van Buren: Our focus is on the emotional aspects or supporting emotional aspects of restorative justice, so less focus on mental health and more focus on process, which is a little different. But we do think a lot about fight and flight responses and things that people need to stay calm and focused.

CL: *How do you approach the trivializing of design?*
DVB: I believe and expect that people are not going to value design very much. These are working communities who are traumatized, and doing a design workshop is not their top priority. That doesn't mean design and the environment is not a hugely important and impactful thing that needs to be addressed. But it's not their responsibility to address it. It's ours as designers and architects to ensure that people have healthy, nourishing, supportive environments for their lives. So you start by building relationships with people and listening to them. It's pretty simple, but it takes some time.

CL: *Where do you see the big gaps, in terms of mental health, or the opportunities?*
DVB: Everything that we've done is primarily focused on restorative justice, economic justice, social justice. So the healing aspects should just be part of it. But we don't sit around and talk about "How does this space heal people? How does space respect people? How does this space support dialogue, difficult dialogue?" And the natural environment is a big part of that.

We've done the evidence-based design research, looking at health-care facilities and education, and we're applying this sort of justice context, given that those places need it more than anybody. And then schools have been a natural place to begin because of the school-to-prison pipeline, and we're focused on addressing the root causes of mass incarceration, and that's one of them. It's not the only one, but it's one of them.

CL: *It seems like a place to begin in terms of starting upstream.*

DVB: And, of course, we should be looking at mental health, given that in our incarcerated population, a vastly disproportionate number are there because of mental health issues and behaviors associated with that.

We have done almost nothing in schools here. Or anywhere, because of the challenges you've noticed. We've had more luck with larger projects like the one we did in Atlanta, which was turning a jail into something else, because of the municipality. The mayor herself was behind it. If there's no political will to do the work . . . and then there's the politics of the school district. You have many buildings instead of one, and the school board, and if everyone isn't in alignment . . . We've tried so hard to work with school districts, and it has just been impossible to pull off.

CL: *It's interesting that you say it's harder than transforming a jail.*

DVB: I know! That's how hard it is. Can you believe it?

CL: *I can! But I'm disheartened that you've had that issue too because I was hoping you'd give me the magic bullet.*

DVB: We're gonna try. We're gonna try again. The magic bullet is just never give up.

CL: *I wanted to ask if you could talk about your most transformative project right now. Is it the Atlanta jail project?*

DVB: I would say so. That is the reimagining of the Atlanta City Detention Center (ACDC). It's a landmark project, not just for us but for the country to look at. It's the city jail there, 475,000 square feet right in south downtown Atlanta. It used to house over a thousand people. We've been talking to the community organizers for almost two years. They contacted us and were like "Hey, we want to close this jail; I think we need an architect." And I was like, "Yep, you do. *And* you need a finance person." So, over the course of late 2018 and early 2019, we worked with the mayor's office and the community organizers as part of the planning team for a process that would engage the City of Atlanta in reimagining what the jail could be.

So the mayor committed to closing it down. She had already done that. The community organizers pushed for that. I mean, community organizers are responsible for all the good stuff. Follow your community organizers.

We worked with them to set up a task force, and we engaged residents of Atlanta both in master planning of that area around the jail and in the jail itself. It's the ACDC for Equity Planning Report. We presented four options to them for what to do with the jail. And it was an incredible process. It is a model process and outcome for what we need to do with our jails. We can close them down and turn them into other things. Or demolish them. And it's necessary. There's a lot of this. We built so much of it. And the jails are interesting because they tend to be located in our urban cores. So what's interesting from a landscape perspective, and to those interested in the public realm, is that you have to look at the entire neighborhood. Because once the jail is gone, you don't need the bail bondsman anymore; that's where the courts are; so what do you do? The ripple effects of that . . . because these justice corridors are like the armpits of our cities.

CL: Because of COVID, social distancing, and awareness, have your priorities shifted at all?
DVB: We just had to amplify, like put it on steroids. It's kind of like proceed as usual because the track we were on is now more right than ever. The amount of advocacy work we're doing has increased, because we're trying in this moment to help folks get clear about what it really looks like to not build prisons, jails, and not invest in policing. What divest/invest really looks like because we have real-world examples. Restore Oakland, ACDC, we have projects in Detroit, the LOVE Building. We just want to keep building the models so people can see the models and replicate the models. And that requires talking about them a lot and sharing them widely.

CL: Given how tough it is to work with schools and school districts . . . what would the ideal version look like? We are in a moment where it feels like we can bring anything to the table. So we need to advocate now for the most extreme version of a good school.
DVB: I agree! I think for schools you're gonna have to look at divest from the police and invest in schools. So what would you be investing in? What kinds of schools are needed? I've always felt like we need different kinds of schools that have different styles. And what's the funding stream . . . so it's no longer the property tax–based model; you need to redesign the financing of schools completely from the ground up. So I would say this

radical reimagining needs to include all the parts, not just design. But the rest of it too. Curriculum, how teachers are trained, what are they doing, you know, the whole thing. And then it also needs to be tied to housing. I like the community school model because I feel like it's starting to support people, like what could a school really be? I would focus on Black and Brown communities, because we need racial equity. So what do they really need in their schools? And every school would have to be different based on who's there. And how can schools do more? I agree with you, it is time for a radical reimagining and proposing those models.

On the Power of Parks and Nature Related to Law Enforcement

Dad, retired Los Angeles County sheriff's deputy with more than thirty-five years of service
Daughter, landscape designer

I worked with the daughter of this father-daughter interview team several years ago, during a time when my son's best friend was shot and killed in Watts. The day before he was killed, I was just a block away from where he would die, walking with a community group and a nonprofit looking for places to plant trees. One of the community members pointed out the irony of planting trees, since the police department regularly cut them down to improve visibility from police helicopters. I wrote an article about it, trying to process this loss and the losses people and communities face every day. I questioned why the police would cut down trees in disadvantaged neighborhoods if we know that trees and nature reduce stress and crime and bring people together. The neighborhoods with the least advantages and most crime needed trees and green spaces the most.

A few days later, the daughter approached me. She told me she'd been shot when she was eighteen. And she invited me to meet her dad, a retired Los Angeles County sheriff's deputy who had served the South Los Angeles neighborhoods, where he grew up, for more than thirty-five years. He knew better than most the challenges and opportunities people face in urban neighborhoods with limited resources. Talking to this father and daughter broadened and deepened my understanding of the challenges Black communities face day to day and over their lifetimes. They agreed to let me share our conversation, on the condition that the father remain anonymous.

CL: Your daughter tells me you were an LA County sheriff?
Dad: I was a county marshal and then a sheriff's deputy. I also worked twenty years at West LA College as a campus police officer. I always looked at it like I get to help people when they really need help. I grew up at 59th and McKinley, three or four miles north of Watts. Everything was South Los Angeles back then.

CL: What was it like growing up there?
Dad: When I was coming up, we had nothing. But our big thing was we would get on our bikes and go to USC Exposition Park, because they had a park there. It was funny, because we were out of the neighborhood. There were twenty kids and we all got out of the neighborhood for a while, and we could relax for a bit, maybe go swimming and go to sleep under a tree; you couldn't do that where I lived. You could kind of relax for a while. I remember how things like that made me feel. Just to get out of where I lived.

CL: Do you think that kind of experience would change things for the people you met as a sheriff's deputy?
Dad: About 10 percent of people really need to be in jail. Ninety percent of people just don't know how to navigate life. I worked Inglewood, Lennox—those are the two toughest areas—and Compton as support. When you work in Compton you talk to people who were charged in Compton, so you get to know them. A man who killed two people, he got the death sentence. He said, "I'd probably live longer in here than I would out there." That's the kind of people.

They had gardens and a farm where they had cows and chickens, over in Wayside [Prison] up by Magic Mountain. This huge land, and the inmates were so different when they could get outside. It was like a farm, and there were trees, and cows grazing. We liked it because it calmed them down. I think they stopped it because of budgets. [The inmates] did everything, they trimmed the trees, anything you did in a farm and park setting. It was totally different, totally different. I'm telling you, those guys were able to come out. There are four prisons there. At Supermax there are long corridors and there are no windows. But at Wayside, there is so much land, and a working farm. The inmates did anything to work there. It gave them purpose, confidence, and calmed them down. These guys would change so much; it was the best thing in the world for us.

Daughter: I think kids want to be outside, but unfortunately in some neighborhoods you can't do that . . . sometimes you can't.

Dad: I went to elementary school in South LA, but after that I went to Audubon Junior High School, and that was like Beverly Hills to me . . . the school is nice, the parks, and it was like a different world, you could walk around, you felt safe; you couldn't do that where I lived. The parks bring people out; there are more eyes and less gangs.

CL: Do you see that same pattern in your neighborhood (West Adams)?

Dad: Yeah, there's a small park over here at Arlington Park, and you see all these families out there having birthday parties, and long tables and stuff. One of the things they do around here is they have a movie night once a month. That place is packed.

Daughter: They redid the park, added new play equipment. There used to be just basketball courts and that was it. There used to be just gang members, and the cops would come and take pictures.

Dad: When they fixed it up, families would come. This is where they hang out now.

CL (to the daughter): Can you tell us about the day you were shot?

Daughter: It was June 22, 2003. That's why I have my tattoo. Across Adams off of Montclair, we were parked outside. We just were hanging out, talking. All of us had just graduated from high school. None of us were bad kids. I was leaning against my friend's car, and I heard two shots. But it was very close to the Fourth of July, so I didn't think about it. I remember looking down the row of cars, and I couldn't see a person, but I could see the red barrel. When my friend Anthony saw it, he tried to dive across the path, and he got shot in the leg. And I got down and tried to get under the car, and I got shot. *(She puts her hand to her chest, where she was shot.)* And I remember everything happened very quickly. And the ambulance came. And I was on a stretcher, and my dad came.

Dad: From a parents' perspective, it affected my wife and me for a long time. I get there and they already have the yellow tape around, and I show the officer my badge, and say she's my daughter, and they say I have to wait here. But the other guy brings me in. She looks up at me and says, "Dad, I don't want to die."

When I go back to work, I'm working court, and we take a break. And all of a sudden, I just start crying . . . I don't know what happened. For, say, a year or more, when we'd watch the news and something . . . we'd turn it off. My wife and I just never talked about it. It affects the whole family.

CL (to the daughter): What was school like for you?
Daughter: In elementary school, I just remember concrete, a huge empty space, though you make the most of what you have. And then Immaculate Heart was the nicest campus I've ever seen. It does matter. You spend a lot of time in school. That does affect how you view the world. There were a lot of trees and grass. And it's unfortunate that those types of campuses sometimes only exist in the private sector. To be able to sit in this nice private campus, and not worry. It's going to affect how you view the world. I remember going to Savannah three months after I got shot. [She earned her BA at Savannah College of Art and Design.] We're flying over Savannah, and it was just covered with trees. To see an entire city, it was so wonderful to be in a place that was so rich, to want to be outside.

Having a nice environment to learn and grow in, that shapes you, and I believe if more schools had that type of green space, it might push kids to want to be in better environments. It might give kids a feeling that "I belong here" (about USC, or anywhere) instead of feeling like "I belong in this barren landscape."
Dad: I think it not only helps kids, but it helps parents. And the kids live with their parents. What if you live in a one-bedroom apartment with your kids, versus what if you can go to a park? For the parents to have a place to decompress . . . that changes how you view the world. It's kind of like once we're out in the park, everyone's the same now. It's an equalizer.

CL: Why would we think helicopter policing is more important than trees?
Dad: A lot of people in government do what's easy. It's easy to cut the tree down. And the other thing is, they don't live there. I bet where they live there are trees. If they cut the trees in their neighborhoods, they'd go crazy. People are looking for simple solutions. If you think about the people in that area, you know it'll take time, but there are always alternatives. There

are ways you could get around that. If you have a park, maybe the solution is to have gravel roads to drive through there, better lighting. The helicopters . . . a lot of times you get this money and think "I gotta use it." "We'll give you money for a helicopter," or military types of guns and battering rams . . . ? "How about $100,000 for planting trees?" "Noooo . . ." They're always looking for a quick fix.

Daughter: Sometimes you can't put logic where there is none.

CHAPTER 9
For the Love of Students

The coronavirus pandemic hit three-quarters into my first year of teaching full-time. When the university closed, we thought we'd be back four days later. We left our offices, colleagues, and students with barely a good-bye.

"See you next Wednesday," I told my studio class.

The days turned into weeks. We scrambled to reimagine the second half of our semester. We moved class to Zoom. My students struggled with different levels of concern for family members, friends, and partners with compromised immune systems. Many lost financial stability as their parents lost jobs or they lost jobs themselves. We learned as a department how close to the edge most of our students lived. Small emergency grants set up through donations to a mutual aid account were quickly depleted. We poured ourselves into making the best learning environment possible for our students, without any physical environment at all. For many of us, faculty and students, that meant setting up an impromptu desk in the kitchen, in the living room, or in a closet, garage, or shed.

At the university level, the class material is relatively easy to deliver remotely. We can record video lectures, set up online discussion boards, share presentations and discussions over Zoom. It was the casual meetings, office-hours drop-ins, and catching up with students, friends, and faculty before and after classes that we missed the most. I started to begin the class videoconference and excuse myself to make a cup of tea to give students a few minutes to catch up informally, as they used to do before class began. We held our final presentations on Zoom. We awarded scholarships and department awards on Zoom. We celebrated our graduating students on Zoom.

Months stretched on.

For younger students and their families, the shift was tougher. Large city school districts serving our most in-need students scrambled to provide free and reduced-price meals. Students without internet or housing or family stability lost touch with teachers and peers. Parents with "necessary" jobs in health care and food service were put in the impossible position of needing to work without school or child care. Millions of others lost their jobs. The fact that Black and Brown communities suffered the most from the pandemic fanned the flames of the fight for civil rights. The social distancing mandate was what we needed to stop the virus. But it was the opposite of what we needed for building a sense of belonging and community resilience. In July 2020, the American Academy of Pediatrics put out a statement strongly recommending that students be "physically present in school" as much as possible, emphasizing the health, socio-emotional, and educational risks of keeping children at home.[1] Even so, public schools in the largest districts across the country decided not to reopen in person. One of the biggest drivers was teachers' health concerns. Very few schools, it turns out, were designed to accommodate social distancing. Even more concerning, most schools' ventilation systems don't meet the fresh-air standards needed to prevent airborne diseases from spreading. Instead of big windows that could open to let in fresh air and sunlight, newer school buildings are sealed tight to save energy in heating and cooling. Technology had advanced with no thought toward the risk of pandemic.

Ironically, it is often the older schools, designed from the 1920s through the 1950s and 1960s, that are best suited to provide fresh air, sunlight, and access to the healing properties of nature. During a webinar between three architects hosted by *Metropolis* magazine, I asked whether the pandemic had changed their idea of sustainable buildings.

Jill Kurtz, director of building sciences for the Page architecture and engineering firm, addressed solutions for climates or seasons that are too hot or too cold for open windows. "We're trying to keep air where people are using it, instead of spreading it around the whole building," she said.[2]

They're also looking at separating ventilation from air-conditioning and humidification systems. Both solutions would help air quality and comfort—pandemic or not.

Kate Diamond, civic design director for HDR, responded: "I studied architecture in Israel at the Technion a very long time ago when in fact there were no air-conditioned buildings in Israel. And the first projects I designed were in Sinai, and you could make them comfortable by thinking about passive design. I come from a generation that always assumed that. Most days in Los Angeles, you can be perfectly comfortable if you can open the windows and get natural air in and survive without any air conditioning so that your power grid can be focused on the things you need operationally. . . . Some of our new technologies are really looking at biophilic processes and applying them to buildings in new ways."[3]

The way forward might be to make the best of two worlds: Younger ages taught predominantly outside. Middle and high school students choosing to learn at their own pace outside and in buildings with plenty of natural ventilation, sunlight, and access to trees and gardens, or in a remote digital environment, whichever serves them and their families best.

The call for action to support our students' and teachers' mental and physical health has become an urgent alarm. Even before the pandemic, public schools were in crisis. Teachers felt unsupported and unfulfilled. Half of them considered leaving the profession in 2019.[4] Months of protests against police brutality and systemic racism during the pandemic laid bare the injustices of our health, criminal justice, environmental, and educational systems. These glaring gaps in resources must be repaired.

Green Schoolyards America; the Lawrence Hall of Science at the University of California, Berkeley; the San Mateo County Office of Education; and Ten Strands partnered to launch the National COVID-19 Outdoor Learning Initiative in the spring of 2020. The goal was to set up schools with the partnerships and infrastructure they need in order to teach students outside on school grounds and in parks. The hope is that after an initial "triage" of quick and free or low-cost outdoor learning solutions, schools can be designed more holistically to truly support public health as a preventive measure.

The nurturing, nature-full, and inspiring environments shared in the previous pages boost mental health, physical health, and immunity. It is no coincidence that this movement began with a hospital study, in which Roger Ulrich documented faster recovery times for patients who had views of nature. Other studies show that sunlight and fresh air have long been shown to heal people with influenza and other viral and bacterial infections.[5] Intuitively, we know this. At the turn of the past century, after industrialization took hold and the world suffered through outbreaks of tuberculosis and Spanish flu, schools redesigned themselves not only to maximize fresh air, sunlight, and views to let the eyes rest but also as community centers and places where experiential and individualized learning could support students' unique strengths.[6] As school districts plan to reopen with social distancing parameters in place, more will likely look to the schoolyard for its multiple benefits of social distance, fresh air, sunlight, and opportunities to learn by doing in nature. The physical and programmatic strategies in this book can support those plans while improving equity and resilience, too.

Students—like the rest of us—need a new vision of the future. We can remake schools into nurturing, nature-full, and inspiring places to learn and be. The world most of us now live in—increasingly paved, loud, chaotic, and absent of relief—isn't healthy for any of us. Education is moving away from prescriptive, lecture-based teaching, but our schools are still shaped that way. The most innovative and supportive businesses and organizations adopt inclusive, democratic structures and processes. It is time to change the trajectory of school design to support students and communities in the same way. By designing schools that heal, we can nurture the most important resource for our collective future: the flourishing minds, hearts, and bodies of our youth.

Resources
A Short List of Resources to Help You
Go a Little Deeper

Background Research

Children and Nature Network Reference Library. https://www.childrenandnature.org
/learn/research/.

Dannenberg, Andrew L., Howard Frumkin, and Richard J. Jackson, eds. *Making Healthy Places: Designing and Building for Health, Well-being, and Sustainability*. Washington, DC: Island Press, 2011.

Goldhagen, Sarah Williams. *Welcome to Your World: How the Built Environment Shapes Our Lives*. New York: Harper, 2017.

Louv, Richard. *Last Child in the Woods: Saving Our Children from Nature-Deficit Disorder*. Chapel Hill, NC: Algonquin Books, 2005.

Community-Led Design Strategies

De la Peña, David, Diane Jones Allen, Randolph T. Hester Jr., Jeffrey Hou, Laura J. Lawson, and Marcia J. McNally, eds. *Design as Democracy: Techniques for Collective Creativity*. Washington, DC: Island Press, 2017.

Hester, Randolph T. *Design for Ecological Democracy*. Cambridge, MA: MIT Press, 2010.

Wilson, Barbara Brown. *Resilience for All: Striving for Equity through Community-Driven Design*. Washington, DC: Island Press, 2018.

Nature-Based Design Strategies

Kimmerer, Robin Wall. *Braiding Sweetgrass: Indigenous Wisdom, Scientific Knowledge, and the Teachings of Plants*. Minneapolis, MN: Milkweed Editions, 2013.

Lyle, John Tillman. *Design for Human Ecosystems: Landscape, Land Use, and Natural Resources*. Washington, DC: Island Press, 1999.

Spirn, Anne Whiston. *The Granite Garden: Urban Nature and Human Design*. New York: Basic Books, 1985.

Thompson, George F., and Frederick R. Steiner, eds. *Ecological Design and Planning*. New York: Wiley, 1997.

Woodward, Joan. *Waterstained Landscapes: Seeing and Shaping Regionally Distinctive Places*. Baltimore: Johns Hopkins University Press, 1999.

School Design

Danks, Sharon Gamson. *Asphalt to Ecosystems: Design Ideas for Schoolyard Transformation*. Oakland, CA: New Village Press, 2010.

Gelfand, Lisa, with Eric Corey Freed. *Sustainable School Architecture: Design for Elementary and Secondary Schools*. Hoboken, NJ: Wiley, 2010.

Green Schoolyards America. https://www.greenschoolyards.org/.

Hip Hop Genius: Remixing High School Education. http://hiphopgenius.org/.

International School Grounds Alliance. https://www.internationalschoolgrounds.org/.

Johnson, Lauri Macmillan, with Kim Duffek. *Creating Outdoor Classrooms: Schoolyard Habitats and Gardens for the Southwest*. Austin: University of Texas Press, 2008.

O'Donnell Wicklund Pigozzi and Peterson, Architects, VS Furniture, and Bruce Mau Design. *The Third Teacher: 79 Ways You Can Use Design to Transform Teaching & Learning*. London: Abrams, 2010.

Striniste, Nancy. *Nature Play at Home: Creating Outdoor Spaces That Connect Children with the Natural World*. Portland, OR: Timber Press, 2019.

Universal Design

The Center for Universal Design: Environments and Products for All People. Raleigh: North Carolina State University, College of Design. https://projects.ncsu.edu/ncsu/design/cud/index.htm.

Morin, Amanda. "What Is Universal Design for Learning (UDL)?" New York: Understood for All. https://www.understood.org/en/learning-thinking-differences/treatments-approaches/educational-strategies/universal-design-for-learning-what-it-is-and-how-it-works.

"Professional Practice: Universal Design." American Society of Landscape Architects, Washington, DC. https://www.asla.org/universaldesign.aspx.

Teacher Training

The Boston Schoolyard Initiative. http://www.schoolyards.org/teaching.overview.html.

Forest School Association. "What Is Forest School?" https://www.forestschoolassociation.org/what-is-forest-school/.

Certifications, Guidelines, and Tools

Climate Positive Design Toolkit. https://climatepositivedesign.com/resources/design-toolkit/.

International Living Future Institute. https://living-future.org/.

International WELL Building Institute. "Register Your Building for WELL Certification." https://www.wellcertified.com/.

Learning through Landscapes (Polli:Nation). "Pollination Toolkit: Learn, Make, Create." http://polli-nation.co.uk/.

National Education Association. *The Six Pillars of Community Schools Toolkit: NEA Resource Guide for Educators, Families, and Communities.* Washington, DC: National Education Association, 2017. https://www.nea.org/sites/default/files/2020-06/Comm%20Schools%20ToolKit-final%20digi-web-72617.pdf.

Safe Routes Partnership. "Safe Routes to School." https://www.saferoutespartnership.org/safe-routes-school.

Seattle Office for Civil Rights. "Race and Social Justice Initiative (RSJI)." http://www.seattle.gov/rsji.

Sustainable Sites Initiative. https://www.sustainablesites.org/.

U.S. Climate Resilience Toolkit. https://toolkit.climate.gov/case-studies.

USDA Forest Service. i-Tree Tools and benefits calculators. https://www.itreetools.org/.

School Funding

"Data: Breaking Down the Where and Why of K–12 Spending." Education Week, September 24, 2019. https://www.edweek.org/ew/section/multimedia/the-where-and-why-of-k-12-spending.html.

"Education Spending per Student by State: 2016." Governing: The Future of States and Localities. https://www.governing.com/gov-data/education-data/state-education-spending-per-pupil-data.html.

Farrie, Danielle, Robert Kim, and David G. Sciarra. "Making the Grade 2019: How Fair Is School Funding in Your State? A Guide for Advocates and Policymakers." Newark, NJ: Education Law Center, 2019. https://edlawcenter.org/assets/Making-the-Grade/Making%20the%20Grade%202019.pdf.

Notes

Chapter 1: Nine Reasons Why We Should Design Schools with Mental Health in Mind

1. Sergio Ocampo, LMFT, SEP, interview with the author, 2018.
2. Ocampo, interview.
3. Alexa Lardieri, "Study: Many Americans Report Feeling Lonely, Younger Generations More So," *U.S. News & World Report*, May 1, 2018, https://www.usnews.com/news/health-care-news/articles/2018-05-01/study-many-americans-report-feeling-lonely-younger-generations-more-so.
4. Jamie Ducharme, "One in Three Seniors Is Lonely. Here's How It's Hurting Their Health," *Time*, March 4, 2019, https://time.com/5541166/loneliness-old-age/.
5. Nikki Graf, "A Majority of U.S. Teens Fear a Shooting Could Happen at Their School, and Most Parents Share Their Concern," Pew Research Center, April 18, 2018, https://www.pewresearch.org/fact-tank/2018/04/18/a-majority-of-u-s-teens-fear-a-shooting-could-happen-at-their-school-and-most-parents-share-their-concern/.
6. US Government Accountability Office, "K–12 Education: Characteristics of School Shootings," GAO-20-455, June 2020, https://www.gao.gov/assets/710/707469.pdf.
7. Barry Svigals, FAIA, interview with the author, 2019.
8. David Yusem, interview with the author, 2018.
9. Deanna Van Buren, interview with the author, 2018.
10. Gerardo "Gerry" Salazar, conversation with the author, 2017.
11. Louis Sahagun, "Just Attracting, Naturally," *Los Angeles Times*, April 16, 2012, https://www.latimes.com/archives/la-xpm-2012-apr-16-la-me-bird-school-20120416-story.html.
12. Rachel Kaplan, "The Role of Nature in the Context of the Workplace," *Landscape and*

Urban Planning 26, nos. 1–4 (October 1993): 193–201, https://doi.org/10.1016/0169
-2046(93)90016-7.

13.Stephanie Leach, conversation with the author, 2018.

14."Designing Resilient Spaces," Metropolis Forums webinar, June 23, 2020, https://www
.metropolismag.com/webinars/metropolis-designing-resilient-spaces/.

Chapter 2: How School Environments Shape Mental, Social, and Physical Health

1.Mary Ellen Flannery, "The Epidemic of Anxiety among Today's Students," *NEA
Today* (National Education Association), March 28, 2018, updated March 2019,
http://neatoday.org/2018/03/28/the-epidemic-of-student-anxiety/.

2.Craig Clough, "Mental Health Screening Results of LAUSD Kids Alarming yet Typical,"
LA School Report, April 10, 2015, http://laschoolreport.com/mental-health-screening
-results-of-lausd-kids-alarming-yet-typical/.

3.Vincent J. Felitti et al., "Relationship of Childhood Abuse and Household Dysfunction
to Many of the Leading Causes of Death in Adults: The Adverse Childhood Experiences (ACE) Study," *American Journal of Preventive Medicine* 14, no. 4 (May 1, 1998):
245–258, https://doi.org/10.1016/S0749-3797(98)00017-8.

4.Alex Shevrin Venet, "The How and Why of Trauma-Informed Teaching," Edutopia,
August 3, 2018, https://www.edutopia.org/article/how-and-why-trauma-informed-teach-
ing.

5.Barnum, Matt. 2019. "New Studies Point to a Big Downside for Schools Bringing In
More Police," Chalkbeat, February 14, 2019, https://www.chalkbeat
.org/2019/2/14/21121037/new-studies-point-to-a-big-downside-for-schools-bringing-in
-more-police.

6.William C. Sullivan, "Landscapes of 20th Century Chicago Public Housing" (paper
presented at the Vernacular Architecture Forum, Savanna, GA, May 1, 2007), https:
//www.researchgate.net/publication/275032357_Landscapes_of_20th_Century_Chicago
_Public_Housing; Rodney H. Matsuoka, "High School Landscapes and Student Performance" (PhD diss., University of Michigan, 2008), https://deepblue.lib.umich
.edu/handle/2027.42/61641.

7.Sullivan, "Landscapes."

8.Matsuoka, "High School Landscapes."

9.Lisa Strong, "Classrooms without Walls: A Study in Outdoor Learning Environments
to Enhance Academic Motivation for K–5 Students" (master's thesis, California State
Polytechnic University, Pomona, 2019).

10.Todd Rose, "The Myth of Average," TEDx Sonoma County video, 18:26, filmed June
19, 2013, https://www.youtube.com/watch?v=4eBmyttcfU4.

11.Peter Barrett, Fay Davies, Yufan Zhang, and Lucinda Barrett, "The Impact of Classroom Design on Pupils' Learning: Final Results of a Holistic, Multi-level Analysis,"
Building and Environment 89 (July 2015): 118–133, http://dx.doi.org/10.1016/j.build-
env
.2015.02.013.

12.Dongying Li and William C. Sullivan, "Impact of Views to School Landscapes on
Recovery from Stress and Mental Fatigue," *Landscape and Urban Planning* 148 (April

2016): 149–158, https://doi.org/10.1016/j.landurbplan.2015.12.015.

13.Matsuoka, "High School Landscapes."

14.Marcella A. Raney, Colette F. Hendry, and Samantha A. Yee, "Physical Activity and Social Behaviors of Urban Children in Green Playgrounds," *American Journal of Preventive Medicine* 56, no. 4 (April 2019): 522–529, https://doi.org/10.1016/j.amepre.2018.11.004.

15.Matsuoka, "High School Landscapes."

16.Sarah Williams Goldhagen, *Welcome to Your World: How the Built Environment Shapes Our Lives* (New York: Harper, 2017).

17.Paula Spencer Scott, "Feeling Awe May Be the Secret to Health and Happiness," *Parade*, October 7, 2016, https://parade.com/513786/paulaspencer/feeling-awe-may-be-the-secret-to-health-and-happiness/.

18.Elizabeth K. Meyer, "Sustaining Beauty: The Performance of Appearance," *Journal of Landscape Architecture* 3, no. 1 (Spring 2008): 6–23, https://doi.org/10.1080/18626033.2008.9723392.

19.John Tillman Lyle, "Can Floating Seeds Make Deep Forms?," *Landscape Journal* 10, no. 1 (Spring 1991): 37–47, https://www.doi.org/10.3368/lj.10.1.37.

20.James Rojas, interview with the author, 2020.

21.Nancy Striniste, interview with the author, 2020.

Chapter 3: Site Design Strategies to Support Mental Health, Safety, and Well-being

1.Gabrielle Bullock, "Designing for Resilient Spaces," Metropolis Forums webinar, June 23, 2020, https://www.metropolismag.com/webinars/metropolis-designing-resilient-spaces/.

2.David Yusem, interview with the author, 2018.

3.Magda Mostafa, "The Autism ASPECTSS™ Design Index," An Architecture for Autism, accessed December 13, 2020, https://www.autism.archi/aspectss.

4.Nina Briggs, interview with the author, 2019.

5.Ian Dillon and Jared Green, "Professional Practice: Universal Design," *American Society of Landscape Architects*, 2020, accessed July 19, 2020, https://www.asla.org/universaldesign.aspx.

6.Diana Fernandez, "Creating New Inclusive Futures One Project at a Time," Heterogeneous Futures, accessed December 13, 2020, https://www.heterogeneousfutures.com.

7.Barry Svigals, FAIA, interview with the author, 2019.

8.Susan Herrington, "Kindergarten: Garden Pedagogy from Romanticism to Reform," *Landscape Journal* 20, no. 1 (January 1, 2001): 30–47, https://doi.org/10.3368/lj.20.1.30.

9.London School of Hygiene and Tropical Medicine, "Improve School Toilets and Reduce Rates of Absenteeism in UK Schools, Advise Hygiene Experts," October 14, 2010, accessed July 2, 2020, https://www.lshtm.ac.uk/newsevents/news/2010/handwashing.html.

10.Kelli Peterman et al., "Mental Health by Design: Fostering Student Emotional Wellness in New York City High Schools by Improving and Enhancing Built Environments," *Journal of Urban Design and Mental Health* 5, no. 5 (September 2018), https://www.urbandesignmentalhealth.com/journal-5---nyc-school-design-for-mental-health.html.

11.Stephen W. Porges, *The Polyvagal Theory: Neurophysiological Foundations of Emotions, Attachment, Communication, and Self-regulation* (New York: Norton, 2011).

12."The Sixth and Seventh Senses: The Vestibular and Proprioceptive Systems," blog post, Eyas Landing, n.d., https://eyaslanding.com/the-vestibular-and-proprioceptive-systems -the-sixth-and-seven-senses/.

13.Robin Wall Kimmerer, *Braiding Sweetgrass: Indigenous Wisdom, Scientific Knowledge, and the Teachings of Plants* (Minneapolis, MN: Milkweed Editions, 2013).

14.Los Angeles Unified School District (LAUSD), *Historic Resources Survey Report*, 2014, prepared by Sapphos Environmental for the LAUSD Office of Environmental Health and Safety.

15.Brad Rumble, "Planting the Seeds of Change (Literally)," Los Angeles Audubon (blog post), July 25, 2019, https://www.laaudubon.org/blog/2019/7/25/qqo6vsc 2aezs70kqbrtpyf2u5xmdlk.

16.Rodney H. Matsuoka, "High School Landscapes and Student Performance" (PhD diss., University of Michigan, 2008), https://deepblue.lib.umich.edu/handle/2027.42/61641.

17.Sharon Danks, personal communication, 2020.

18.Marcella Raney, personal communication, 2015.

19.Richard Louv, *Last Child in the Woods: Saving Our Children from Nature Deficit Disorder* (Chapel Hill, NC: Algonquin Books, 2005).

20."Ripping Up the Playground Rule Book Delivers Incredible Results," Essential Kids, n.d., accessed March 2020, http://www.essentialkids.com.au/education/school/starting-school /ripping-up-the-playground-rule-book-delivers-incredible-results-20140203-31wc2.

21.Michelle Lani Shiota, "How Awe Transforms the Body and Mind," video, 34:22, August 2016, *Greater Good* magazine, https://greatergood.berkeley.edu/video/item/ how_awe _transforms_the_body_and_mind.

22.Khaled S. Almansour et al., "Playground Lead Levels in Rubber, Soil, Sand, and Mulch Surfaces in Boston," *PLoS ONE* 14, no. 4 (April 25, 2019): e0216156, https://doi .org/10.1371/journal.pone.0216156.

23.Kimmerer, *Braiding Sweetgrass*.

Chapter 4: Leveraging Schools for Public Health, Equity, and Climate Resilience

1.National Center for Education Statistics, "Characteristics of the 100 Largest Public Elementary and Secondary School Districts in the United States, 1999–2000," https://nces .ed.gov/pubs2001/100_largest/discussion.asp.

2.Manal Aboelata, MPH, interview with the author, 2019.

3.Rachel A. Davis, MSW, Howard Pinderhughes, PhD, and Myesha Williams, MSW, "Adverse Community Experiences and Resilience: A Framework for Addressing and Preventing Community Trauma" (Oakland, CA: Prevention Institute, February 2016).

4."What Are Park Prescriptions?," ParkRx, Institute at the Golden Gate, https://www .parkrx.org/about.

5.Arthur Neslen, "Access to Nature Reduces Depression and Obesity, Finds European Study," *Guardian*, March 21, 2017, https://www.theguardian.com/society/2017/mar/21 /access-nature-reduces-depression-obesity-european-report.

6.School Nutrition Association, "School Meal Trends and Stats," 2019, https://school nutrition.org/aboutschoolmeals/schoolmealtrendsstats/.

7.Juliana F. W. Cohen et al., "School Lunch Waste among Middle School Students: Nutrients Consumed and Costs," *American Journal of Preventive Medicine* 44, no. 2 (February 1, 2013): 114–121, https://dx.doi.org/10.1016%2Fj.amepre.2012.09.060.

8.Prevention Institute's Moving Upstream, "Community Organizing to Prevent Violence," video, 41:58, 2019, https://soundcloud.com/user-676580582/community-organizing-to -prevent-violence.

9.Norman Garrick, "Burying a 1950s Planning Disaster," Bloomberg CityLab, September 1, 2016, https://www.citylab.com/transportation/2016/09/burying-a-1950s-planning-disaster /498203/.

10.Patrick Lohmann, "Exclusive: New York Selects 'Community Grid' Alternative for I-81 in Syracuse," Syracuse.com, April 22, 2019, updated April 23, 2019, https://www .syracuse.com/news/2019/04/exclusive-new-york-selects-community-grid-alternative -for-i-81.html.

11.Angie Schmitt, "Street Grid to Replace Old I-81 in Syracuse, NYS Decides," Streetsblog USA, April 22, 2019, https://usa.streetsblog.org/2019/04/22/street-grid-to-replace-old -highway-in-syracuse-state-decides/.

12.Natalia Rommen, "Syracuse's Proposed Community Grid Could Right a Decades-Old Wrong," Next City, August 13, 2019, https://nextcity.org/daily/entry/syracuses-proposed -community-grid-could-right-a-decades-old-wrong.

13.Gabrielle Bullock, "Designing for Resilient Spaces," Metropolis Forums webinar, June 23, 2020, https://www.metropolismag.com/webinars/metropolis-designing-resil ient -spaces/.

14.United States Congress Joint Economic Committee, "Zoned Out: How School and Residential Zoning Limit Educational Opportunity," November 12, 2019, https://www. jec .senate.gov/public/index.cfm/republicans/2019/11/zoned-out-how-school-and-residential -zoning-limit-educational-opportunity.

15.Joint Economic Committee, "Zoned Out."

16.National Education Association, "The Six Pillars of Community Schools," 2019, accessed July 2020, http://www.nea.org/communityschools.

17.Barbara Brown Wilson, *Resilience for All: Striving for Equity through Community-Driven Design* (Washington, DC: Island Press, 2018).

18.Wilson, *Resilience for All.*

19.Bioneers, "Fania Davis' Trailblazing Restorative Justice Approach," Medium, September 25, 2017, https://medium.com/bioneers/fania-davis-trailblazing-restorative-justice -approach-bda874a6d4af.

20.American Civil Liberties Union, "Cops and No Counselors: How the Lack of School Mental Health Staff Is Harming Students," n.d., accessed 2020, https://www.aclu.org /sites/default/files/field_document/030419-acluschooldisciplinereport.pdf.

21.Deanna Van Buren, interview with the author, 2018.

22.Adele Peters, "This Atlanta Jail Will Transform into a Center for Justice and Equity,"

Fast Company, June 15, 2020, https://www.fastcompany.com/90515296/this-atlanta
-jail-will-transform-into-a-center-for-justice-and-equity.

23.Lisa Fujie Parks, in Prevention Institute's Moving Upstream, "Community Organizing
to Prevent Violence," video, 41:58, 2019, https://soundcloud.com/user-676580582
/community-organizing-to-prevent-violence.

24.Federal Highway Administration, "National Household Travel Survey: Travel to
School: The Distance Factor," January 2008, https://nhts.ornl.gov/briefs/Travel%20To
%20School.pdf.

25.Andrea Faber Taylor and Frances E. Kuo, "Children with Attention Deficits Concentrate Better after Walk in the Park," *Journal of Attention Disorders* 12, no. 5 (March 1,
2009): 402–409, https://doi.org/10.1177%2F1087054708323000.

26.Safe Routes Partnership, "Safe Routes to School," https://www.saferoutespartnership
.org/safe-routes-school.

27.Los Angeles Unified School District (LAUSD), *Historic Resources Survey Report*, 2014,
prepared by Sapphos Environmental for the LAUSD Office of Environmental Health
and Safety.

28.Danielle Slabaugh, "Construction Documents for Climate Justice: Democratic Design
Methods for Climate Resilient Communities" (master's thesis, California State Polytechnic University, Pomona, 2020).

29.The Nature Conservancy, "Funding Trees for Health: An Analysis of Finance and Policy
Actions to Enable Tree Planting for Public Health," accessed April 12, 2020, https:
//www.nature.org/content/dam/tnc/nature/en/documents/Trees4Health_FINAL.pdf.

Chapter 5: How to Communicate for the Best Chance at Change

1.Kerry Patterson et al., *Crucial Conversations: Tools for Talking When Stakes Are High* (New
York: McGraw-Hill, 2012).

2.David Yusem, Oakland Unified School District Restorative Justice program manager,
personal communication, 2018.

3.Taylor Allbright, PhD, assistant professor in educational leadership, California State
Polytechnic University, Pomona, personal communication, 2020.

4.Lisa Strong, "Classrooms without Walls: A Study in Outdoor Learning Environments
to Enhance Academic Motivation for K–5 Students" (master's thesis, California State
Polytechnic University, Pomona, 2019).

5.Jaime Zaplatosch, personal communication, 2019.

6.US Department of Education, IDEA: Individuals with Disabilities Education Act,
"About IDEA," n.d., accessed December 2020, https://sites.ed.gov/idea/about-idea/.

7.Emma García and Elaine Weiss, "Student Absenteeism: Who Misses School and How
Missing School Matters for Performance," Economic Policy Institute, September 25, 2018,
https://www.epi.org/publication/student-absenteeism-who-misses-school-and-how
-missing-school-matters-for-performance/.

8.Mateja Mihinjac and Gregory Saville, "Third-Generation Crime Prevention through
Environmental Design (CPTED)," *Social Sciences* 8, no. 6 (2019): 182, https://doi
.org/10.3390/socsci8060182.

9.William C. Sullivan, "Landscapes of 20th Century Chicago Public Housing" (paper presented
at the Vernacular Architecture Forum, Savanna, GA, May 1, 2007), https://www.researchgate

.net/publication/275032357_Landscapes_of_20th_Century_Chicago_Public_Housing.

10. "Varsity Odds 2020," http://www.scholarshipstats.com/varsityodds.html; "Pro Odds 2020," http://www.scholarshipstats.com/odds-of-going-pro.htm.

11. SHAPE America—Society of Health and Physical Educators, "Guidance Document: The Essential Components of Physical Education," 2015, https://www.shapeamerica.org //upload/TheEssentialComponentsOfPhysicalEducation.pdf.

Chapter 6: Money Doesn't Grow on Trees . . . or Does It?

1. Re-Build America's School Infrastructure Coalition, "Education Equity Requires Modern School Facilities: The Case for Federal Funding for School Infrastructure," September 2018, http://www.cacsfc.org/documents/EducationEquityRequiresModernSchool Facilities-BuildUSSchools.orgSept2018.pdf.

2. Planning for PK–12 School Infrastructure National Initiative, "Adequate & Equitable PK–12 Infrastructure: Priority Actions for Systemic Reform," June 2017, http://citiesandschools .berkeley.edu/uploads/PK12_Infrastructure_Priority_Actions_Report_06152017.pdf.

3. Politico and Harvard T.H. Chan School of Public Health, "Americans' Views of President Trump's Agenda on Health Care, Immigration, and Infrastructure," March 2018, https://www.politico.com/f/?id=00000162-20dc-d21f-abe7-feddbc1f0000.

4.   E. Gregory McPherson, Natalie van Doorn, and John de Goede, "The State of California's Street Trees," USDA Forest Service, Pacific Southwest Research Station, Davis, CA, April 2015, https://www.fs.fed.us/psw/topics/urban_forestry/documents/20150422CAStreetTrees.pdf.

5. Marcella Raney, PhD, student activity researcher, personal communication, 2020.

6. The Center for Health and Health Care in Schools, "A Guide to Federal Education Programs That Can Fund K–12 Universal Prevention and Social and Emotional Learning Activities," May 2014, http://healthinschools.org/wp-content/uploads/2016/10 /SEL-Federal-Funding-Guide_v2.pdf.

7. Emma García and Elaine Weiss, "Student Absenteeism: Who Misses School and How Missing School Matters for Performance," Economic Policy Institute, September 25, 2018, https: //www.epi.org/publication/student-absenteeism-who-misses-school-and-how-missing -school-matters-for-performance/.

Chapter 7: Ten Schools to Inspire and Guide You

1. GreatSchools, "Eagle Rock Elementary and Magnet Center," https://www.greatschools .org/california/los-angeles/2042-Eagle-Rock-Elementary-And-Magnet-Center/.

2. Rachel Kaplan, Stephen Kaplan, and Robert L. Ryan, *With People in Mind: Design and Management of Everyday Nature* (Washington, DC: Island Press, 1998).

3. Marcella A. Raney, Colette F. Hendry, and Samantha A. Yee, "Physical Activity and Social Behaviors of Urban Children in Green Playgrounds," *American Journal of Preventive Medicine* 56, no. 4 (April 1, 2019): 522–529, https://doi.org/10.1016/j.amepre .2018.11.004.

4. Kenneth Pletcher, "Japan Earthquake and Tsunami of 2011," in "Japan Earthquake and Tsunami of 2011" by John P. Rafferty, *Encyclopaedia Brittanica*, 2011, https://www .britannica.com/event/Japan-earthquake-and-tsunami-of-2011/Aftermath-of-the-disaster.

5. Yoshiyuki Nagata, "A Critical Review of Education for Sustainable Development (ESD)

in Japan: Beyond the Practice of Pouring New Wine into Old Bottles," *Educational Studies in Japan: International Yearbook*, no. 11, March 2017, 29–41, https://files.eric.ed.gov /fulltext/EJ1147530.pdf.

6. David Bressan, "How Century-Old 'Tsunami Stones' Saved Lives in the Tohoku Earthquake of 2011," *Forbes*, March 11, 2018, https://www.forbes.com/sites/davidbressan /2018/03/11/how-century-old-tsunami-stones-saved-lives-in-the-tohoku-earthquake-of -2011/#6b47529b44fd.

7. Bressan, "'Tsunami Stones.'"

8. Mitsunari Terada, personal communication, October 25, 2019.

9. Tomohiro Ichinose, "The Reconstruction of Transportation and Environmental Infrastructure in Rural Areas," *IATSS Research* 36, no. 1 (July 2012): 24–29, https://doi .org/10.1016/j.iatssr.2012.05.002.

10. Masahito Abe, "Educational Challenges and ESD in Disasters and Reconstruction," trans. Hiromitsu Suetake, in *Academic Trends*, special feature 1, *Disaster and Environmental Education*, 2013, https://www.jstage.jst.go.jp/article/tits/18/12/18_12_27 /_pdf/-char/ja.

11. Matthew Nolan, "The Village," 2020, https://shelteredstorm.com/11-the-village/.

12. Barry Svigals, FAIA, personal communication, October 22, 2020.

13. Svigals, personal communication.

14. Margaret Rhodes, "The New Sandy Hook Elementary School Is All About Invisible Security," *Wired*, November 14, 2014, https://www.wired.com/2014/11/new-sandy -hook-elementary-school-invisible-security/.

15. Oakland Planning History, "The Planning History of Oakland, CA," accessed July 6, 2020, https://oaklandplanninghistory.weebly.com.

16. Oakland Planning History, "The Great San Francisco Earthquake, 1906–1945," accessed July 6, 2020, https://oaklandplanninghistory.weebly.com/the-great-san-francisco -earthquake.html.

17. Nailah Morgan, "Searching for the Middle: The Disappearance of the Black Middle Class," Oakland North, December 10, 2015, accessed July 6, 2020, https://oaklandnorth .net/2015/12/10/searching-for-the-middle-the-disappearance-of-the-black-middle-class/.

18. Morgan, "Searching for the Middle."

19. Roland G. Fryer Jr. et al., "Measuring Crack Cocaine and Its Impact," Harvard University Society of Fellows and NBER, April 2006, accessed July 6, 2020, https://scholar .harvard.edu/files/fryer/files/fhlm_crack_cocaine_0.pdf.

20. Morgan, "Searching for the Middle."

21. Ash Vasudeva et al., "Oakland Unified School District New Small Schools Initiative: Evaluation," Stanford Center for Opportunity Policy in Education, June 1, 2009, https://edpolicy.stanford.edu/library/publications/259.

22. Vasudeva et al., "Oakland Unified School District."

23. Vasudeva et al., "Oakland Unified School District."

24. Vasudeva et al., "Oakland Unified School District."

25. Barry Svigals and Sam Seidel, notes on the class, 2020.

26. Los Angeles Unified School District (LAUSD), *Historic Resources Survey Report*, 2014, prepared by Sapphos Environmental for the LAUSD Office of Environmental Health

and Safety.

27. LAUSD, *Historic Resources Survey Report.*

28. LAUSD, *Historic Resources Survey Report.*

29. LAUSD, *Historic Resources Survey Report.*

30. Council for Watershed Health, "Daniel Webster Middle School: A DROPS Campus Tour," ArcGIS StoryMaps, October 1, 2020, https://storymaps.arcgis.com/stories/a555a6295c7d44849daf2ce58447474b.

31. LAUSD, *Historic Resources Survey Report.*

32. Amy Tikkanen, "Spandau," in *Encyclopaedia Brittanica*, December 21, 2008, accessed July 11, 2020, https://www.britannica.com/place/Spandau.

33. Tikkanen, "Spandau."

34. City of Berlin, Germany, "Neighborhood Management in Berlin: Information on the Program 'Socially Integrative City,'" Referat Soziale Stadt (Socially Integrative City Unit) for the Senate Department for Urban Development Communication, 2010.

35. City of Berlin, "Neighborhood Management."

36. City of Berlin, Germany, Senate Department for Education, Youth and Science, "Report for Inspection of the B. Traven School 05K05 (Community School)," 2015.

37. Grün macht Schule, Berlin, Germany, accessed July 11, 2020, http://www.gruen-macht-schule.de/index.php/de/.

38. Manfred Dietzen, in-person tour of Grün macht Schule schoolyards with the International School Grounds Alliance, Berlin, September 2017.

39. City of Berlin, "Report for Inspection."

40. Mireya Navarro and Sindya N. Bhanoo, "Teaching Green, beyond Recycling," *New York Times*, January 10, 2010, https://www.nytimes.com/2010/01/11/nyregion/11green.html.

41. Lacey Harris, Environmental Charter Schools website, accessed April 2020, https://ecsonline.org/.

42. US Department of Education, "A 'Snapshot' of Environmental Charter High School's Green Efforts, Strengths, and Accomplishments," Environmental Charter High School for the US Department of Education Green Ribbon School Application, 2020.

43. Jose Guadalupe Gutierrez, personal communication, July 10, 2020.

44. Jeff Litz, personal communication, 2017.

45. Fairfax County, Virginia, "Stormwater Management," in *FY 2019–FY 2023 Adopted Capital Improvement Program, Fairfax County, Virginia*, 2019.

46. US Department of Energy, Better Buildings Beat Team, "Better Buildings Summit Showcase Tours: Marshall High School," June 29, 2017, https://betterbuildingssolutioncenter.energy.gov/beat-blog/better-buildings-summit-showcase-tours-marshall-high-school.

47. Patricia Leslie, "Fairfax County Public Schools Cuts Ribbon on New Marshall HS Building," *Falls Church (VA) News-Press*, March 30, 2015.

48. Elaine Tholen, personal communication, 2017.

49. Anna Vecchio, "Three Fairfax County Schools Awarded Eco-Schools USA Green Flag for Exceptional 'Green' Achievement," National Wildlife Federation press release, June 6, 2017, https://www.nwf.org/Latest-News/Press-Releases/2017/6-6-17-Fairfax-County-Schools-Receive-National-Environmental-Award.

50. Susan M. Baum, Robin M. Schader, and Steven V. Owen, *To Be Gifted and Learn-*

ing Disabled: Strength-Based Strategies for Helping Twice-Exceptional Students with LD, ADHD, ASD, and More (Waco, TX: Prufrock Press, 2017), 7–8.

51.National Education Association, *The Twice-Exceptional Dilemma* (Washington, DC: National Education Association, 2006).

52.Bridges Academy, "Our Philosophy," accessed July 16, 2020, https://www.bridges.edu /philosophy.html.

53.City of Los Angeles, "Corvallis High School Historic District," January 15, 2013, in *SurveyLA: The Los Angeles Historic Resources Survey*, prepared for the City of Los Angeles Department of City Planning, Office of Historic Resources, by Historic Resources Group, accessed July 18, 2020, http://historicplacesla.org/reports/f193a7a9-5802-4248-a1ba-388adc2b1a5e.

54.City of Los Angeles, "Sherman Oaks–Studio City–Toluca Lake–Cahuenga Pass Community Plan Area," 2013, in *SurveyLA: The Los Angeles Historic Resources Survey*, prepared for the City of Los Angeles Department of City Planning, Office of Historic Resources, by Historic Resources Group.

55.Robert Douglass, "Bridges Academy Campus Landscape Master Plan," LA6121L Studio Project, California State Polytechnic University, Pomona, 2020.

Chapter 9: For the Love of Students

1.Dana Goldstein, "Why a Pediatric Group Is Pushing to Reopen Schools This Fall," *New York Times*, June 30, 2020, https://www.nytimes.com/2020/06/30/us/coronavirus -schools-reopening-guidelines-aap.html?auth=login-google.

2.*Metropolis*, "Designing Resilient Spaces," Metropolis Forums webinar, June 23, 2020, https://www.metropolismag.com/webinars/metropolis-designing-resilient-spaces/.

3.*Metropolis*, "Designing Resilient Spaces."

4.Carolyn Phenicie, "'We've Got a Real Crisis': Half of U.S. Teachers Have Considered Leaving Profession, PDK Poll Finds," *LA School Report*, August 5, 2019, http://laschoolreport. com/weve-got-a-real-crisis-half-of-u-s-teachers-have-considered-leaving-profession-pdk -poll-finds/.

5.Richard A. Hobday and John W. Cason, "The Open-Air Treatment of Pandemic Influenza," *American Journal of Public Health* 99, suppl2 (October 2009): S236–S242, https://doi.org/10.2105/AJPH.2008.134627.

6.Los Angeles Unified School District (LAUSD), *Historic Resources Survey Report*, 2014, prepared by Sapphos Environmental for the LAUSD Office of Environmental Health and Safety, 44–45.

Acknowledgments

There is not enough room in this book to adequately thank all of the people who helped me understand and communicate the topics written about in *Schools That Heal*. The following are most of those who directly contributed to the preceding words. I'm certain I've left some out.

To my editor, Courtney Lix, thank you for making a dream come true by inviting this book. You have a gift for seeing clear solutions through muddy drafts. I hope this work makes a difference for your little Cyrus and his generation and all the generations to come. Thank you and the rest of the Island Press team for your expert guidance and production of a book I am incredibly proud of: Annie Byrnes, Sharis Simonian, and Patricia Harris. I'm also incredibly grateful for the special care given to this content by Yasmin A. McClinton, editor at Tessera Editorial, and to the Island Press book team for supporting a cultural competency review.

Thank you to Adrian Chi Tenney for committing your time, talent, and design thinking to the beautiful drawings in chapter 7. They bring the schools and the design strategies alive. I cherished our Saturday drawing sessions (which were so much more than that!) during a time of social distancing, social unrest, and general uncertainty.

Barbara Deutsch and the Landscape Architecture Foundation: thank you for creating the Fellowship for Innovation and Leadership (and everything you do to further our understanding of natural processes). To

Lucinda Sanders, for conceiving it . . . I am forever grateful for the experience and exploration it allowed. To you and Laura Solano, Lisa Switkin, Jenn Low, Brice Maryman, Alpa Nawre, Harriett Jameson Brooks, Nicole Plunkett, and Scott Douglas . . . our yearlong journey truly was transformational. The ideas formed from our collaboration became the foundation of *Schools That Heal*. All of you, plus Rachel Booher, Christina Sanders, Megan Barnes, Heather Whitlow, and the entire LAF family, provided a buoy when I needed it most. Your deep work and support systems pull landscape architecture forward.

To Lise Bornstein, Jana Wehby, and the Association for Women in Architecture Foundation: the Mid-Career Fellowship provided the impetus and mentorship to first name the design strategies that now anchor this book. Thank you to the women of AWAF and its sister organization, the Association for Women in Architecture + Design: you are my sisters and my mentors. And to the LALAs—who've heard and supported these ideas from the beginning and been my design family and community for the past ten years and then some—my home is your home.

Thank you, Manal Aboelata, for connecting the dots between public health and planning and design, and for your continuous support in this mission. From our first conversation, your collaboration and partnership has done what we need so much more of: bringing health, equity, education, and design practitioners together around the same table to effect change.

Sharon Danks—you paved the way for so many of us with *Asphalt to Ecosystems*. Thank you for inviting me into your Green Schoolyards America circle. Nancy Striniste and Elaine Tholen: your wisdom in design and education led me to many of the schools and resources included in this work. To the partners of the National COVID-19 Outdoor Learning Initiative—as well as the COVID-19 Emergency Schoolyard Design Volunteers—thank you for seeing and acting upon an opportunity to build equity and raise awareness of the promise of outdoor learning amid a pandemic.

To my students, who give me hope for a healthier, more equitable and just future. A special thank-you to those who tested and refined the design strategies in this book. Spring 2019: Sancho Cagulada, Ava Cheng, Jordan Henry, Lana Jeries, Patricia Kaihara Arce, Kay Kite, Chris Konieczny, Lauren McKenna, Raquel Reynolds, Morgen Ruby, Dan

Scheir, Brittney Seman, Laurel Skinner, and Dani Slabaugh. Spring 2020: Colleen Cochran, Robert Douglass, Sarah Fisher, Philip Gann, Graham Goldich, Linley Green, José Guadalupe Gutierrez, Michelle Shanahan, Adrian Chi Tenney, and Chris Weathers. Your work moved this book forward in important and tangible ways. And to our school design studio collaborators, Eileen Alduenda, Taylor Allbright, Bevin Ashenmiller, Stephen Carroll, Adrian Hightower, Lara Killick, Amanda Millett, Susan Mulley, Sergio Ocampo, Marcella Raney, Matilda Reyes, Gerardo "Gerry" Salazar, Kenny Tang, and Jean Yang.

Lauren McKenna, your extra support as teaching assistant, student mentor, and past educator meant so much when our studio went online during the pandemic. Your environmental ethic, humility, and grace shine bright.

To Viviana Franco, channa grace, Ashley Hart, Monique López: you shared insights that shaped the direction of this work early on. Thank you for your guidance and for sharing your own lived experiences.

To Willie Nakatani and Jeff Mailes for sharing your past and present work in the Eagle Rock Junior/Senior High School horticultural garden. Your work points to opportunities for an optimistic future—or at least, to steal Jeff's term, gives us tools to survive the zombie apocalypse.

To José Guadalupe Gutierrez, for inviting me on your high school tour and sharing your insights about environmental education, community organizing, and lived experiences: thank you for giving me the words to define "Honor lived experiences and abilities."

To Lori A. Harris for opening the door to the world of juvenile justice and for your fierce advocacy for children and youth. And thank you to the group of brilliant women legal, environmental, health, and spiritual minds who brought us all together for Sunday brunches: Foongy, Carrie, Denise, Pamila, Karen, Tori. I'm honored by your friendship.

Thank you, Deanna Van Buren, for beginning a conversation three years ago about how design can support restorative justice and mental health, and for graciously picking it back up amid a summer of unrest and many requests for your expert voice. I am in awe of your work in showing the way to justice through design.

To the Los Angeles County sheriff's deputy and his daughter: thank you for sharing your expert and lived observations of human behavior and humanity and for your courage and dedication to community.

To Sergio Ocampo for sharing your deep knowledge of somatic therapy with class demonstrations as well as in conversation. You introduced me to a world of mind-body-environment work I didn't know was out there.

Thank you, Allan and Linda Mangold, for your expertise in security design and your commitment to prioritizing students' mental health and well-being over armoring a school site, despite its being the softer, less lucrative path. And to Andy Thompson, principal at DLR Group, for championing the topic and inviting me into your interdisciplinary conversations.

To the schools that partnered with our CPP LA 6121 Studio—Cleveland Charter High School, Eagle Rock Junior/Senior High School, Willard Elementary School, Jackson Elementary School, and Bridges Academy—for opening your campuses. Willard Elementary: Principal Angela Baxter, Ingrida Grabis, Joan Stevens, Shirly Barrett, and the students of Mrs. Grabis's Green Team. Cleveland Charter High School: Jennifer Macon, Enzo LaConte, Principal Cindy Duong, and the student leadership team. Jackson Elementary School: Principal Rita M. Exposito, Brooke Kind, Raquel Pedroza, and Amigos de Los Rios. Bridges Academy: Director Carl Sabatino, Carmen Sevilla, Amanda Millett, Daniel Watson, Rajab Sayed, Caroline Maxwell, Tyler Peck, Dylan McKenzie, and students of the Sustainable Campus Design enrichment cluster and architectural design classes for partnering with Cal Poly Pomona students to envision healthier school environments.

Thank you to the school teams who shared resources and images for the schools in chapter 7.

Eagle Rock Elementary School: Amanda Millett for writing the grant and pouring your heart and soul into giving students the nurturing environments they deserve. Principal Stephanie Leach for believing in the vision and championing the outcome for other schools, everywhere. Los Angeles Beautification Team (LABT) founder Sharyn Romano for your transformative program hiring youth and for managing the grant and never giving up. Site manager Sal Lopez for welcoming us on-site, showing us the ropes, and answering random questions via text message whenever they came up during drawings and construction. Jeff Hutchins for teaching the LABT team irrigation to Matt Lysne and Rebecca Schwaner for your contributions to the drawings. Marcella Raney and Bevin Ashenmiller for including me in your journey to research and communicate the extraordinary benefits of the living schoolyard. Thank you to Mirta Muscaroles for sharing your classroom and the many parents, teachers, staff, students, and community members who donate(d) sweat equity, creative capital, and heart and soul to bring an asphalt schoolyard to life.

Kesennuma Shiritsu Omose Primary School: immense thank-yous to participatory landscape planner Mitsunari Terada and Principal Tomohiro Taniyama for answering endless questions and sending so many images, many of which, sadly, didn't make it into this book, and to CPP LA faculty Keiji Uesugi and CPP LA student Hiromitsu Suetake for translating the Japanese.

Sandy Hook Elementary School and ASCEND Elementary School: Barry Svigals for the many deep conversations about how to make schools safe and warm and welcoming. Thank you to the Svigals + Partners architecture team (Julia McFadden and Cheryl Hart) for sending images and meeting last-minute requests.

Daniel Webster Middle School: the Los Angeles Unified School District (Christos Chrysiliou, Jan Ducker, Guelsy Gomez), Eileen Alduenda at the Council for Watershed Health, Michelle Bagnato from TreePeople, and the whole Studio-MLA team.

B. Traven Community School: Thank you to the Grün macht Schule team (Manfred Dietzen, Edeltraud Schmoelders, Ulrike Wolf, Ulf Schroeder) for the site visit and many e-mails to answer follow-up questions and send additional resources. Your work sets the standard for schoolyards that heal.

Environmental Charter High School: Eddie Cortes, José Guadalupe Gutierrez, and Julie Vo for sharing your time, expertise, and resources, and founder Alison Diaz for creating and maintaining a new model of education that puts students, environment, and community first.

George C. Marshall High School: Principal Jeff Litz for sharing your expertise and your deep commitment to your students' mental health; Elaine Tholen for the tour and introductions; and the teachers whose names are lovingly inscribed in my notebook, trapped in my office, which is locked up because of COVID-19.

Bridges Academy: Director Carl Sabatino for the interview and invitation to tour campus and Amanda Millett for your inexhaustible ability to bring people and ideas together to make things happen.

Redwood Park Academy: Ed Bond for the tour and insights and many follow-up resources. Thank you, Learning through Landscape's Mary Jackson, for setting it all up and sharing work that has established a precedent for so many of us elsewhere. And thank you to all the students who made and take care of that wonderful school garden.

Andy Wilcox, thank you for inviting me to teach fifteen years ago and always making Cal Poly Pomona feel like home. Your early support of the Designing Schools to Support Mental Health workshop launched many of the relationships and explorations mentioned in these pages. To Kris Penrose, for supporting this work in so many ways, and for keeping us going while also caring for your family through pandemic and wildfire season. To Dean Lauren Bricker and Associate Dean Alyssa Lang, for sending me on what would become the last school field trip I could make before we all went home . . . and for your enthusiasm and belief in design with mental health in mind. To my landscape architecture faculty colleagues and students; and the students, faculty, and staff of the Cal Poly Pomona. I truly believe that by continuing our tradition of learning by doing, and beginning a tradition of honoring students' lived experiences and supporting their mental health and well-being, we can create a new model of higher education for design.

For Nina Briggs and Maryam Escandari, whose work and friendship inspire mine: your honesty and encouragement during the spring, summer, and fall of 2020 meant the world. Thank you for the laughter, the tears, the outrage, and being real. #squad

To Brad McKee (*Landscape Architecture Magazine*), Jared Green (The Dirt), and Vinayak Bharne (My Liveable City) for uplifting and amplifying this work and work like it. Michael Todoran, thank you for your support and for lifting up Cal Poly Pomona students, faculty, and alumni through *The Landscape Architecture Podcast* and in real life. Remember to breathe.

Deep thanks to the Los Angeles Living Schoolyards Coalition: Tori Kjer (Los Angeles Neighborhood Land Trust—LANLT), Robin Mark (The Trust for Public Land—TPL), Marcella Raney (Occidental College), Bevin Ashenmiller (Occidental College), Anna Gruben (LANLT), Mikaela Randolph (Randolph Consulting Group), Damon Nagami (NRDC), Sharyn Romano (LABT), Eileen Alduenda (Council for Watershed Health), Ariel

Whitson (TreePeople), Michelle Bagnato (TreePeople), Matilda Reyes (TPL), Teresa Dahl (chair, Carthay Environmental Studies School Garden Science Program), Tracy Bartley (LAUSD parent and green schoolyard advocate), Jonathan Pacheco Bell (LANLT), Rosa Romero (Urban & Environmental Policy Institute), Melissa Guerrero (Kounkuey Design Initiative), Lauren Elachi (Kounkuey Design Initiative), and Joe Laskin (North East Trees). Our collaboration over the past year (but in many cases much longer) and commitment to creating equitable, just, and thriving school environments keeps me going.

And to the Green LA Coalition—not only did you provide a sounding board for the earliest versions of this work; you also brought me into your environmental community and shared knowledge that informs this book. Conner Everts, all the feels for all the wisdom and opportunities you've brought. And to Liz Crosson, Meredith McCarthy, Rita Kampalath, Melanie Winters, and Claire Robinson for your collaboration and for all that each of you do to make Los Angeles healthier and greener.

To Mia Lehrer for the mentorship and opportunity to dive into this and other advocacy through design work. Thank you for your infinite vision and leadership. And to the whole Studio-MLA team for your friendship and collaboration. I'm especially thankful for the feedback on and support of much of this work by Holly Kuwayama, Margot Jacobs, and Jean Yang.

For Nord Erickson, Stephen Carroll, Matthew Hall, Scott Horsley, and the EPTDESIGN team, who taught me how to practice landscape architecture in a family-friendly, employee-centered environment. Thank you for supporting this work in practice and in theory. Your belief and encouragement helped me through the most difficult years of my life.

Thank you, Joan Woodward. Your kind and inclusive leadership in the CPP MLA program in 2003 was the reason I moved to California. You've been a constant and honest mentor and friend ever since. Your influence is everywhere in this book, but especially in the parts concerned with maintenance, resilience, and climate-appropriate design. Thank you for encouraging me to apply to the LAF Fellowship and for helping me rethink my proposal, the night before it was due, to be true to my strengths instead of someone else's. And to Tori Kjer, my dear friend from that first day we met on the bench outside Building 7, thank you for your early review of chapter 3 and for all you do to bring parks, schools, and communities to life.

To the mom communities who kept me (mostly) sane during this work and the long years leading up to it. And to the friends I lean on daily and weekly as well as those whose reconnection, even after years, makes it feel like we never left. Thank you. There aren't enough words to express my deep love and appreciation. And for the second moms who helped raise me and my siblings, while also paving the way for women, equality, and education: I love, admire, and thank you.

To my siblings: Julia, who knows me better than anyone and has supported me through the good, the bad, and the ugly. You and Jasper are my anchors and my creative heroes. Thank you, Robin, for sharing your fierce belief in and action toward righting wrongs and restoring relationships. Your gift with words fills my earliest and most recent memories. To Felicity, Jacob, and Levi for making me laugh, cry, and everything in between. I am eternally grateful and proud to be your mom. And, of course, to my mom, Jane Latané, who nurtured my love of reading and writing and taught by example that it is never too late to go to school, get a new job, move, or rewrite your story. I look forward to the next transformation.

About the Author

Claire Latané is a landscape architecture professor at California State Polytechnic University, Pomona (Cal Poly Pomona). Her teaching and scholarship apply research connecting the mind, body, and environment to design places and processes that support mental health and well-being. The principles and guidelines in *Schools That Heal* began with support from the Landscape Architecture Foundation, the Association for Women in Architecture Foundation, Prevention Institute, and Cal Poly Pomona Department of Landscape Architecture. Claire has practiced landscape architecture since 2006. She lives in Los Angeles, where her own garden is an experiment in what will grow wild with little care but lots of love. Her three children—who are very loved and not too wild—are all grown.

Index